Melody strikes again and hits at *Daring to Ask for More, Daring* Christian walk. Carefully researched, power-packed with strong biblical content and interwoven with engaging stories; this book is a thought-provoking read. Anyone who is seeking to experience a greater and more meaningful life as a Christ-follower should prayerfully read and study *Daring to Live by Every Word*. And as you do, prepare to be transformed!

Kandus Thorp, cofounder, Hope Channel International

Are you satisfied with a superficial relationship with Jesus? If so, this is *not* the book for you! But if you are hungry for a deeper authentic relationship with Jesus and are willing to be broken and made into His image, then I dare you to read this book! It will change your life!

Gary Blanchard, World Youth director, General Conference

Prepare for your relationship with Jesus to grow in amazing ways as you learn what it means to love and worship God with heart, body, mind and soul. This book is not just dry theory! We have walked with Melody as close friends and ministry partners for a number of years, and have seen firsthand the authentic joys, struggles, and precious victories she has experienced in her own love relationship with Jesus. These experiences have prepared her to beautifully share God's deepest heart passion for His last day people. We encourage you to prayerfully read *Daring to Live by Every Word*, then live it, and let the power of the Holy Spirit change your life!

Jerry and Janet Page, General Conference Ministerial Association

I am in tears this morning as I read *Daring to Live by Every Word*. What a powerful, life-changing book! What moving testimonies! I'm especially touched as I read about well-respected leaders being real about their struggles to surrender. Already I sense a wonderful love and conviction from the Holy Spirit as I read, and it moves me to pray for God to do a more thorough work in my own heart and life. I admire Melody's courage in writing this book. This is a timely message, and I know it's going to change many lives . . . including mine!

Kristin Hutchison, wife and busy mother of four

Blitzed 24-7 by the siren song of an electronic culture, there isn't one of us who hasn't experienced a gnawing hunger for something deeper, something—anything with the fingerprints of God on it. My friend Melody taps that longing in her new book about the one Book that can leave His fingerprints on us too. Radical. Countercultural. What a new generation of Jesus' followers needs to live as He did: "It is written."

Dwight Nelson, senior pastor, Pioneer Memorial Church, Andrews University

Humans have nothing for which to live until they've found a cause for which they're willing to die. This book gives us a cause worth dying for while propelling readers on an exciting journey of Christian living through humble surrender and radical faith. In *Daring to Live by Every Word*, Melody gets to the heart of things as she shares about the struggles we all face, and the victories that are possible in Jesus. This book will be a life-changer for every reader who takes the messages seriously!

Nicole Parker, adjunct professor,
School of Religion, Southern Adventist University,
and author of the Tales of Exodus series

If you love Jesus and want to be ready for His soon return, you should read this encouraging book! *Daring to Live by Every Word* overflows from Melody's personal experience with God. This book will not only guide you into a deeper, more intimate relationship with Jesus, but it will also help you learn how to love Him more, as you prepare for His second coming.

Pavel Goia, editor, *Ministry* magazine

This beautiful book, so well written, will lead you into the Word—and through the study of the Word—will change your life. *Daring to Live by Every Word* encourages faith through short inspiring testimonies, guides the reader through a series of biblical passages, and leads the reader to a deeper connection with the Infinite Creator God. As such it reaches the core need of every person, scholar or simple Bible student, to live in Christ and for Christ and experience the joy He offers! This book has been a tremendous blessing to me personally.

Michael G. Hasel, PhD, director,
Institute of Archaeology and professor of Near Eastern Studies
and Archaeology at Southern Adventist University

God's Word is worth dying for but it is also worth living by. In this inspiring volume Melody practically applies the principles of God's Word to our daily lives. She calls us to a deeper commitment to the Word through the power of Christ. This book is worth reading!

Mark Finley, assistant to the president, General Conference

Have you felt God drawing you to Himself lately? Can you hear His gentle whisper, "I want to bring you deeper into My presence?" I have—and Melody Mason's new book, *Daring to Live by Every Word* is binding my heart tighter to God with every page. If you long for a faith (walk with Jesus) that will see you through what's just ahead for planet Earth, *don't miss this book*!

Cindy Tutsch, associate director (retired), Ellen G. White Estate

In this inspiring book, Melody shows through practical, real-life examples how to live for Jesus in a way that actually works! This book is not about a "try harder" paradigm. It's about core heart issues and how they impact daily life. Everyone should read this book!

Mark Paden, freelance filmmaker, photographer, and young-adult leader

So many have been inspired by *Daring to Ask for More*. In this sequel volume, Melody Mason challenges us all to courageously move to the next level in our walk with Jesus. I encourage you to read *Daring to Live by Every Word* with much prayer! As you do, the blessings you will receive will flow out like rivers of living water to bless the lives of those around you!

Derek Morris, president, Hope Channel International

God has done it again! He was obviously with Melody as she composed each chapter of this book, for it's evident that His fingerprints are everywhere. This book reintroduces us to the intimacy that God desires with His people, and shows us the sweetness of surrender and the joy that full obedience brings. From the very first chapter, I've been convicted and I desire that He will take me deeper.

Gem Castor, missionary and prayer leader

In *Daring to Live by Every Word*, Melody makes the journey of righteousness by faith and surrender to the indwelling Christ, practical, real, and appealing. In these pages, readers are taken back again and again to "It is written," the heart of the Christian experience! I enjoyed this book and you will too!

John Bradshaw, president, It Is Written

Loving God With Heart, Body, Mind, and Soul

DARING TO LIVE

BY EVERY WORD

MELODY MASON

Pacific Press®
Publishing Association
Nampa, Idaho | www.pacificpress.com

Cover design by Gerald Lee Monks
Cover design resources from iStockPhoto.com | neyro2008 (Bible) | wingmar (Background)

The author assumes full responsibility for the accuracy of all facts and quotations as cited in this book.

Purchase additional copies of this book by calling toll-free 1-800-765-6955 or by visiting http://www.adventistbookcenter.com.

ISBN: 978-0-8163-6632-3

February 2020

Dedicated

To those who *long* to be more like Jesus!
To those who *wait* in hope for His soon return!

When he shall appear, we shall be like him;
for we shall see him as he is. And every man that hath
this hope in him purifieth himself, even as he is pure.
—1 John 3:2, 3, KJV

Contents

THE WORD THAT TRANSFORMS

THE WORD THAT EMPOWERS

RESOURCES

Introduction

The year was A.D. 320. Emperor Constantine had just issued an edict legalizing Christianity throughout the Roman Empire. For a time, his coruler and rival, Licinius, who controlled the eastern half of the region, conceded to Constantine's wishes, allowing Christians religious freedom. However, eventually, the Emperor Licinius broke his alliance with the West and determined to stamp out Christianity in his part of the empire. As Licinius prepared his army for battle, he realized that he should remove all Christians from his army, lest there be mutiny among his ranks.

As the story goes, during this time, there was a company of one hundred soldiers, which included many Christians, camped by a lake outside the city of Sebaste (now Sivas in modern-day Turkey). These brave soldiers had distinguished themselves in service to Emperor Licinius, but now their true allegiance was to be put to the test.

Late one cold winter evening, a messenger arrived at their camp. He had a message for the company's captain. The captain took the message and read it by the flickering light of a nearby campfire. The message read, "It is commanded by the Emperor that when our messenger arrives, the bugle be sounded to call the men into line. Then shall an altar be built in the midst of the camp and each soldier as he passes by shall pour upon it a cupful of wine as an offering to the Emperor. And it is decreed that all who refuse so to honor the Emperor shall be killed."[1]

After the captain had finished reading the order, the messenger asked, "What shall I tell the Emperor?"

The captain responded, "You can tell the Emperor that we will obey his command!"

However, even as the captain pledged obedience, he struggled with what he should do. While he was not a Christian himself, he admired his Christian men. He didn't want to see them die. But what could he do? The Emperor's orders must be obeyed!

So the captain gave a signal, and the bugle was sounded. Once all his men were in line, an altar of crude stones was built in front of them, and the men were told of the Emperor's command. Then each soldier was given a cup of wine.

One by one, the men began taking turns marching around the altar and pouring their wine out in honor to the Emperor. However, as the fourth man approached the altar, he hesitated, then turned away and poured his wine on the ground. Immediately he was ordered to step aside.

Despite knowing that disobedience to the Emperor's orders meant death, forty out of those one hundred soldiers bravely remembered the first of the Ten Commandments, "You shall have no other gods before me," (Exodus 20:3) and decided to "obey God rather than men" (Acts 5:29). They knew that they could not *even pretend* to worship anyone but God.

As a result of their choice, the men were stripped of their clothes and sent out onto the cold, icy lake to die. However, as the stillness of night began to settle over the camp, something surprising happened. Beautiful music began to come from the lake. The men were singing, bravely, boldly, in allegiance to their Lord and Savior Jesus Christ.

The captain, hoping that some would change their mind, prepared warm baths and fires near the edge of the lake. But the men did not come. As the night wore on, the singing gradually grew fainter and fainter. At long last, a lone form crept across the ice back to the lake's edge. He collapsed near one of the warm baths. However, seeing the failing faith of this one deserter, the guard who had been stationed to keep watch over the martyrs threw off his clothes, and declaring his faith in Jesus, ran out to join the remaining men on the ice.[2]

The next morning, when the sun came up, the bodies of forty Christian men lay frozen on the cold icy lake. They had faced the ultimate test, being forced to choose between obeying the authority of a worldly emperor and staying true to God, and they had passed their test. They had kept their eyes fixed on Jesus, and as a result, God had given them the victory.[3]

Today, more than 1,700 years later, we are still in the midst of a great spiritual controversy, and we are again facing the same test. The test is over whom we will worship and whom we will ultimately obey. While the world fights over political authority, parental rights and authority, and even ecclesiastical authority, the most serious battle of all is waged daily between "self" and the authority of God and His Word. The whole universe is watching this very personal battle! Who will bend? Will we bend to the Word in humble submission and obedience, or will we seek to bend God's Word to suit our own human desires and preferences?

God tells us in the Bible, "If you love Me, keep My commandments" (John 14:15). He tells us, "Be doers of the word, and not hearers only, deceiving yourselves" (James 1:22). Again and again, He asks, "Why do you call Me 'Lord, Lord,' and not do the things which I say?" (Luke 6:46).

When we read the Bible but don't follow it or apply it to our daily life, it is like we are building a house without a foundation (Luke 6:49). Unfortunately, many Christians in our world today are building with little or no Biblical foundation.

The famous researcher George Barna, in a survey of religion in America, once wrote, "Our rejection of orthodox Christian beliefs, coupled with a relativistic culture, has led millions of adults to embrace a world view totally at odds with the faith they allegedly embrace. The irony is that most of the individuals who are caught up in their own contradictions[4] are completely unaware of those conflicts."[5]

While we belong to a church that is known for its firm commitment to Scripture, it is foolish to think that we have not been influenced by the "relativism" sweeping through our world and culture. That's why it's time that we as Christians take a renewed stand upon the authority of God and His Word. While it may not be popular, and at some point, it might even cost us our very life, it's time we once again choose whom we will worship and whom we will obey.

In the book *The Great Controversy*, we read, "None but those who have fortified the mind with the truths of the Bible will stand through the last great conflict. To every soul will come the searching test: Shall I obey God rather than men? The decisive hour is even now at hand. Are our feet planted on the rock of God's immutable word? Are we prepared to stand firm in defense of the commandments of God and the faith of Jesus?"[6]

While we might hope to be spiritual "superheroes" when the rough times hit, author Ellen White tells us, "It is not a conclusive evidence that a man is a Christian because he manifests spiritual ecstasy under extraordinary circumstances. Holiness is not rapture: it is an entire surrender of the will to God; it is living by every word that proceeds from the mouth of God; it is doing the will of our heavenly Father; it is trusting God in trial, in darkness as well as in the light; it is walking by faith and not by sight; it is relying on God with unquestioning confidence, and resting in His love."[7]

Are you hungry for a deeper walk with Jesus? Are you eager to experience the genuine joy of a life fully submitted to Him? Then let me invite you along for this exciting journey.

In case you are wondering, this book is not written to give you a long list of dos and don'ts on how to live the Christian life. Yes, I will be talking about some specific issues and by so doing may step on a few toes along the way (*forgive me if they happen to be yours*). However, the main focus of this book will be on the beauty of the Word and what it really means to *love* and *worship* the Living Word, the One who has created us, rescued us, and redeemed us. Of course, the reality we will discover along the way is that we actually *love and worship God* by how we choose to live our lives today. As one author so beautifully writes, "God's commandments are the shoes in which our love for God walks and finds its faithful expression."[8]

With this in mind, we will be asking ourselves, "How can we love and worship God more through the honor of His Word? How can we align our heart, body, mind, and soul with Scripture, so we will be ready to meet Jesus when He comes?" We will also be asking ourselves, "How can we love others more?" for our love and treatment of those around us is one of the strongest indicators of our love for God.

The Bible tells us, "Love suffers long and is kind; love does not envy; love does not parade itself, is not puffed up; does not behave rudely, does not seek its own, is not provoked, thinks no evil; does not rejoice in iniquity, but rejoices in the truth; bears all things, believes all things, hopes all things, endures all things. Love never fails" (1 Corinthians 13:4–8).

While I do not claim to be the perfect role model for all the topics I will address (there's only one perfect role model, and that is Jesus), I will be real as I talk about the normal daily struggles we all face. I will also be real as I share how we can experience joyful victory—not through self's work, for all our righteousness is as filthy rags (Isaiah 64:6), but through the power of the Holy Spirit and Jesus' finished work!

At the end of each chapter, you will find a short section called "Going Deeper." This can be studied as a small group or on your own. But if you truly desire a more intimate walk with Jesus, don't skip it. Pray over it, and take what you learn to heart and, most important, to daily life. I've also included a song with each chapter, so you don't forget to worship and sing praises to God as you go!

The time for lukewarm Christian living is over (Revelation 3:16). The time for business as usual is over. The Bible tells us, "Choose for yourselves this day whom you will serve" (Joshua 24:15). If we profess to be a people preparing for heaven, preparing for Jesus' soon coming, it's time we get serious about how we love and worship God—not just on Sabbath, but during every day of the week, not just in our theology, but in nitty-gritty everyday life.

So come, pick up your Bible, and join me as we begin an exciting journey learning what it means to love and worship God with heart, body, mind, and soul, daring to live by His every Word!

Part 1

THE WORD THAT BREAKS

Chapter 1

The Beauty in Brokenness

Roof Off, Walls Down

The sacrifices of God are a broken spirit, a broken and a contrite heart—these, O God, You will not despise.
—Psalm 51:17

I will never forget the time several years ago, as I was preparing to lead a prayer service for a large event the next day, how the Holy Spirit convicted me of something specific in my life that I needed to make right with God. Overwhelmed, I sank to my knees on the floor that night as I prayed, "Oh Lord, please forgive me . . ."

However, while I confessed my sin to God, certain steps were necessary to make proper amends. But I couldn't take these steps immediately, so I wasn't sure what to do. Should I still go forward with my prayer ministry responsibilities, or should I get someone else to fill in for me until I had made things right?

As a respected leader in ministry, it was very humiliating to think of admitting to others that I had failed God in a specific area. I didn't want to make a stir and appear spiritually weak to my teammates, or to the many strangers that were in attendance at the meetings. So with a heavy heart and tears in my eyes, I went to sleep that night determined that I would ask someone else to lead the prayer service the next day.

However, the next morning as I set out to find someone to take my place, God stopped me in my tracks as the Holy Spirit began speaking to my heart. "Melody, you need to lead the prayer service this morning. Don't get someone to replace you!"

"Wait, God . . . You can't mean this," I said as fresh tears came to my eyes. But the Holy Spirit continued to speak to my heart.

"Yes, I want you to lead. However, you are not to lead it as *the person you want everyone to think you are*. Don't you see? I'm not looking for people to lead who cover up their sins and go on as if everything is OK. I'm looking for *yielded, broken vessels*; vessels that will humble themselves to such a degree that pride is gone. Only then can I use them for My glory. I know this hurts, but you need to share with the congregation what I convicted you of last night. Be honest about how you've failed Me! Then invite them to come with you to the Cross to put away all sin and compromise. You see, if people wait to come until they have everything in order, they will never come."

Again, I began to protest. "I can't do this, Lord! What will everyone think when they see how I've failed You?"

The Holy Spirit spoke softly to my heart as He turned my eyes toward heaven. "It doesn't matter what they think. This is not about protecting your reputation. This is about bringing glory to God. But if He is to work, you must humble yourself."

Oh, how I did *not* want to obey the Holy Spirit's promptings that morning. If I could have run away like Jonah, or crawled in a cave, I would have done so immediately. But I knew what I must do. I had to obey.

Shaking and with tears in my eyes, I went before hundreds of people that morning and shared what the Lord had laid on my heart. You could have heard a pin drop in the room as everyone listened. "Jesus tells us to come as we are," I said softly as I continued to wipe tears away from my eyes. "So I'm coming as I am, and I'm inviting you to join me at the foot of the Cross."

At this invitation, everyone got out of their chairs and came forward to the front of the room. There was soft weeping here and there as different people asked God's forgiveness for those areas of sin and compromise that had crept into their lives. And the Holy Spirit was there.

In hindsight, I think it was one of the most sweet, sacred prayer services I've ever experienced, for God did a deep work of cleansing among all of us that morning. Many hearts were broken, but how beautiful and healing the brokenness was.

In the book *Steps to Christ,* we are told:

> If you see your sinfulness, do not wait to make yourself better. How many there are who think they are not good enough to come to Christ. Do you expect to become better through your own efforts? "Can the Ethiopian change his skin, or the leopard his spots? Then may ye also do good, that are accustomed to do evil." Jeremiah 13:23. There is help for us only in God. We must not wait for stronger persuasions, for better opportunities, or for holier tempers. We can do nothing of ourselves. We must come to Christ just as we are.[1]

Of course, in general, private sins should be kept private. What happens in secret, between God and us, is always more significant than what happens in public.[2] However, since the Holy Spirit convicted me to share, I knew I needed to be transparent and open that morning with those present.

I will never forget one elderly gentleman who came forward after the service. He told me how he had come to the meetings with a crusty heart of skepticism and doubt, but seeing me honestly share my struggles and my need of the Savior had convicted him of his own need, and as a result, that morning he decided to give his heart to the Lord.

"I've never seen leaders on the platform be real before like you were today, Melody," he told me through moist eyes. "It always seems like such a performance at religious events. But you showed me today that God is real because I saw how He was convicting you, breaking you, and changing you. Thank you." His voice was cracking as he spoke.

Roof off and walls down

Ellen White writes, "We shall often have to bow down to weep at the feet of Jesus, because of our shortcomings and mistakes. But we are not to be discouraged. . . . As we distrust our own power, we shall trust the power of our Redeemer."[3]

Thankfully, God is a God of mercy, and He understands our

weaknesses. It's because His mercies are new every morning that we are not consumed (Lamentations 3:22, 23). However, repentance is only genuine if we surrender ourselves to be genuinely changed.

I love what author Norman Grubb writes in his book *Continuous Revival: The Secret to Victorious Living*:

> All Christian relationships are *two-way*, not *one-way*. They are *horizontal* as well as *vertical*. . . . We cannot, for instance, say that we have become righteous before God through faith in Christ and yet continue to be unrighteous among men.[4]

Let me put it this way. We can liken a man to a house. It has a roof and walls. So also man in his fallen state has a roof on top of his sins, coming between him and God; and he also has walls up, between him and his neighbor. But at salvation, when broken at the cross, not only does the roof come off through faith in Christ, but the walls fall down flat, and man's true condition as a sinner-saved-by-grace is confessed before all men.

Unfortunately, the trouble soon begins again after conversion— and here lies the basic hindrance to continued revival. Continued revival is continued brokenness; but brokenness is two-way, and that means that the walls [must be] kept down as well as roof off. But man's most deep-rooted and subtle sin is the subtle sin of *pride*: self-esteem and self-respect. Though hardly realizing it, while we are careful to keep the roof off between ourselves and God through repentance and faith, we soon let those walls of respectability creep up again between ourselves and our brethren. We don't mind our brethren knowing about the success we have in our Christian living. If we win a soul, if we lead a class, if we have a prayer answered, if we get good ideas from Scriptures—we don't mind if they hear about these things, because we get a little reflected credit because of them. . . . [But] if God has to deal with us over our impatience or temper in the home, over dishonesty in our business, over coldness or some other sin, by no means do we easily bear testimony to our brethren of God's faithful and gracious dealings in such areas of failure. Why not? Just because of pride. . . . The fact is, we love the praise of men as well as of God, and that is exactly what the Scriptures say stops the flow of confession before men (John 12:42–43).[5]

Life lessons from Corrie

Corrie Ten Boom, along with her family, helped save the lives of more than 800 Jews during the Nazi Holocaust of World War II. As a result of her family's underground work in Holland, the entire family was arrested and sent to Ravensbrück, one of the most brutal concentration camps in all of Germany. Thousands died there!

By the time Corrie was miraculously released from the concentration camp in December of 1944, all of her closest family members had died while in prison. However, instead of nursing her wounds or growing bitter, Corrie went on to spend the remaining years of her life traveling the world, sharing the love of Jesus.

Corrie was known and loved for her compassion and her sweet spirit of grace and humility. And many were brought to Jesus by her testimony. Yet, she was still very human, just like you and me.

One time, while traveling in Cuba, Corrie shared how she had been struggling sitting through a long evening of meetings. She had just given a message about the love of God and then had to wait on the platform while two more men shared lengthy presentations. It was very hot and humid, pesky bugs were everywhere, and it was getting late. Corrie was tired, and her patience was wearing thin as the last speaker began to make a lengthy appeal.

"Surely, no one is in the mood to do anything but go home," Corrie grumbled to herself. "I hope no one comes forward. I'm aching for my bed."

But to her great surprise, many people began coming forward, responding to the call. Some had tears in their eyes. Suddenly, Corrie recognized the selfishness of her heart. Here she had hoped people would not give their life to Jesus that night simply because she was tired, hot, and weary. Immediately, she confessed her sin to God and asked His forgiveness, then she got up to pray with those who had come forward.

The next day, Corrie was asked to speak at a large church in an upper-class area of Havana. Many prominent and affluent people were present. As she came into church that morning, they handed her the program booklet that contained her flowery introduction. It read: "Corrie Ten Boom is a most popular world evangelist. . . . She is tireless and completely selfless in her absolute dedication to the cause of the gospel." As she read the introduction, her heart sank. "Oh Lord," she prayed, "if only these people knew who the real Corrie Ten Boom is, they would not have come to hear me speak this morning."

"Why don't you tell them who the real Corrie is . . . " the Holy Spirit answered. Immediately, Corrie began to protest. "But Lord, if I tell them, what if they reject me?" Again she heard the soft but firm voice, "Can I bless a lie?"

So that morning, Corrie opened her heart and told her audience the truth. As a result, many hearts were broken, and the foundation for genuine revival was laid.[6]

Roy Hession writes, "To be broken is the beginning of revival. It is painful, it is humiliating, but it is the only way."[7]

Unfortunately, there aren't a lot of resources out there on how to be broken. It's not as if you can look on Amazon and find a selection of books on how to mourn and weep over your sins, or on how to humble yourself. Besides, who really wants to be broken?

"Our culture is obsessed with being whole and feeling good. This drive affects even the way we view the Christian life. We want a 'painless Pentecost'; we want a 'laughing' revival. We want gain without pain; we want resurrection without going through the grave; we want life without experiencing death; we want a crown without going by way of the cross. . . . But in God's economy, the way up is down. You and I will never meet God in revival until we first meet Him in brokenness."[8]

What is true brokenness? you might wonder. Some think it is constant morbid introspection. Others think it's about being overly emotional in religious services, or depressed in spirit while everyone else is happy. Let me assure you, it is none of the above. While heart searching is needed, and at times the emotions will be stirred, these things in and of themselves are not the signs of true brokenness. The reality is that many people have cried their hearts out and never yet experienced true genuine brokenness.

"True brokenness is a moment-by-moment lifestyle of agreeing with God about the true condition of my heart and life—not as everyone else thinks it is, but as He knows it to be. Brokenness is the shattering of my self-will—the absolute surrender of my will to the will of God.

It is saying, 'Yes, Lord!'—no resistance, no chafing, no stubbornness—simply submitting myself [no matter the pain or cost] to His direction and will in my life."[9]

While the shattering of "self-will" is often a painful process, one of the recurring themes that we see again and again throughout Scripture is that God always does His best work through broken humble people. Just consider the stories of Abraham, Isaac, Jacob, Joseph, Moses, David, Naomi, Ruth, Esther, and many of the prophets.

Priceless dust

Brokenness is truly the most sacred offering and sacrifice we can give to God. Indeed, it is the only sacrifice we have to give. The Bible tells us, "The sacrifices of God are a broken spirit, a broken and a contrite heart—these, O God, You will not despise" (Psalm 51:17).

If you look up the verb "contrite" in Psalm 51:17, you find that it comes from the Hebrew word *dâkâh*, which means *to crumble, to beat in pieces, to break, to crush to powder, to dust, to utterly destroy.*

Think about it. If something is broken, you might be able to glue it back together, but you can't glue dust back together. And that's what we are in reality—dust, broken vessels!

"What an exalted privilege!" we are told. "Finite beings, of dust and ashes, admitted through the mediation of Christ, into the audience chamber of the Most High."[10]

And to think, not only do we have an audience with God, but dust is the very ingredient that God uses again and again to work His best miracles.

In the beginning, God planted all the beautiful trees and plants in the Garden of Eden in dust so they would grow and produce fruit (Genesis 1:11). Then God formed man, His crowning work of creation, from dust and breathed into him the breath of life so that he would produce fruit (Genesis 2:7; Genesis 1:28).

Pause for a second here. Do we recognize that all our best fruit and labors, all our best works, apart from the breath of life, the blood of Jesus, and the power of the Holy Spirit, are nothing more than dust? And yet, frequently, we get so arrogant that we glory *in our dust*!

Thankfully, even after the curse of sin fell upon the world, Jesus still cared about the dust. And so He returned to earth to continue His work among broken humanity (1 Samuel 2:8). While He used dust to restore the blind man's sight (John 9:5, 6), it is the dust and brokenness of life that He often uses today to restore our spiritual sight. He was good at mixing water with dust to make clay. And it is as moldable clay (mud) in the hands of the Master Potter that we become all that He's created us to be even in this fallen world (Jeremiah 18:6).

As one author so eloquently writes, "Dust doesn't have to signify the end. Dust is often what must be present for the new [life] to begin."[11]

Yes, dust truly can become beautiful if it is in the hands of a loving God. And surrendered dust is priceless!

As we begin this journey, daring to live by every word, let's give God our dust—the dust of genuine brokenness from a heart that says, "Yes, Lord! All I have to offer You is broken and flawed. Even my best efforts are merely dust, but I'm willing to give all my *dust* to You and become clay in the hands of the Master Potter. Roof off, walls down, whatever You say, I'm Yours."

Daring to Live by Every Word—Going Deeper!
Roof Off, Walls Down: Psalm 51:1–19

If you've ever raised a horse, you know that the horse has to be broken in—meaning it's will must be broken so that it will be submissive to its master. The same must happen to our self-will before God can truly work in us. And that will only happen as we learn to yield to the Word. So open your Bible and pick up a pen and notebook as you consider the following "going deeper" Bible study questions.

- Isaiah 57:15—Where does God dwell?
- Psalm 51:17—How can we worship God more fully with our brokenness?
- 2 Corinthians 7:9–11—What are the results of godly sorrow?
- Psalm 51:1–19—What did David ask for in his prayer of repentance?
- 1 John 1:5–9—How does God respond to genuine repentance?
- Luke 15:11–32—What does the prodigal son's story tell us about God's heart?

- Psalm 139:23, 24—Write down a prayer in your own words, patterned after this psalm, as you seek God for genuine repentance and humility.

Along with each Going Deeper segment, I'm going to suggest a song taken from the *Seventh-day Adventist Hymnal*. I encourage you to sing each song shared and soak in the message it brings. If you are not a singer, then find the song and reflect on the words. For this chapter, as you contemplate what you've read, I encourage you to sing or reflect on the well-known favorite, "Just as I Am,"[12] hymn no. 313.

To go even deeper, consider downloading the document "Clearing the Way for the Holy Spirit," by Scott Griswold.[13] And may our prayer truly be, "Roof off, walls down, whatever You say, Lord, I'm yours!"

Time to dig deep into God's Word, get on our knees, and allow the Holy Spirit to take this message deeper into our hearts!

Chapter 2

Our Greatest and Most Urgent Need

Real, Raw, and Spiritually Weak

> *But God has chosen the foolish things of the world*
> *to put to shame the wise, and God has chosen the weak things*
> *of the world to put to shame the things which are mighty.*
> —1 Corinthians 1:27

The date was October 11, 2010, and many of the Seventh-day Adventist church leaders from around the world were gathered together for the Annual Council[1] meetings, which are held at the General Conference headquarters in Silver Spring, Maryland, each fall. Some of the leaders had been earnestly praying that God would do something special for the church during this Annual Council. I believe God heard those prayers.

It was Monday morning worship, and everyone was listening intently to Pastor Dwight Nelson, who was the guest speaker of the day. He was giving a message based on Zechariah 12:10 and 13:1—God's appeal for spiritual leaders to seek forgiveness and cleansing at the foot of the cross.

The previous morning during worship, another speaker had shared a personal testimony and given an urgent appeal for the leaders to put away all sin, sins such as bitterness and fault finding as well as private sin. *Preach it!* Pastor Dwight had thought to himself. *Tell them like it is!*

This is what our church leaders need to hear!

However, at the end of the message, as everyone knelt to pray, Pastor Dwight was deeply convicted of his own sin of envy that he had held in his heart for many years against another church leader. Later that night, in the privacy of his hotel room, the conviction deepened: "Oh Lord, You aren't going to ask me to share and confess this publicly are You?" he questioned as he prayed.

But the next morning, the conviction had not lessened. So that Monday morning, as Pastor Dwight was speaking to all the church leaders, he paused as he was nearing the end of his sermon. Even while his message was being broadcast on live television, he turned to address a man that was sitting behind him on the platform. It was another well-known leader in ministry. "I need to apologize to you today," he told the man. "I have held something in my heart against you over the years. Today I want to confess this to you—even as I have confessed it to God."

It was a sacred moment, and there were tears in many eyes as Pastor Dwight stepped away from the podium to meet the fellow leader who was already walking toward him with outstretched arms.

While most speakers would have chosen to confess privately to maintain professional respectability, Pastor Dwight was modeling in living reality what it means to take the roof off and put the walls down. As a result, the Holy Spirit was able to draw very near that morning.

"Away with this false dignity," Ellen White urged the church leaders in years past. "Fall on the Rock and be broken, and Christ will give you the true and heavenly dignity. Let not pride, self-esteem, or self-righteousness keep anyone from confessing his sin. . . . The humble and broken heart can appreciate something of the love of God and the cross of Calvary."[2]

Of course, no one knew what Pastor Dwight was going to share that morning, nor did they know what was on the meeting agenda for that day. However, not long after Pastor Dwight finished speaking, as some were still wiping tears out of their eyes, General Conference president, Elder Ted Wilson, got up and made a heartfelt appeal.

"Jesus has been waiting to come back for many years. But we're still here, friends. We've tried everything, and we've failed. If we want to go home, something has to change. We have to do something different . . . just like what happened here this morning."

Not long after, a document was passed out to all the leaders titled: "An

Urgent Appeal for Revival, Reformation, Discipleship, and Evangelism."[3] This powerful and moving document appealed to church leaders to make personal revival a priority, to set aside time daily to spend with God and His Word, and to spend time examining their hearts and asking the Holy Spirit to convict them of anything that may be hindering their walk with Jesus. Then it encouraged leaders to use every means possible to share the urgency for "revival and reformation" with others, and to take time in their own meetings and organizations to study and pray together.

God was working, and hearts were ripe. The vote to move forward with the new revival and reformation emphasis was unanimous. However, few would imagine the far-reaching ripple effect that would soon touch the lives of church members all around the world. Thousands have since fallen in love afresh with the daily reading of God's Word, and countless lives, including my own, have been forever changed through the power of prayer. Work in difficult territories has expanded as more and more people have accepted the call to sacrificial missions. In addition, personal and corporate evangelism efforts have exploded. History is being made as millions are joining the faith. But is this enough? Is God content? Not as long as there are still billions yet unreached—not as long as there are still many cities and villages that have not yet heard about Jesus.

While we celebrate the growth and the millions that have given their lives to Jesus, we have to be honest and recognize that our best evangelism efforts have still only been a drop in the bucket compared to the vast need that remains. So what are we still missing as a church? What are we still missing personally? Is there something that is holding back the full outpouring of the Holy Spirit?

I think we find our answer in the following statement:

"The Lord can do more in one hour than we can do in a whole lifetime, and when He sees that His people are fully consecrated, let me tell you, a great work will be done in a short time, and the message of truth [will] be carried into the dark places of the earth, where it has never been proclaimed."[4]

Oh, that God would strip away all pretense and half-hearted commitment to Him and teach us afresh what it means to be fully consecrated for His glory.

The pineapple story

I love stories. In fact, some of my favorite memories as a child are those long, cold winter evenings when we would gather around the warm stove in the living room, curl up with our blankets, and listen to my father read us stories. How I treasure those precious memories.

One story will never be forgotten, for it continues to shape and impact my life—even to this very day.

Back in the early 1960's, Otto Koning and his wife, Carol, traveled to Irian Jaya, Indonesia (formerly Dutch New Guinea), where they served fourteen years as missionaries to a primitive jungle tribe. From the very beginning, they had big plans and hopes about all that they were going to do for these jungle dwellers.

However, during their first years of service, they experienced anything but success. Rather than seeing souls brought to Jesus, the Koning's fought fatigue, frustration, and mounting anger toward the local people, who turned out to be chronic thieves and stole everything from safety pins and silverware (which they turned into various forms of jewelry) to the Koning's prized pineapples growing in the garden behind the mission house.

Now the pineapples were especially precious, for Otto had imported the plants in by airplane, and it took three long years before the plants matured enough to produce fruit. But the local villagers would steal the fruit before it was even ripe.

Otto tried everything he could to stop the stealing but to no avail. The people called him the angry, stingy, white man with the box, for he often went from house to house in the village with a big box gathering up items and fruit that had been stolen.

Finally, after years of very little success, and with health and nerves nearly breaking, Otto and his wife returned home on furlough. There it was, while attending a retreat for missionaries, that Otto heard a message that forever changed his life.

"Give your possessions to God, because He can take better care of your property than you can," the speaker implored everyone. "Whatever you surrender to God, you will never lack. The people you fight with, you can never win for Christ."

Otto was deeply convicted and broken as he recognized the error of his ways. "People are dying without Jesus. And here I am, just foolishly fighting for my pineapples and my rights. Oh, Lord, please forgive me," he prayed with breaking heart. Pride and anger flowed out of his soul as he recommitted his heart and his pineapples to God.

Upon returning to their mission station in the jungles of Indonesia, one of the first things Otto did was to go out into his pineapple field and pray: "God, I can't take care of this pineapple garden anymore, so I'm giving it to You. I give myself to You."

While things did not change overnight, Otto began to learn what it means to die daily, to surrender daily, to yield to Jesus and His agenda daily. As a result of Otto's continued prayers of surrender, a spirit of peace began to take the place of frustration, and soon the locals began noticing significant changes about the angry white man.

"Otto, you've become a Christian!" a young man said excitedly one day. "What do you mean?" Otto asked in shock. "Well, you've been preaching to us all these years about what Christians act like, and we hoped to meet one someday, but now you've become one." Otto's heart was pierced afresh as he realized how foolish he must look to those watching, but it was from this point of broken pride that Otto and Carol's true ministry began to grow and flourish.

As it turned out, God did take care of their pineapple field, and soon the stealing stopped. But what was most beautiful was that as Otto and Carol experienced deep personal revival in their walk with God, the Holy Spirit started opening the hearts of the indigenous people, who soon began turning from spirit worship and cannibalism to faith in God. Within just a short time, Otto and Carol's mission station was ten years ahead of all the other mission stations in the region as God worked miracle after miracle on their behalf. If you have never heard this amazing testimony, I encourage you to take the time to hear their full story.[5]

Our greatest need!

John 15:5 tells us, "I am the vine, you are the branches. He who abides in Me, and I in him, bears much fruit; for without Me you can do nothing."

Do we realize that without Jesus, we truly can *do nothing*?

The problem is that many of us assume we are abiding in Jesus just because we call ourselves Christians when in actuality, we are barely attached to the Vine. It's no wonder our spiritual fruit is so meager. It's no wonder that we are constantly falling prey to temptation. However, once we recognize our great need and cast ourselves on Jesus, He opens the doors of heaven on our behalf.

We read in *The Desire of Ages*, "From the soul that feels his *need*, nothing is withheld. He has unrestricted access to Him in whom all fullness dwells."[6]

Just pause a few moments with me to ponder the significance of this amazing passage: *Nothing withheld. Unrestricted access to Him in whom all fullness dwells!*

Think of the unlimited spiritual possibilities that are within our reach if we would stop trying to pretend we have it all together and just cast ourselves wholeheartedly upon Jesus, acknowledge our *real sin, and our desperate raw need.*

Unfortunately, it is pride that keeps us from admitting our great need. In fact, we often tend to look down upon those who can't seem to pull their life together, while at the same time, we overlook the spiritual pride and character defects that eat out the godliness of our own souls.

The following passage from the book *Steps to Christ* gives even more clarity as to why pride is so deadly for the spiritual life of a believer:

> However trifling this or that wrong act may seem in the eyes of men, no sin is small in the sight of God. Man's judgment is partial, imperfect; but God estimates all things as they really are. The drunkard is despised and is told that his sin will exclude him from heaven; while *pride, selfishness*, and *covetousness* too often go unrebuked. But these are sins that are especially offensive to God; for they are contrary to the benevolence of His character, to that unselfish love which is the very atmosphere of the unfallen universe. He who falls into some of the grosser sins may feel a sense of his shame and poverty and his need of the grace of Christ; but pride feels no need, and so it closes the heart against Christ and the infinite blessings He came to give.[7]

This is why I believe our greatest and most urgent need today is that *we recognize our desperate spiritual need!*

As one author writes, "We must know our real condition, or we shall not feel our need of Christ's help. We must understand our danger, or we shall not flee to the refuge. We must feel the pain of our wounds, or we should not desire healing."[8]

Do we recognize our true condition? Do we understand our danger?

Do we feel the pain of our wounds and thirst for deeper spiritual healing and victory?

God tells us, "For I will restore health to you, and heal you of your wounds" (Jeremiah 30:17). He also tells us,

"For I will pour water on him who is thirsty,
And floods on the dry ground;
I will pour My Spirit on your descendants,
And My blessing on your offspring" (Isaiah 44:3).

Naturally, we don't like to come across as *wounded*, *needy*, and *thirsty!* It goes against our pride and ego, which desires to appear strong and in control. But being *thirsty* and *needy* is actually the very soil where deep, authentic Christianity takes root. Being *hungry* and recognizing that only Jesus can fill us each day is the very key that opens the windows of heaven on our behalf.

In the book *Ministry of Healing*, we are reminded, "Our only claim to [God's] mercy is our *great need*"![9]

It doesn't matter our age, the color of our skin, whether we are male or female, the success we've achieved, or the long titles that come after our name. It doesn't matter whether we hold multiple positions in ministry or none at all. All we have to offer God today (and every day) is the reality of our desperately helpless condition and our simple raw need.

"We have nothing to recommend us to God; the plea that we may urge now and ever is our utterly helpless condition, which makes His redeeming power a necessity. Renouncing all self-dependence, we may look to the cross of Calvary and say: 'In my hand no price I bring; Simply to Thy cross I cling.' "[10]

Dear friends, it's time we go to the cross and truly lay down our all. Whatever Jesus asks us to surrender, whatever our sin—pride, selfishness, unbelief, pineapples, or the shame and guilt of the years—let's give it all to Jesus. He has all we need and so much more!

Daring to Live by Every Word—Going Deeper!
Humility Versus Pride: 1 Corinthians 1:18–31

In the book *Gospel Workers*, we are told, "I saw that the strength of the children of God is in their humility. When they are little in their own eyes, Jesus will be to them their strength and their righteousness, and God will prosper their labors."[11]

It's time to open our Bibles as we consider the following "going deeper" questions.

- 1 Corinthians 1:18–31—Why is God's way foolishness to the world?
- Luke 18:9–14—What is the difference between true humility and false humility?
- Psalm 34:18—How can we avoid growing "proud" in our humility?
- James 4:6–10—What counsel does God give to help us overcome pride?
- Mark 14:27–31—Why did Peter deny Jesus, and how are we often like Peter?
- Philippians 2:5–8—How did Jesus demonstrate humility?
- Psalm 95:6–11—How can we worship God in deeper humility?
- Sing or reflect on the song, "Fill My Cup Lord," hymn no. 493.

If you desire to take this message even deeper, I invite you to prayerfully read through the Humility "Heart Challenge," which I've included in Appendix 1 in the back of this book. As you go through this heart challenge, ask God if there are any *pineapples* in your life that you need to surrender or anyone in your sphere of influence (family, friends, work colleagues) of whom you need to ask forgiveness. Then obey the Holy Spirit's leading (Psalm 66:18; Matthew 5:23, 24; Proverbs 28:13; Matthew 6:14, 15).

Andrew Murray, in his book *Humility and Absolute Surrender*, writes: "It is easy to think we humble ourselves before God: but humility towards men will be the only sufficient proof that our humility before God is real."

Let's clear the way and submit to the Holy Spirit so that God can do His work!

Time to dig deep into God's Word, get on our knees, and allow the Holy Spirit to take this message deeper into our hearts!

Chapter 3

The Call to Holiness

God's Ideal and Our Reality

*For He made Him who knew no sin to be sin for us,
that we might become the righteousness of God in Him.*
—2 Corinthians 5:21

I t's not unusual for weddings to run a little late getting started, but this was getting ridiculous. The wedding was supposed to start forty-five minutes ago, and Jeff, the groom, still hadn't shown up. What was taking him so long? Had he changed his mind?

Janice tried to be patient, but as the waiting guests began whispering among themselves, even she was getting a bit worried.

Jeff, on the other hand, had been doing his best to prepare for their big day. That morning he had gotten up extra early to drive two hours to the cabin he had reserved for the first few days of their honeymoon. He wanted every romantic detail to be just right. After he placed two-dozen red roses in the cabin and assembled wood in the fireplace so it would be ready to light when they arrived, he left to return for the wedding.

He still had plenty of time, but then unexpectedly, his tire went flat. Since cell phones had not been invented, he couldn't call his bride

35

to tell her what was happening, nor could he call for a repair truck. So Jeff changed the flat tire himself.

After changing the tire, Jeff drove to meet his cousin Brent, who helped him hide his getaway car so it would not be sabotaged. Then they left in Brent's car to get ready. But then Brent's car had a flat tire. After changing this flat tire, they arrived at Jeff's sister's home for showers. Now the time was running out!

They quickly took showers only to discover that there was not a single towel in the entire house, as all the towels had been dropped off at the laundromat. So in desperation, Jeff and his cousin Brent dried themselves with the living room curtains.

As if they hadn't had enough mishaps for one day, on the way to the church, Brent's car had a second flat tire. Once again, they worked to change and repair the flat tire. Now they were dreadfully late. With no place to wash their black, grease-stained hands, Jeff and Brent drove on to the church. However, when they arrived at the church, Jeff's soon-to-be mother-in-law grabbed him furiously. "What has been keeping you so long?" she hissed. Dragging him toward the dressing room, he told her, "Wait! I have to wash my hands!" Unfortunately, there was no soap in the bathroom, and there wasn't time to find any.

And so, almost an hour late, a breathless Jeff, dressed in a white tuxedo with still-grease-stained hands, strolled into the church sanctuary to marry his lovely bride. You and I may be laughing about this unbelievable yet very true story, but can you imagine what all the guests must have been thinking that day?

On your wedding day, you obviously want to be on time and look your best! You also want to smell your best. And you certainly want to act your best.

If this is how we are for our wedding day, why are we less concerned with preparing to meet our heavenly Groom, who is pure and spotless? The Bible tells us, "When he shall appear, we shall be like him; for we shall see him as he is. And every man that hath this hope in him purifieth himself, even as he is pure" (1 John 3:2, 3, KJV).

While my friend Janice did marry Jeff that day, even with his greasy hands, the reality is that we aren't going to heaven with the grease and stains of sin upon our hands or heart.

Charles Spurgeon once wrote, "Dost thou think to go [to heaven] with thine unholiness? God smote an angel down from heaven for sin, and will he let man in with sin in his right hand? God would sooner extinguish heaven than see sin despoil it."[1]

Now, before you close this book in despair, take courage. While we are stained with sin, Jesus has provided a way! He's given us His perfect, spotless wedding garment to wear, which gives us the right to enter heaven (Matthew 22:11). We are told, "At an infinite cost to heaven, provision has been made for all . . . [but] the wedding garment must be put on in this life. In this life, we are to be clothed with the righteousness of Christ."[2]

Think about it! Just as the groom longs to see his beautiful bride, "so the Lord Jesus anticipates the day when we will appear before Him, free from all defilement, clothed in His righteousness, to be His holy bride forever. And as an engaged woman eagerly, lovingly prepares for her wedding, desirous to be her most beautiful for her groom, so the thought of being wedded to our Holy Groom should motivate us to spend our lives here on earth in pursuit of holiness that we know is our ultimate end and His greatest desire for His bride."[3]

What is true holiness?

Let's take a few minutes to look deeper into the theme of holiness. Contrary to public opinion, holiness is not just for a few spiritual giants or pious Christians that do nothing but read their Bibles all day. It's for you and me, and all who are preparing for heaven! The Bible tells us, "Be holy, for I am holy" (1 Peter 1:16).

But what does true holiness look like? you might be wondering. Here's the simple answer. It looks like Jesus!

Since we don't look like Jesus, what are we to do? We are to put on the wedding garment He offers, and keep it on at all times. In practical terms, this means we surrender our hearts to Jesus each day, and ask that His righteousness cover our life. Then we ask that He abide in us and live in us through the Holy Spirit. The Holy Spirit was given to lead us in a deep, abiding, fruitful experience (Ephesians 2:22). As we stay under the covering of Jesus' robe of righteousness, with hearts fully submitted to His will, we will begin to look and act more and more like Jesus.

While I cannot begin to lay an adequate foundation for the subject of holiness in just a few brief paragraphs, remember that holiness is the essence of God's nature and character. Sin cannot exist in the presence of God. That's why we cannot stand in the presence of a holy God unless covered by the righteousness of Jesus. God is completely good, with no evil. He is just. He is pure! He is also love! In fact, His love and holiness are inseparable, and we can be thankful for that. As one author writes, "Without God's holiness, His love would be in danger of sentimentalism; without His love, God's holiness would be stern and unapproachable. Both attributes, His love and His holiness, are foundational to His nature."[4]

However, if holiness is foundational to God's character and intertwined with His nature of love, why does His call to holiness in our own lives bring such trepidation to our hearts? Does some of our fear come from our lack of understanding?

In *Christ Object Lessons*, we read, "True holiness is wholeness in the service of God. This is the condition of true Christian living. Christ asks for an unreserved consecration, for undivided service. He demands the heart, the mind, the soul, the strength. Self is not to be cherished. He who lives to himself is not a Christian."[5]

You see, it is not our actions that God is most concerned about, but our heart, our attitudes, and our motives. He knows that if He has our heart and if our motives are pure (sanctified through the power of the Holy Spirit), our actions will naturally demonstrate our love. He knows that if we allow Jesus to abide in us, we will bear holy fruit (John 15:4). If the inside of the cup is clean, the outside will be clean as well (Matthew 23:25). So rather than focusing on mere externals, our first task each day is to give Jesus our heart. We must daily behold Him through time in His Word and time in prayer. As we do this, His character will become ours. This is the beautiful process of sanctification that will continue until we reach heaven.

Nancy DeMoss Wolgemuth, in her book *Holiness,* describes God's call to holiness as being seen in two distinct facets—to be set apart and to be morally clean. She writes the following:

Throughout the Scripture, we find that God set apart certain things and places and people for Himself; they were consecrated for His use. They were not to be used for common, ordinary, everyday purposes; they were holy (See Ex. 16:23, Lev. 27:30, Ex. 26:33). . . .

The second facet of holiness has to do with being pure, clean, free from sin. In this sense, to be holy is to reflect the moral character of a holy God. . . .

. . . [God] wants us to understand that He is holy, and that holiness is not an option for those who belong to Him. He wants us to know that He is concerned with every detail and dimension of our lives. He wants us to understand the blessings of holiness and the consequences of unholy living.[6]

So if holiness is the call for every Christian, and if Jesus' character is to be ours, why do we not experience holiness more easily in daily life now? Author Jerry Bridges attempts to answer this question with three simple thoughts:

Our first problem is that *our attitude toward sin is more self-centered* than God-centered. We are more concerned about our own "victory" over sin than we are about the fact that our sins grieve the heart of God. . . . Our second problem is that *we have misunderstood "living by faith"* (Gal. 2:20) to mean that no effort at holiness is required on our part. . . . We must face the fact that we have a personal responsibility for our walk of holiness [in other words, we have to choose to do something, and that is give God our will. We will talk about this more in coming chapters]. . . . Our third problem is that *we do not take some sin seriously.* We have mentally categorized sins into that which is unacceptable and that which may be tolerated a bit.[7]

And it's those sins "which may be tolerated a bit" that are constantly tripping us up!

However, let's be honest, even if we were doing everything exactly right, according to the letter of the law, we all know that we still would not be holy.

The Bible tells us, "The heart is deceitful above all things, and desperately wicked; who can know it?" (Jeremiah 17:9). Ungodliness is so natural for us that we drink iniquity like water (Job 15:16). In fact, the more we read the Bible, the more clearly we see the contrast between the holiness of God and our own unholy wretchedness. That's why I take comfort when I remember, "For He made Him who knew no sin to be sin for us, that we might become the righteousness of God in Him" (2 Corinthians 5:21). That's why God's call to pursue holiness (Hebrews 12:14) is, most important, a call to pursue Jesus.

"The call to holiness is a call to follow Christ. A pursuit of holiness that is not Christ-centered will soon be reduced to moralism, pharisaical self-righteousness, and futile self-effort. Such pseudo-holiness leads to bondage, rather than liberty; its unattractive to the world and unacceptable to God. Only by fixing our eyes and our hope on Christ can we experience that authentic, warm, inviting holiness that He alone can produce in us."[8]

Are you discouraged in your journey, feeling far from where you know you should be? Do you feel overwhelmed with life and struggle to find the time with God that you need?

Ellen White writes,

Look up; it is fatal to look down. . . . A divine hand is reached toward you. The hand of the Infinite is stretched over the battlements of heaven to grasp your hand in its embrace. The mighty Helper is nigh to help the most erring, the most sinful and despairing. Look up by faith, and the light of the glory of God will shine upon you. Do not be discouraged because you see that your character is defective. *The closer you come to Jesus, the more faulty you will appear in your own eyes; for your vision will be clearer, and your imperfections will be seen in distinct contrast with his perfect character.* Be not discouraged; this is an evidence that Satan's delusions are losing their power, that the vivifying influence of the Spirit of God is arousing you, and that your indifference and ignorance are passing away.[9]

With this beautiful quote in mind, let me share another one of my favorite stories. It's the story of John Bunyan.

My righteousness is in heaven!
John Bunyan, an energetic and outspoken preacher from the mid-1600s, would probably have been forgotten long ago if he had not written one of the most famous classics of all time, *Pilgrim's Progress.* Outside of the Bible, it may be one of the most powerful portrayals of

the Christian journey ever written. What makes this classic additionally special is that Bunyan wrote it while in jail for his bold preaching and witness for Jesus.[10]

However, long before John Bunyan ever went to Bedford jail, he was in another prison, a prison of depression and discouragement because of his continual failure at living a victorious Christian life.

Although his parents had him christened[11] in a small parish in Elstow, England, not long after his birth in the year 1628, John Bunyan grew up with such disregard for God and words of cursing upon his lips that he was a terror to all that he encountered.

Yet hidden under his hard coarse exterior, there began to grow a deep hunger for God and holiness. As time went on, he began to make repeated efforts at self-reformation. As a result, bad habits were abandoned, and his swearing ceased, much to the admiration of his companions. Crimes and mischief that he had led out in previously, he just watched, and then soon left altogether.

However, still overcome by his many spiritual shortcomings, he was often filled with deep despair. He once reflected, "It is miserable to sin, and yet miserable not to sin."[12] He was sure he had committed the unpardonable sin and began to think that probably there was no more hope for him.

However, the light of truth came into his heart one day when, grasping hold of John 6:37, he read, "The one who comes to Me I will by no means cast out." This was good news! Relieved that he still had an open door to God, he began seeking God more earnestly and working even harder to reform his life.

Not long after, as he was walking through a field, the amazing thought struck him, "Thy righteousness is in heaven." For the first time, he recognized that it was not his good works that made his righteousness better nor his sins that made his righteousness worse. His righteousness and salvation rested alone in *Jesus*.

With relief, Bunyan recognized that it was Jesus' work at the cross and His being High Priest in heaven that gave him salvation. In the same way, it was Jesus living *in him* that gave him the ability to live a holy life. As the truth burst upon his heart, the chains of discouragement fell off, and the affliction of his soul, at last, fled away.[13]

After five years preaching the glorious liberty found in Jesus, John

Bunyan saw much fruit in his ministry. Then for the third time, he was thrown into prison, where he stayed for over twelve long years. But being shackled in these difficult chains only opened the door for God to be glorified more fully, for it was through this difficult prison experience that the story of *Pilgrim's Progress* went out to touch millions of lives around the world, even to this day.

As we reflect on Bunyan's life, I'm reminded of a profound statement that Charles Spurgeon once made. He said, "My faith rests not in what I am, or shall be, or feel, or know, but in what Christ is, in what He has done, and in what He is now doing for me."[14]

Power for sanctification!
We are going to make these concepts more practical in the coming chapters, but for now, let me ask, Where is your faith? Have you discovered that your righteousness is in heaven? I pray so! However, I would be doing everyone a great injustice if I ended this chapter here, for this righteousness is not merely for our justification. It's also the key to our sanctification.

As the author Paul Washer writes, "It is a long-standing gospel truth that the greatest evidence of having been justified is that we presently are being sanctified. We have assurance that God has saved us from the condemnation of sin because He is currently saving us from its power."[15]

The Holy Spirit and the grace of God are given to make us holy—not holy in theory, but holy in practice. And the same grace that brings salvation also leads us to renounce unholy living. We don't receive God's grace in part. "If we have experienced it at all, we will experience not only forgiveness of our sins but also freedom from sin's dominion."[16]

It's interesting that whenever you bring up the topic of holiness or obedience to God's law and standards, everyone shouts legalism. But legalism is a problem of incorrect motives, not incorrect standards. Obedience to God is not legalism but faithfulness. Of course, our obedience to the law does not save us. The law simply shows us our great need and leads us in the path of righteousness (Romans 7:6; Joshua 22:5). It leads us to see our need for Christ.

However, perhaps the lines are blurring in your mind between Jesus' gift of righteousness in our justification versus our journey of sanctification. Understanding these concepts is foundational to what I will share in the remainder of the book, so bear with me as I briefly explain.

In *Messages to Young People*, we are told, "The righteousness by which we are justified is imputed; the righteousness by which we are sanctified is imparted. The first is our title to heaven, the second is our fitness for heaven."[17]

"What is the difference between *imputed* and *imparted*?" you might be wondering.

Imputed means to ascribe/credit or put to another's account. This is the gift of justification. This is the spotless robe of righteousness we are given because of Jesus' perfect life and death. We do not deserve it. We did not earn it. As I've heard it said, "Even our tears of repentance need to be washed in the blood of the Lamb."

Imparted, on the other hand, means to "give" or to "infuse." Imparted righteousness is the gift Jesus gives, via the work of the Holy Spirit in the heart. This is the result of the abiding experience, and it is what makes the journey of sanctification possible.

In the book *The Desire of Ages*, we read, "Christ was treated as we deserve, that we might be treated as He deserves. He was condemned for our sins, in which He had no share, that we might be justified by His righteousness, in which we had no share. He suffered the death which was ours, that we might receive the life that was His. 'With His stripes, we are healed.' "[18]

Unfortunately, many Christians thank God for the gift of justification, and then move forward thinking that the work of sanctification is now left up to them. As a result, there are a multitude of professed Christians today "who show the working of no greater power" in their lives than that of their own flesh.[19]

Oswald Chambers, in his book *My Utmost for His Highest*, brings all this confusion into clarity. "The one marvelous secret of a holy life lies not in imitating Jesus, but in letting the perfections of Jesus manifest themselves in my mortal flesh. Sanctification is 'Christ in you.'. . . Sanctification is not drawing from Jesus the power to be holy; it is drawing from Jesus the holiness that was manifested in Him, and He manifests it in me."[20]

What courage this brings to me! While we each have to choose to surrender, no amount of striving or self-effort can make us righteous or holy. "The righteousness of God is embodied in Christ. We receive righteousness by *receiving Him*."[21] So let us seek Jesus!

Remember, God did not give just *any gift*, "He gave the choicest gift of heaven, and [as a result] the treasures of Heaven are at our command."[22]

Daring to Live by Every Word—Going Deeper!
A Faith That Works: 2 Corinthians 5:17–21

As we reflect on the message of this chapter, let's consider the following passage from the book *The Acts of the Apostles*:

Before the believer is held out the wonderful possibility of being like Christ, obedient to all the principles of the law. But of himself man is utterly unable to reach this condition. The holiness that God's word declares he must have before he can be saved is the result of the working of divine grace as he bows in submission to the discipline and restraining influences of the Spirit of truth. *Man's obedience can be made perfect only by the incense of Christ's righteousness*, which fills with divine fragrance every act of obedience. The part of the Christian is to persevere in overcoming every fault. Constantly he is to pray to the Saviour to heal the disorders of his sin-sick soul. He has not the wisdom or the strength to overcome; these belong to the Lord, and He bestows them on those who in humiliation and contrition seek Him for help.

The work of transformation from unholiness to holiness is a continuous one. Day by day God labors for man's sanctification, and man is to co-operate with Him, putting forth persevering efforts in the cultivation of right habits. He is to add grace to grace; and as he thus works on the plan of addition, God works for him on the plan of multiplication. Our Saviour is always ready to hear and answer the prayer of the contrite heart, and grace and peace are multiplied to His faithful ones. Gladly He grants them the blessings they need in their struggle against the evils that beset them.[23]

Time to open your Bible once again as you consider the following questions:

- Habakkuk 1:13; Isaiah 6:1–5; Isaiah 40:25; James 1:13; 1 John 1:5—What do these passages teach us about the holiness of God?
- Romans 7:12; 1 Timothy 1:8–11—What do these passages teach us about the law and the purpose of the law?
- Psalm 15; Ephesians 2:19–22; 2 Timothy 2:21—What do these passages teach us about God's dwelling place?
- 1 Samuel 13:13, 14; Psalm 51:4; Ezekiel 39:7; Romans 6:14; Revelation 22:11—What do these passages teach us about our call to holiness?
- Matthew 23:25—What is the significance of this passage for our lives today?
- 1 Chronicles 16—How can we worship God with thanksgiving for His great gift?
- Sing or reflect on the song, "Holy, Holy, Holy," hymn no. 73.

To take this message even deeper, I invite you to prayerfully read "What You Are in Christ!" found in Appendix 2 in the back of the book. While Satan constantly tries to discourage us with our short comings and sins, let's not forget that we are Heaven's beautiful, glorious bride! That means it's time to put our wedding garments on!

Time to dig deep into God's Word, get on our knees, and allow the Holy Spirit to take this message deeper into our hearts!

Chapter 4

Dying to Self in a Selfie Generation

Where All Battles Begin

> *"If anyone desires to come after Me, let him deny himself,*
> *and take up his cross daily, and follow Me."*
> —Luke 9:23

Y ou should go be a student missionary," the campus pastor told Richard one day.

Richard was busy with college life, and being a student missionary was really not what he had in mind. *Why would I leave my friends and go away to some strange place for a whole year?* he thought to himself.

"There's a need for a chaplain in the Bella Vista Hospital in Mayaguez, Puerto Rico," the pastor continued. "Didn't you spend some of your childhood there? It would be like going home."

It was true. Richard's father had been the hospital administrator at Bella Vista back when Richard was in elementary school. Richard had a lot of great memories from those days in Puerto Rico. "Perhaps, I should go back. And it would be a great opportunity to go snorkeling and scuba diving!"

Three months later, for all the wrong reasons, Richard found himself on a plane headed to Puerto Rico as a student missionary.

The first day at his new job, Richard was greeted warmly by Chaplain Fred Hernandez. "This is the perfect place to start your career in chaplaincy," he said, his face beaming.

In the first room they visited, they were met by a happy family surrounding the crib of a newborn baby. Everyone was all smiles. They prayed, shook hands, and then left.

This is going to be easy, Richard thought to himself.

As they were heading to the next room, Chaplain Hernandez suddenly remembered an appointment he had in twenty minutes. "I feel bad leaving you on our first day, Richard, but you will do fine." And with that, he was gone.

Now alone, Richard wasn't sure what to do. Opening the door to the next room, he found a young unwed mother who was giving her baby up for adoption. Richard quickly prayed in English and then rushed out of the room as if the young woman might be contagious.

Downstairs, Richard started looking for "easier patients" to approach. However, the next woman he talked to asked him boldly if he could pray in Spanish. "No," he responded, embarrassed that he had been caught pretending to be what he was not. "Sit down and let me teach you to pray in Spanish," she told him.

In the weeks that followed, as he followed Chaplain Hernandez around the hospital, Richard's nervousness began to fade as his Spanish slowly improved. Gradually, he began to gain confidence and feel more like a chaplain.

One day, Richard was finishing up hospital rounds alone when the call came to visit Mrs. Rodriguez. Grandma Rodriguez, as she liked to be called, had been battling cancer, and it looked as though the cancer was winning. It was likely that she would pass away any day. She and Richard had talked some and become friends, and he was sad to see her go. But since she was the last patient visit for the day, his mind was already on other things, things such as eating supper and going for a dive. He was eager to be off duty, and already his scuba gear was packed and ready.

Richard grabbed his Bible and rushed upstairs for a quick visit with Grandma Rodriguez. However, as he stepped into her room, he froze as eight pairs of eyes searched his face. "What will you say that will make it easier for us to let her go?" they seemed to be asking. It was Grandma Rodriguez's family gathered around for her final moments.

With shame, Richard realized he had nothing to give. While he was a student chaplain in training to be a pastor, and he knew enough about God to get by, he knew it wasn't enough, for he had been living a life of spiritual pretense. Right then, they needed more than memorized words or rote Scripture verses. They needed to feel God's embrace, and Richard's heart was empty.

In shame, Richard fell to his knees beside the bed as he prayed, "God forgive me. I have nothing to give. I am empty. Help me!"

Then he got up and quickly left the room. Suddenly, supper and scuba diving were not important anymore. He was humiliated, and his pride was broken. He knew he had let the Rodriguez family down, he had let the hospital down, and most important, he had let God down.

A few hours later, after many tears and much confessing of his sins to God, Richard returned to the hospital with his head hanging low. He knew it was all over, and he was probably going to be handed a return ticket home to the states.

When he arrived at the hospital, just as he feared, the head doctor approached him. "Richard! What did you say to the Rodriguez family?" the doctor asked earnestly.

With tears, Richard broke down and told the doctor everything, begging forgiveness. At that moment, the Rodriguez family came down the steps, stopping to hug Richard as they went by. After they were gone, the doctor quizzed him again. "Did you pray in English or Spanish?"

"Just English," Richard replied sheepishly.

"That's not what they said," the doctor responded with surprise. "They praised God for the wonderful, compassionate prayer that you prayed. They told me your words were perfect and just what they needed to hear to let Grandma go to her rest. They said you prayed in perfect Spanish. That's why I wanted to ask what you said!"

As the doctor walked away, young Richard Duerksen sat down, stunned as he thanked God for sending him as a student missionary to Puerto Rico.[1]

Our *selfie*-focused generation!

God is so patient and tender with us. While Richard did not realize the danger of living a life of spiritual pretense, God had a beautiful way of waking him up to his true need and then showing him that although his motives had been selfish and self-centered, he still could be used. As a result, Richard's life was forever changed.

But what will it take before we wake up to our true need?

More than a hundred years ago, Ellen White wrote to the church, "The time demands greater efficiency and deeper consecration. O, I am so full of this subject that I cry to God, 'Raise up and send forth messengers in whose hearts *self-idolatry, which lies at the foundation of all sin,* has been crucified.' "[2]

I think our church pioneers would probably roll over in their graves if they saw the society of today. We have become a completely self-focused generation, a culture built upon self-preservation, self-actualization, and self-glorification. This "selfie-focused" mentality is killing us—quite literally.

Gregory Jackson, author of the book *Surrender: The Secret to Perfect Peace and Happiness*[3] writes, "Today we hear much talk about self-actualization or the development of self to the point that self has been exalted to the position of a god. This so-called New Age thinking has not only dominated secular thought, but also it has made its way into the religious world. The concept of 'sin' has become outdated and outmoded. To this 'enlightened' way of thinking, there is no sin, only what's right or wrong for an individual. God's law is no longer the standard for righteousness . . . self [has become] the ultimate authority."[4]

What a dangerous way to live! There is never safety in looking to self to determine truth! Our only safety is in looking to Jesus and His unchanging Word (Malachi 3:6; Psalm 119:89; Isaiah 8:20).

Unfortunately, many in God's church are dozing in a state of Laodicean lethargy, while the king of all liars, and the leader in self-idolatry, is actually taking over our world by storm. Satan knows the seriousness of this battle over self. But do we?

In *Steps to Christ,* we are told, "The warfare against self is the greatest battle that was ever fought. The yielding of self, surrendering all to the will of God, requires a struggle; but the soul must submit to God before it can be renewed in holiness."[5]

The call to take up our cross

Brad was a good kid, and he'd been raised in a good Adventist home.

But he hadn't totally surrendered to God. In fact, he wasn't sure that he even wanted to surrender. He was already going to church and doing the right things, for the most part. But he was afraid that if he surrendered, God might ask him to be a missionary in some dark jungle, and he might never get to marry. Life would be boring and dry.

But God kept working on Brad. Because of his parents' prayers and that of many others, slowly Brad's heart softened. During his junior year at Pacific Union College, he was convicted to read *The Great Controversy*. During his reading, he decided to give his life completely to Jesus.

After this, God began addressing different areas in Brad's life, one of which was a specific unhealthy activity that he would often do with his friends on weekends. Although he knew it wasn't best, he reasoned that after studying hard all week, he deserved the break. And going along with what his friends wanted to do was much better than spending Saturday evenings alone in his dorm room. But Brad's conscience bothered him, and he realized that God was calling him to start making better choices.

Although it wasn't easy, Brad finally made the firm decision that he was going to honor God, even if that meant the rest of his life was boring, and even if that meant every Saturday evening would be spent alone. His friends didn't understand, but he stuck to his resolve.

That first Saturday night, after his friends had gone to have their fun, Brad told God, "Okay, God, I have done what You wanted me to do. Now, here I am alone with nothing to do. No social life!" As he thought about his sad state of affairs, suddenly the phone rang. It was another friend inviting him to an evening get-together. Rather than being bored, Brad ended up having a wonderful evening, and he wondered why he had been so worried about surrendering to God.

As providence would have it, not long after, he also met a beautiful, godly woman named Michelle, who would eventually become his wife. Michelle would never have been interested in the old Brad, but God knew and was preparing Brad's heart. Today, Brad and Michelle are happily married with three children, and Brad enjoys serving in his local church. He is so glad that he made the decision all those years ago to say yes to God.

Just like Brad, we often struggle with the concept of surrender and taking up our cross as we picture people who carry crosses as being sad and heavy burdened and living dry, boring, uninteresting lives. We are also afraid of what this type of surrender might mean.

First, we are afraid that if we die to self and truly surrender to God's will, we are going to miss out on a better and happier life. Second, we are afraid that if we take up our cross, we will lose complete control of our lives, and we could even end up being very humiliated in the process. And third, we are afraid that whatever God asks us to do will actually limit our personal growth and glory.[6] This is the same fear that Eve gave ear to.

However, contrary to popular thinking, the sweet reality is that when we take up our cross, it frees God's hands to remove those roadblocks in our life that are hindering us in our heavenward journey.

In the book *The Ministry of Healing*, we read, "We are never called upon to make a real sacrifice for God. Many things He asks us to yield to Him, but in doing this, we are but giving up that which hinders us in the heavenward way. Even when called upon to surrender those things which in themselves are good, we may be sure that God is thus working out for us some higher good."[7]

Unfortunately, we often approach surrender from a selfish point of view. We give to God because we want the spiritual reward here and now. However, what God wants most of all is us. The call to die to self and take up the cross is not just a call to sacrifice *something*—although many things will be sacrificed. The call to take up the cross is most importantly a call to sacrifice someone, and that someone is *you*. He wants our heart, He wants our body, He wants our mind, and our will, so that He can give us eternal rewards.

The sweet reality that Brad discovered is that when we choose to give ourselves to Jesus and take up His cross, something amazing happens. Rather than the cross becoming a burden, we discover that "as we lift this cross . . . [the cross actually] lifts us."[8]

"Come to Me, all you who labor and are heavy laden, and I will give you rest," Jesus pleads with us. "Take My yoke upon you and learn from Me, for I am gentle and lowly in heart, and you will find rest for your souls. For My yoke is easy and My burden is light" (Matthew 11:28–30).[9]

Perhaps you are struggling with a secret sin or spiritual stronghold in your life that you can't seem to get the victory over. As one author writes, "The key isn't how committed you are to the battle—it's how surrendered you are to God."[10]

Let us remember that for the believer, waving the white flag of "surrender" does not mean "I'm a loser in this battle!" It means "I've found victory at last, in Jesus!"[11] It means "Welcome to the Promised Land of spiritual plenty!" It means "Help yourself to the fountain that never runs dry!"

"Are we ready to sit down and count the cost, and conclude that heaven is worth the sacrifice of dying to self? . . . We cannot retain self and yet be filled with the fullness of God. We must be emptied of self. If heaven is gained by us at last."[12]

Paul wrote, "Yet indeed I also count all things loss for the excellence of the knowledge of Christ Jesus my Lord, for whom I have suffered the loss of all things, and count them as rubbish, that I may gain Christ" (Philippians 3:8).

Daring to Live by Every Word—Going Deeper!
Where All Battles Begin: Luke 9:23, 24

Ellen White writes, "The Christian's life is not a modification or improvement of the old, but a transformation of nature. There is a death to self and sin, and a new life altogether. This change can be brought about only by the effectual working of the Holy Spirit."[13]

As you reflect on the message of this chapter, ask yourself the following questions:

- How have I been catering to the "selfie" mentality of living?
- What ways might *self* be holding back my complete devotion to Jesus?
- What fears are keeping me from trusting God's complete goodness?
- What lies of the enemy have I swallowed and made my own?
- Do I really want Jesus, or is it primarily His blessings I seek?

Now open your Bible as you consider the following "going deeper" Bible study questions. Take your time and pray as you study!

- Luke 9:23, 24—What does "taking up my cross" look like practically here and now?
- Romans 7:18–25—Why is the battle against self so difficult?
- 2 Corinthians 10:3–5—Where is true victory won?
- 1 Corinthians 10:12–14—What warnings and what promises did God give in these texts?
- John 6:37, 38; John 14:10—What model of living did Jesus leave for us?
- Genesis 22:1–18; Deuteronomy 30:20—How can we worship God through our surrender?
- Sing or reflect on the song, "All to Jesus I Surrender," hymn no. 309.

I love the following thought from Inspiration. It brings everything into clear focus!

"When the soul surrenders itself to Christ, a new power takes possession of the new heart. A change is wrought which man can never accomplish for himself. It is a supernatural work, bringing a supernatural element into human nature. The soul that is yielded to Christ becomes His own fortress, which He holds in a revolted world, and He intends that no authority shall be known in it but His own. A soul thus kept in possession by the heavenly agencies is impregnable to the assaults of Satan."[14]

As we know, God will not live in a divided heart or rule from a divided throne. Every rival must be dethroned! The Bible says, "He who is not with Me is against Me" (Matthew 12:30). Let's surrender our selfie mentality to Jesus today!

Time to dig deep into God's Word, get on our knees, and allow the Holy Spirit to take this message deeper into our hearts!

Chapter 5

Willing to Be Made Willing

The First Steps to Spiritual Victory

> *But as many as received him, to them gave he power to become the sons of God, even to them that believe on his name.*
> —John 1:12, KJV

Millie was ninety-two years old but still very active. She had been a leader in the church for more than seventy years, and she controlled everything that went on in the church. When committees met together, if Millie voted one way, then everyone would vote the same. If she came up with some new plan, then everyone would go along with the plan. Everyone knew that it was futile to go against her. After all, she had money—lots of it. And she knew how to use it.

When my friend Pastor Pavel Goia moved into the area and became Millie's new pastor, Millie wasted no time in letting him know who was in charge. The first time she met Pavel, she stuck her finger in his face. "You do as I say, and everything will be okay. If you don't do as I say, things will not go well. The previous pastors I have moved, and I can move you too!"

Pavel had learned from his days living in Communist Romania that we serve a big God, and because of that, there's no reason ever to be afraid of anyone. He unflinchingly stood his ground. "You cannot move me unless God moves me, and if He moves me, that will be fine. If not, He's going to move you."

Millie walked away fuming, and for the next three months, made life a living hell for Pavel. Constantly, she called the conference, the union, even the division offices complaining about him. She twisted his words from his sermons; she criticized and maligned his character as she spread lies and rumors, trying to get the members to unite against him.

As he faced the difficult situation, Pavel wasn't sure what to do, but he remembered a specific quote from the book *Thoughts From the Mount of Blessing* that had touched him.

The victory is not won without much earnest prayer, without the humbling of self at every step. Our will is not to be forced into co-operation with divine agencies, but it must be voluntarily submitted. Were it possible to force upon you with a hundredfold greater intensity the influence of the Spirit of God, it would not make you a Christian, a fit subject for heaven. The stronghold of Satan would not be broken. The will must be placed on the side of God's will. You are not able, of yourself, to bring your purposes and desires and inclinations into submission to the will of God; but if you are "willing to be made willing," God will accomplish the work for you.[1]

Recognizing that prayer was the only solution, to change Millie's heart, Pavel and his wife, Dana, began earnestly to fast and pray.

After three months, the church members started secretly knocking on Pavel's door. "We are on your side, Pastor Goia!" they told him. "We just want you to know."

"There are no sides in God's church," Pavel responded firmly. "Sides come from Satan; unity comes from God. Let's sacrifice self and focus on the ministry. We must put God's church above ourselves. He's in control, and the victory must be won in prayer."

However, even while Pavel spoke these positive words of encouragement to his church members, in his heart, he was still struggling to sacrifice self. After all, Millie was making his life absolutely miserable.

Not knowing what else to do, he and Dana kept praying.

Not long after, word came that Millie had fallen on the ice and broken her hip as well as one of her arms. She had been taken to the hospital. After hearing the news, Dana told her husband immediately, "You need to go to the hospital to visit her!"

"I'm not going to go visit her! I don't like her. She's made my life miserable," Pavel argued.

But Dana persisted. "You are a pastor. You are supposed to love those that hate you, not those that love you. Now, go visit her."

Finally, Pavel agreed, although his heart wasn't in it. "When you go, take some flowers!" Dana encouraged.

Pavel looked at his wife incredulously. "Why should I buy her flowers? She's not worth that!"

"If she's worth the blood of Jesus, she's worth buying flowers for," Dana replied. Reluctantly, Pavel went to the market and found the cheapest flowers he could find, and then he went to the hospital.

Millie scowled when she saw him. She took the flowers and then hit him over the head with them, breaking their stems. "Get out of here! I hate you!" she yelled.

Well, I don't like you either, Pavel thought to himself as he obediently turned and left.

Upon arriving home, Dana asked him how things had gone. "She took the flowers and hit me over the head with them," Pavel told her.

"Did you pray with her for her salvation?" Dana queried.

"No. She told me to go!" Pavel replied with irritation.

"Then you need to go back! God brought you here for her. Forget about everyone else. Unless you work with her and love her enough to help her find salvation, you are not a true pastor."

The words stung, but Pavel knew that what his wife said was true. If he couldn't love Millie, how could he say that he loved God? After spending more time praying, Pavel mustered up his courage and went back to the hospital, this time with a fresh batch of cookies that Dana had made. "Don't come back until you save her!" his wife told him.

Back at the hospital, Millie was shocked to see Pavel again. "What are you doing back here? I told you to get out!"

"Well, I admit that I don't want to be here. But my wife pushed me to come back," Pavel told her. "Honestly, I don't like you, and I have a hard time praying for you. But I think we both need to repent. When there is a conflict, that means repentance is needed because I need to love you, and you need to love me. So let me pray for you."

"Well, you are the first pastor that has come back!" Millie told him. "But it's no use praying for me. The Holy Spirit left me long ago."

"Why do you say that He has left you?" Pavel asked.

"Because I sinned 72 years ago, a big sin, and I've prayed and prayed for forgiveness, and He never gave it to me," Millie said miserably.

"What you have is a faith problem, not a sin problem," Pavel told her. Pavel then proceeded to help Millie see how if she confessed her sin to Jesus, He forgives. She simply needed to believe His Word.

After a few minutes, Millie agreed for Pavel to pray, and she slowly repeated his prayer. At the end of the prayer, she smiled as tears came down her cheeks. "Can I give you a hug?" she said. "You are my first real pastor."

A few days later, Millie died, but she died in peace. And as for Pavel, what joy he experienced surrendering to God's plan.[2]

We have a choice!

Most Christians, if you ask them, will admit that they want to surrender self and live for Jesus, but they don't know how. Their flesh is too strong, their hate too deep, their cravings for sinful pleasure too overpowering. And so they settle down for a life of spiritual mediocrity, accepting that holy living is not possible.

The problem, however, is usually because of one of two errors in their thinking. First, they have sought to live a holy life in their own strength and willpower—and they've failed miserably. Or they have sought to live a holy life simply by faith.

Writing of the second thinking error, Jerry Bridges states, "After experiencing a great deal of failure with our sinful nature, we are told that we have been trying to live the Christian life in the energy of the flesh." We need to "stop trying and start trusting," or to "let go and let God." We are told that if we "just turn our sin problem over to Christ and rest in His finished work on Calvary, He will then live His life in us, and we will experience a life of victory over sin."[3]

While initially this new perspective is a breath of fresh air to the weary soul, after a while, if we are honest with ourselves, we will find that we are still experiencing defeat. We still struggle with pride, impatience, a judgmental spirit, hatred, materialism, gluttony, and more. So what is the problem? What are we missing?

In Romans 6:12, we find our answer. The Bible tells us, "Therefore do not let sin reign in your mortal body, that you should obey it in its lusts." In this verse, we see that we have something specific to do—we are not to let sin rule.

Now you may be wondering, how does this play out in daily practical life? We will talk about that in the coming chapters. But first, we have to understand some foundational theology.

You see, while God has made ample provision for us to live a holy life, He's given us distinct responsibilities. Holiness is not a gift we receive, like justification, but something that we have to work at.

Let's look at Romans 6 more closely. Notice the connecting word in verse 12, "Therefore." In other words, we are not to let sin rule because certain previously stated facts are true.

Romans 6:1–11 gives us these facts. We have died to sin as a result of our union with Jesus. Because Jesus died to sin, we have died to sin also. Dying to sin is not something we do, but what Jesus has already done, "the value of which accrues to all who are united with Him."[4] This does not mean that we have been removed from sin's ability to touch us. It means we have been removed from sin's dominion and power. It is a fact, a fact that was settled at the cross. While we were once slaves to the prince of darkness and sin (Acts 26:18), now we have become servants of righteousness (Romans 6:17, 18). Jesus has set us free. But whether we live in that freedom is still our choice!

As Bridges writes so beautifully, "The responsibility for resisting is ours. God does not do that for us. To confuse the potential for resisting (which God provided) with the *responsibility* for resisting (which is ours) is to court disaster in our pursuit of holiness."[5]

Of course, the apostle Paul knew what it meant to struggle. He wrote, "For I delight in the law of God according to the inward man. But I see another law in my members, warring against the law of my mind, and bringing me into captivity to the law of sin which is in my members. O wretched man that I am! Who will deliver me from this body of death? I thank God—through Jesus Christ our Lord!" (Romans 7:22–25).

As we consider the battle Paul was having here, we must understand that indwelling sin remains, even though it has been dethroned. It's like a country where two sides are fighting a battle. With the help of an outside force, eventually, one side wins the war and assumes control of the government. However, the other side does not stop fighting but now resorts to guerrilla warfare. So the battle continues, even though the losing side has been dethroned.

If we are to wage a successful war against the enemy within, we must understand something of our enemy's guerrilla battle tactics.

First, the Bible tells us that the seat of indwelling sin is the heart. "For from within, out of the heart of men, proceed evil thoughts, adulteries, fornications, murders, thefts, covetousness, wickedness, deceit, lewdness, an evil eye, blasphemy, pride, foolishness. All these evil things come from within and defile a man" (Mark 7:21–23; see also Genesis 6:5).

Because of this, we need to ask God daily to search and purify our heart (Psalm 139:23, 24; Isaiah 59:1, 2). As we ask God to put His spotlight on our heart, we must expose ourselves to the searching of His Word, for it is the double-edged sword of God's Word that brings our sin to light (Hebrews 4:12). It is also His Word that leads us to our only source of hope: Jesus!

Second, we need to recognize that indwelling sin gains control largely through the manipulation of our desires. The next time you face temptation, notice the battle between your reasoning and your desires. We tend to act according to our feelings and desires. If we are honest, like Pavel shared in his testimony, we seldom feel like doing what we should do. That's why, through the power of the Holy Spirit, we have to take control of our bodies and make them our servants instead of our masters. Of course, not all our desires are evil, but James 1:14 tells us, "But each one is tempted when he is drawn away by his own desires and enticed."

Third, we need to recognize that indwelling sin seeks to manipulate the truth and often deceives our understanding or reasoning. That's why Satan's greatest strategy is to keep us out of God's Word and to take control of our thinking patterns.

The path downward is slow and subtle. Satan gradually leads us away from watchfulness and prayer, and then he draws us away from obedience by subtle spiritual compromises, and by leading us to question what God says in His Word. Then he gives us self-confidence in our own strength and wisdom. And then, as a capstone on it all, he teaches us how to justify our disobedience through the abuse of God's grace. "That's no big deal. God will overlook that!" And on the battle goes. However, if we are continually immersing ourselves in God's Word, we won't be deceived by Satan's lies.

Understanding the power of the will

If we are struggling with something in our hearts, a wrong attitude, an addiction, or anything else, what should we do? We should choose to serve God and give Him our will. The Bible says, "But as many as received him, to them gave he power to become the sons of God, even to them that believe on his name" (John 1:12, KJV).

I love the following passage from the book *Steps to Christ*. It has forever changed my view of the importance of a submitted will.

Many are inquiring, "*How* am I to make the surrender of myself to God?" You desire to give yourself to Him, but you are weak in moral power, in slavery to doubt, and controlled by the habits of your life of sin. Your promises and resolutions are like ropes of sand. You cannot control your thoughts, your impulses, your affections. The knowledge of your broken promises and forfeited pledges weakens your confidence in your own sincerity, and causes you to feel that God cannot accept you; but you need not despair. What you need to understand is the true force of the will. This is the governing power in the nature of man, the power of decision, or of choice. Everything depends on the right action of the will. The power of choice God has given to men; it is theirs to exercise. You cannot change your heart, you cannot of yourself give to God its affections; but you can choose to serve Him. You can give Him your will; He will then work in you to will and to do according to His good pleasure. Thus your whole nature will be brought under the control of the Spirit of Christ; your affections will be centered upon Him, your thoughts will be in harmony with Him.

Desires for goodness and holiness are right as far as they go; but if you stop here, they will avail nothing. Many will be lost while hoping and desiring to be Christians. They do not come to the point of yielding the will to God. They do not now choose to be Christians.

Through the right exercise of the will, an entire change may be made in your life. By yielding up your will to Christ, you ally yourself with the power that is above all principalities and powers. You will have strength from above to hold you steadfast, and thus through constant surrender to God you will be enabled to live the new life, even the life of faith.[6]

Everything, in essence, depends on the right exercise of the will, for our "will is the spring of all [our] actions."[7] So first, we choose to serve God. Next, we choose to give Him our will (and this is a daily choice and sometimes a moment-by-moment choice as situations arise). Then we choose to act on the belief that He has heard our prayer, and His power is ours for the taking, even before we *feel* the strength or answer to our prayer.

However, even as we give God our will, let us remember that it is not the "right exercise of our will" that gives us victory or transforms us. In *Christ Object Lessons,* we read one more significant statement:

In all who will submit themselves to the Holy Spirit a new principle of life is to be implanted; the lost image of God is to be restored in humanity. But man cannot transform himself by the exercise of his will. He possesses no power by which this change can be effected. The leaven—something wholly from without—must be put into the meal before the desired change can be wrought in it. So the grace of God must be received by the sinner before he can be fitted for the kingdom of glory. All the culture and education which the world can give, will fail of making a degraded child of sin a child of heaven. The renewing energy must come from God. The change can be made only by the Holy Spirit. All who would be saved, high or low, rich or poor, must submit to the working of this power.[8]

Have you ever been in the situation where the Holy Spirit was convicting you that you needed to let go of some sin or compromise that was coming between you and God, but when you got on your knees to pray, you realized you just couldn't let go? That's when we need to pray *to be made willing to be made willing.*

Surrendering our will does not come naturally or without a battle. But each time we choose to surrender, the next surrender is easier to make.

Be still my soul

Many of us probably have a favorite life song that is particularly meaningful as it represents something God has done or is doing in our lives. God gave me just such a song almost twenty years ago when I was walking through a very dark valley. The song was "Be Still My Soul," and ever since, this has been one of my favorite songs.

I love the lyrics to "Be Still My Soul," for they speak about a God who is on our side, a God who is still in charge of the storms, and a God who leads us through thorny ways to bring us to a joyful end. Whenever I'm feeling discouraged, I remind myself of this song, and immediately hope comes back to my heart.

However, several years ago, I found myself walking through another dark valley. This valley was not just a few down days. It was a few down weeks. At the time, I was already working with the General Conference Prayer Ministries and had a packed speaking itinerary. From all appearances, my life and ministry were going well. But a deep pain was silently wearing away the courage of my heart. "Lord, are You still by my side?" I cried day after day. As time went on, it seemed the darkness of discouragement only thickened.

One day, feeling sorry for myself as well as very much alone, I decided to go shopping. I treated myself out, splurged on some unhealthy food, and wasted money that I didn't have on an expensive dress that I didn't need. Basically, I took a trip to pity-party city, but the sweet indulgences only temporarily distracted me from the pain, and afterward, I felt even worse.

The next morning (which happened to be a Sabbath), I woke up early as usual to have my devotions. But I found that I could not pray. I tried, but my mind was blank. Finally, I cried out, "Dear Jesus, why can't I pray?" It was then that He, through the Holy Spirit, spoke softly to my heart. "You have not surrendered, Melody. Here you are having a pity party because you think that I've forgotten you. So you wasted money on this and that . . . and now you've taken back things you once surrendered to me." Immediately, I began to argue with the Holy Spirit, justifying my actions. But then, He was silent.

At that moment, I realized that I could continue to resist and fight stubbornly, or I could surrender. Ultimately, I knew I would have no peace until I surrendered.

Finally, a reluctant prayer of surrender came to my lips. It went like this: "Dear Jesus, I don't want to do what You are asking me to do, but I choose to give You my will, and I'm asking that You change my heart. Make me willing to be made willing." It was as simple as that.

Then I got up from my knees and took my new expensive dress that I had just purchased the day before, off the hanger in my closet, and put it in a bag, determined that I would return it after Sabbath. Next, I took a piece of paper, and I wrote down different things that I had taken control of in my life—things that rightfully belonged to God. Then I handed the paper to God in my prayer. "Here, God, I give these things back to You!" I told Him.

As I took these simple active steps of surrender, tears began coursing down my cheeks, but peace once again filled my mind, and the prayers began to flow effortlessly from my heart and lips. For two hours, I worshiped and prayed, but I hardly noticed the passing of time. It was beautiful.

After finishing my devotions, my heart was light. As I turned my cell phone back on, almost immediately, I got a text message from an acquaintance, Nina, I had met four months earlier. Although Nina and I had met only once, we had instantly connected at our first meeting and had decided to exchange phone numbers for keeping in touch. But we had not been in communication since, so I was surprised to be getting a text message from her so early in the morning.

"Melody, I feel a little awkward sharing this," she wrote. "But last night I had a dream about you. In my dream, the Lord came to me and asked me to pray for you." She then listed the things that God had impressed her to pray about for me, and to my amazement, they were some of the exact issues I'd been struggling over that very morning in my prayer. Then she told me that even after she had woken up, she had felt impressed to continue praying for me. So she had. She had been praying for me during the precise time I'd been on my own knees, two hours before, wrestling in prayer for spiritual victory.

I sat on my bed in amazement as I read the text message, hardly believing that God had sent Nina a message from heaven just for me.

But then came the clincher to the dream. "Melody, there was a song playing in my dream," she told me. "The song was 'Be Still My Soul.'"

Nina, who has since become a very dear friend, had no idea that morning what I was going through, nor what I'd been struggling with over the previous weeks. But God saw, and God knew. And when I finally gave Him my will, He changed my heart by giving me one of the most precious gifts that I have ever received. I still get tears in my eyes, just writing this testimony.

Yes, I admit that these kinds of miracle stories don't happen in my life every day. However, the same God who heard my desperate cry for help hears your cry today as well. And even when we don't feel His immediate presence, we can take courage because He is bending very near. "To all who are reaching out to feel the guiding hand of God, the moment of greatest discouragement is the time when divine help is nearest."[9]

The Bible tells us that He works in us "both to will and to do for His good pleasure" (Philippians 2:13). That means, if we allow Jesus freedom to work, He "will so identify Himself with our thoughts and aims, so blend our hearts and minds into conformity to His will, that when obeying Him we shall be but carrying out our own impulses. The will, refined and sanctified, will find its highest delight in doing His service."[10]

What a promise! Let's give God our will today. Let's pray to be willing to be made willing. As the martyr Jim Elliot once said, "He is no fool who gives up what he cannot keep to gain what he cannot lose."[11] How can we lose when God has already given us His all?

Daring to Live by Every Word—Going Deeper!
The First Steps to Spiritual Victory: John 1:12, 13

As we take some time to let the message of this chapter sink in, I encourage you to reflect on the following passage from *Christ Object Lessons.*

No outward observances can take the place of simple faith and entire renunciation of self. But no man can empty himself of self. We can only consent for Christ to accomplish the work. Then the language of the soul will be, Lord, take my heart; for I cannot give it. It is Thy property. Keep it pure, for I cannot keep it for Thee. Save me in spite of myself, my weak, unchristlike self. Mold me, fashion me, raise me into a pure and holy atmosphere, where the rich current of Thy love can flow through my soul.

It is not only at the beginning of the Christian life that this renunciation of self is to be made. At every advance step heavenward it is to be renewed. All our good works are dependent on a power outside of ourselves. Therefore there needs to be a continual reaching out of the heart after God, a continual, earnest, heartbreaking confession of sin and humbling of the soul before Him. Only by constant renunciation of self and dependence on Christ can we walk safely.[12]

Now it's time to open our Bible and dig a little deeper.

- John 1:12, 13, KJV—Based on this passage, who receives the power of God?
- Does the "will of our flesh" have anything to do with us receiving this power?
- Isaiah 50:4–6—In this prophecy, how did Jesus demonstrate obedience and surrender of His will?
- Matthew 26:39—How did Jesus demonstrate laying down His will at the cross?
- Romans 13:1–7—How does our relation to human authority and our relation to God's authority overlap?
- Ezekiel 36:25–27—How can we learn to obey and surrender to God joyfully?
- Romans 6:16—How can we worship God through our submitted will?
- Sing or reflect on the song, "Have Thine Own Way, Lord," hymn no. 567.

As we move forward on our knees, may our daily prayer be, *Have Your own way, Lord! Take my heart! Take my will! I'm Yours!*

Time to dig deep into God's Word, get on our knees, and allow the Holy Spirit to take this message deeper into our hearts!

Part 2

THE WORD THAT RESTORES

Chapter 6

Captivated by His Love

Discovering Our Heart's True Desire

> *You have captivated my heart with one glance of your eyes.*
> —Song of Solomon 4:9, ESV

Had Oswald Chambers been given the opportunity to choose a life motto, it probably would have been *Excelsior*—a Latin word that's often translated to mean "ever upward" or "still higher." Chambers was never content with mediocrity but was continually striving for higher goals and pursuits. Maybe that's why I find his testimony so inspiring. The passion of his soul was only for Jesus, and he wanted nothing to hinder his spiritual journey—even if that meant turning down scholarships to study at prestigious schools abroad.

However, it was not until Chambers was attending a Bible college in Dunoon, Scotland, that his personal walk with God began to thrive. There he learned that God answers prayer and that through daring faith in God's promises, his daily needs would be supplied. As his spiritual hunger grew, he learned that climbing higher is not accomplished by running but by kneeling, by surrender and not by determination.

One day, Dr. F. B. Meyer, a pastor and evangelist in England involved in ministry and inner-city mission work, came to visit Dunoon College and spoke powerfully about the gift of the Holy Spirit. Oswald Chambers determined then and there that this was what he needed. He went immediately to his room and begged God for this gift. But for four years, nothing exceptional happened, and his sense of soul depravity continued to grow.

Growing more and more desperate, Chambers continued to pray. Finally, one day during a public prayer meeting, he stood up and spoke passionately. "Either Christianity is a downright fraud, or I have not got ahold of the right end of the stick."[1] Then and there, he again asked God for the gift of the Holy Spirit, claiming Luke 11:13.

Later, Chambers wrote about this experience and what happened soon after:

> I had no vision of heaven or of angels, I had nothing. I was as dry and empty as ever, no power or realization of God, no witness of the Holy Spirit. Then I was asked to speak at a meeting and forty souls came to the front. Did I praise God? No, I was terrified and left them to the workers, and went to Mr. MacGregor (a friend) and told him what had happened and he said: "Don't you remember claiming the Holy Spirit as a gift on the word of Jesus, and He said, 'Ye shall receive power . . .' ? This is the power from on high." Then like a flash something happened inside of me, and I saw that I had been wanting power in my own hand, so to speak, that I might say—Look what I have by putting my all on the altar.[2]

Recognizing his sin, Chambers begged forgiveness from God. Not long after he wrote, "Glory be to God, the last aching abyss of the human heart is filled to overflowing with the love of God. Love is the beginning, love is the middle and love is the end. After He comes in, all you see is 'Jesus only, Jesus ever.' "[3]

Chambers was captivated by the love of God, and this changed every dimension of his life and ministry. He became highly sought after as a teacher, speaker, and writer. His most popular work, *My Utmost for His Highest*, has sold over 13 million copies since its first printing in 1927. But it was not for self that he labored but for Jesus.

Others, later reflecting on his life, wrote,

He was a man of prayer, interceding, imploring, and believing. He had rare insight into the meaning of the Scripture, and from this came pointed and practical preaching. . . .

". . . His enthusiasm knew no bounds. He could never do anything by halves. . . ."

He was passionately devoted to the Lord Jesus Christ. He walked with God and inspired all who knew him to believe that real life was to know God and Jesus Christ whom He had sent. Because he himself walked with the Highest, his students learned also to follow in that pathway. One of them declared: "He introduced us to Jesus Christ, never to himself . . . he never made it easy, never offered us an alternative."

The absorbing passion of his life was utter abandonment to the Lord Jesus and to His will.[4]

How often have we sought the Lord and the Holy Spirit, not because we want the Lord Himself, but rather because we want the power that knowing Him brings? And yet, have we discovered what it means to be truly captivated by His love?

Discovering my heart's true desire

Now it's time to share a personal, heart-to-heart confession. The reality is that I have been a hopeless and incurable romantic for as long as I can remember. It's okay if you want to roll your eyes. Yes, the truth is that I started dreaming about romance and my Prince Charming when I was only five years old. I started planning my wedding not long after. By the time I was ten, I had my life all figured out. I would finish high school, marry my childhood sweetheart (just as my parents had done), and then the two of us would go off into the sunset to serve the Lord together. We would be so happy.

Well, as it turned out, life did not go according to my little-girl plans. There was no childhood sweetheart. As the years went by, I watched all my friends marry and start families of their own as I continued to work for God *alone*. It wasn't easy. While I kept serving the Lord, deep in my heart, the haunting question was always, "Does God still have a beautiful love story for me?"

Millions around the world are asking this same question today as they look in vain for the answers. The sweet reality I finally discovered is that while God may not take away our human desires, He longs to give us much more than we can imagine. While we try to find fulfillment in possessions, relationships, and even our achievements, He wants to give us our heart's true desire—*Himself!* As one author writes, "The Almighty creates no desires deep in the human soul that He cannot Himself satisfy."[5]

I will never forget when the beauty of God's divine, heavenly romance first captured my heart. If you've read my first book, *Daring to Ask for More*, you've probably already heard some of my testimony. However, in a nutshell, let me share it again briefly here as well as a few additional details that I've not shared before.

I was raised in the church by loving parents. While there were normal challenges, for me, life was good. I didn't struggle with rebellion in my youth. My struggles were more subtle and private—and as such, everyone thought I was the model Christian. (*I thought I was too!*)

However, while I gave my life to Jesus at a young age, and I sought out ministry opportunities to serve Him, I never really experienced the full beauty or power of the gospel.

Of course, I understood that Jesus had died for my sins, but the sacrifice of Jesus at Calvary did not break my heart personally because, honestly, I didn't feel as though I was that great a sinner. Oh yes, I had my struggles (and I asked forgiveness for these), but as I looked around at the struggles my companions had, I thought I was doing pretty good *by comparison*. (As I look back, I'm ashamed of the spiritual pride that engulfed me!)

As my story goes, not long after graduating from Southern Adventist University, with an impressive resumé and multiple ministry opportunities opening up before me, suddenly my picture-perfect world fell apart. Because of a deep, heartbreaking disappointment, I was completely broken—broken spiritually, emotionally, mentally, and even physically. To be honest, I felt as if God had failed me, and as a result, I wasn't sure if I could trust Him anymore. For a time, I struggled reading my Bible and even praying.

I will spare you the details of all that happened during this dark time. I will just say that for close to two years, I fell into such deep depression that at times I didn't even want to go on living.

Thankfully, God did not give up on me. And slowly, He began to open my eyes to my true spiritual condition. All pride and self-sufficiency were stripped away, and for the first time, I truly saw my desperate need of my Savior. When I realized what He had done for me on Calvary, a work that only a supernatural God could do, and how desperately lost and filthy I was without His robe of righteousness—a gift I could never earn—and how He wanted to fill me with His Holy Spirit and make me like Him, my heart was broken in a new way. I wept and wept, as I had never cried before, as the reality of His love consumed me.

In hindsight, I recognize that God had a beautiful purpose in this painful experience, for it was through this dark valley, the death of my vision, the death of my dreams, and the death of my plans, that He became even more real in my life. Suddenly, with overwhelming clarity, I realized how much God loved me and how much He longed for me to truly be in love with Him. I also recognized for the first time that He was my heart's true desire, and I could be perfectly satisfied in His love.

When we talk about what Jesus has done on Calvary, we must keep in mind that the Cross is not just a plan that God and Jesus came up with in ages past to rescue us from the depths of sin. The wonder of the gospel that should cause us all to stand in complete awe is that we are forgiven and justified through the blood of Jesus on the cross so we can *come back to God.* God is the ultimate treasure and reward. God is the end. Forgiveness is not the end. Justification is not the end. Sanctification is not the end. Marriage is not the end. Having a good life is not the end. Our going to heaven and no longer having a sick body is not the end. All pain and suffering being forever wiped away is not the end. All of these are just a road of blessings—a road to seeing Him, knowing Him, loving Him, becoming more like Him, and being satisfied and complete in Him.[6]

As John Piper likes to say, "God is most glorified in us when we are most completely satisfied in Him."[7]

As God's love captivated my soul more and more, I longed for a deeper walk with Him. In fact, this is where my *daring to ask for more journey* really began, for it was this difficult experience that made me realize I couldn't live a normal, mediocre Christian life any longer. I wanted more—I especially wanted more of Jesus!

As the psalmist says,

> One thing I have desired of the LORD,
> That will I seek:
> That I may dwell in the house of the LORD
> All the days of my life,
> To behold the beauty of the LORD,
> And to inquire in His temple (Psalm 27:4).

Of course, I still have normal heart longings and struggles, just like everyone. And we are told, "So long as Satan reigns, we shall have self to subdue, besetting sins to overcome."[8] But each day, God keeps giving me the grace I need, and I'm learning to trust His goodness in the middle of my life story, even when I cannot see what He is doing. Although the journey hasn't been easy, I would not change my story, for it is the difficult parts that have helped shape me into the person I am today. It is these experiences that have helped me love Jesus more!

Have you truly fallen in love with God? Has love for Jesus captured *your heart*?

Inspiration tells us, "There is a peculiarly close union between the transformed soul and God. It is impossible to find words to describe this union. It is a treasure worth infinitely more to the true believer than gold and silver."[9]

This was the treasure I discovered, and it is priceless!

Daring to Live by Every Word—Going Deeper!
Captivated by His Love: Song of Solomon 4:9

As we reflect on the message of this chapter, let's ask ourselves, "How can we learn to delight in Jesus' presence and find our true fulfillment in Him? How can we worship with deeper love and greater devotion?" To help you delight in your love relationship with Jesus, I encourage you to take some time gazing into His face. Gazing is natural for young lovers, but it's not always natural for us, especially if we haven't made this a spiritual habit. But if we cultivate the discipline of gazing, our love for Jesus will grow.

Ellen White writes, "It would be well for us to spend a thoughtful hour each day in contemplation of the life of Christ."[10] If you've ever wondered how this might look practically, consider getting the book *A Thoughtful Hour: Tracing the Final Footsteps of Jesus*, by Jerry D. Thomas. However, for today, perhaps the following passages will help you gaze more deeply at the One who gave His all for you!

- Song of Solomon 4—How the Bridegroom adores His bride— contrast this with what Jesus might be looking for in us
- Isaiah 53—Jesus' life and suffering prophesied
- Luke 2; Matthew 27—Jesus' birth and crucifixion realized
- Psalm 96; Psalm 103—Jesus worshiped and praised
- Sing or reflect on the song, "My Jesus, I Love Thee," hymn no. 321.

If you'd like some additional inspiration, download "Seeing Jesus With New Eyes" from www.revivalandreformation.org. This beautiful collection of Bible verses covers some of the biblical names and characteristics of Jesus. It is awe-inspiring, and as you read, you will find yourself longing to worship Jesus more deeply.

Time to dig deep into God's Word, get on our knees, and allow the Holy Spirit to take this message deeper into our hearts!

Chapter 7

Singing the Sweeter Song

Fullness of Joy at Jesus' Feet

You will show me the path of life; in Your presence is fullness of joy; at Your right hand are pleasures forevermore.
—Psalm 16:11

While I'm not the greatest singer, I love to sing. It's a gift I inherited from my father. He sang to us kids when we were little, and he continues to sing to us today. He sings while he works, drives, or hikes— even while he rappels over dangerous mountain cliffs! He and my mom have been married almost fifty years now, and he still sings my mom love songs in the kitchen. But he doesn't sing just for the love of his family. He sings because he loves Jesus. And because of that, he can sing about God's goodness, even in the dark times of life, when pain and suffering are threatening to steal his joy. How my courage and faith has grown over the years, as I've watched my daddy sing, even in the times of pain.

In the book *Ministry of Healing*, we read, "[God] has a song to teach us, and when we have learned it amid the shadows of affliction we can sing it ever afterward."[1]

Unfortunately, many of us are struggling to sing that song of praise to

God through life's afflictions, because our hearts have been drawn away by other dangerous but alluring songs. The song of *worldly wonder*, the song of *unbelief*, the song of *doubt*, the songs of *bitterness* or *busyness*, the song of *superficial pleasures*, or the song of *self-sufficiency*. These songs don't seem deadly at first, for the enemy has covered them in a beautiful, attractive disguise, but they are dangerous because they lead us away from Jesus. As I consider the enemy's deceptive songs, which are leading so many to shipwreck of faith, I'm reminded of a story told by the ancient Greek poet Homer.

Homer wrote in his legendary work the *Odyssey* about the singing Sirens. As legend had it, these mythical mermaid-like creatures lived on an island in the western sea between Sicily and Italy, and as ships would pass, they would lure the sailors in with their sweet seductive songs, until coming too close to shore, the ships would be dashed to pieces on the rocks.

However, as the story goes, one captain named Ulysses came up with a brilliant idea. To avoid the danger, he ordered his men to fill their ears with wax so that they could not hear the Sirens' song. While the men obeyed, everyone was miserable, for they knew they were missing out on incredible music. But Captain Ulysses knew it was the only way to save the ship and his men.

However, not far behind Ulysses's ship was another ship and another captain who had an even better idea.

As this second ship neared the coastline of the dangerous Sirens, Captain Orpheus took out a beautiful instrument and began to play. Everyone on board the ship drew near spellbound by the beautiful melodious song coming from his instrument. As he played, in no time, without his crewmen even realizing what had happened, the dangerous Siren coastline had passed by out of sight. It was only then that the captain concluded the beautiful song that he had composed. As a result of his beautiful music, not a single person on board the ship had been tempted by the Sirens' song. In fact, no one had even heard it.[2]

Yes, the Sirens' music was alluringly sweet, but the all-wise and loving Captain Orpheus had played for his men a *sweeter song*, and in so doing, had saved their lives.

Learning to hear the sweeter song
"So how do we learn to hear and sing the sweeter song?" you may be asking. "How do we avoid getting swept away by the alluring music of the enemy of our souls?"

The answer is simple! We learn to hear and sing the sweeter song when we spend time at Jesus' feet. As I've heard it said, "Seeing Christ for who He is awakens such a sweet savor for God that sin completely loses its power."

You see, Jesus is singing us a sweeter song. And when we turn our eyes and ears toward heaven and listen to the Master Musician's sweeter song, we will no longer be taken captive by the deadly allurements of the world around us. We will no longer lose our spiritual focus in the afflictions of life. The temptations of our flesh will no longer overcome us.

Let me share some divine keys that, if applied to your life each day, will help you learn to hear and sing heaven's sweeter song.

Start your day at Jesus' feet and stay with Him all day! That's your only safety! You wouldn't fight a physical battle if you hadn't taken your body-guard with you, or if you hadn't eaten food to give you strength. Yet how often we try to fight our spiritual battles each day on empty spiritual stomachs and with no heavenly bodyguard around? And we wonder why God isn't working and why our ship keeps getting dashed to pieces on the rocks of sin. We must have *time* in God's Word and *time* in prayer. We must have *time* at Jesus' feet if we hope to hear the sweeter song of heaven and have victory against the alluring temptations of the enemy.

Many, even in their seasons of devotion, fail of receiving the blessing of real communion with God. They are in too great haste. With hurried steps they press through the circle of Christ's loving presence, pausing perhaps a moment within the sacred precincts, but not waiting for counsel. They have no time to remain with the divine Teacher. With their burdens they return to their work. These workers can never attain the highest success until they learn the secret of strength. They must give themselves time to think, to pray, to wait upon God for a renewal of physical, mental, and spiritual power.[3]

As you spend time with Jesus, drink deeply of the Living Water. Dig deeply in His Word, and learn what it means to really pray. (I will talk more in-depth about how to study God's Word and how to go deeper in prayer in the following chapters.)

Whatever you do, don't settle for superficial blessings. Don't *diet* spiritually. Even if you are a busy mom with children around your feet, do your best, and God will make up the difference. When we make quality time with Jesus a daily priority, He will become our greatest Treasure. And our priceless Treasure will become our source of pure joy.

Treat Jesus with reverence as the King He is: Turn off all distractions (put your cell phone in airplane mode if needed) and focus on your King. The Bible tells us, "Holy and reverend is his name" (Psalm 111:9, KJV).

True reverence for God is inspired by a sense of His infinite greatness and a realization of His presence. Ellen White writes, "In prayer we enter the audience chamber of the Most High; and we should come before Him with holy awe. The angels veil their faces in His presence. The cherubim and the bright and holy seraphim approach His throne with solemn reverence. How much more should we, finite, sinful beings, come in a reverent manner before the Lord, our Maker!"[4]

Give Jesus your heart and will each morning and again when needed throughout the day—not in a vague way, but in all the specific ways that affect your daily life, even the painful, confusing parts.

Pastor Gregory Jackson writes, "If we wait until the moment of temptation [or crisis] to give our choice to Jesus, that means He didn't have our choice before the temptation came. It's like trying to change drivers while the car is going 120 miles an hour. It's very difficult, if not impossible. But if you start with the right driver, in the beginning, the problem is solved."[5]

Remember that whoever has your heart—has you! As my friend Maria once said to me, "If God is not the Lord of your mundane, then He's not the Lord of your life, because the mundane [and the difficult] is where you live." Our seemingly small choices of obedience matter. Let us never "despise the day of small things" (Zechariah 4:10).

In *Steps to Christ*, we are told,

Consecrate yourself to God in the morning; make this your very first work. Let your prayer be, "Take me, O Lord, as wholly Thine. I lay all my plans at Thy feet. Use me today in Thy service. Abide with me, and let all my work be wrought in Thee." This is a daily matter. Each morning consecrate yourself to God for that day. Surrender all your plans to Him, to be carried out or given up as His providence shall indicate. Thus day by day you may be giving your life into the hands of God, and thus your life will be molded more and more after the life of Christ.[6]

Learn to worship God and sing praises to His name! Often it seems we come to heaven's throne room to receive—but God longs to receive our gifts of adoration and praise as well. That's why the Bible tells us, "Sing to Him, sing psalms to Him; talk of all His wondrous works!" (1 Chronicles 16:9).

It doesn't matter whether we are good singers or not and whether we are in the midst of good times or bad, when we sing in praise and thanksgiving, it brings God pleasure. Remember, "Singing is as much an act of worship as is prayer. Indeed, many a song is prayer."[7] And we are told that the Almighty inhabits the praises of His people (Psalm 22:3).

I love to sing during my morning worship, and I often sing as I go through my day. But I don't believe we should sing just when we are happy. The most beautiful songs of praise are sung during times of great trial and pain. When I'm hurting, discouraged, or feeling afraid, I've learned from my daddy that one of the best things I can do is sing—yes, even through my tears. As I do this, the whole atmosphere around me changes. It's amazing!

Remember how Paul and Silas sang in prison, even in their chains? We have much to learn from their story (Acts 16:25). Satan and his evil angels cannot stand to stay in the presence of those who are worshiping and praising God's name.

Ellen White writes, "When the enemy comes with his darkness, sing faith and talk faith, and you will find that you have sung and talked yourself into the light."[8]

My friend Frank Hasel, in his new book *Living for God*, shares how we can learn to practice gratitude and praise in very real and practical ways, even in the midst of trials and suffering. How? By spending a few moments every day writing down ten different things that we are grateful for. If we are hurting, perhaps all we can think of at first is our toothbrush, our bed, or the fact that we can read, but that's a good start. Next, we should ask ourselves why these things are important and what they mean to us. Then we should take each gratitude and make a sentence of praise to God, speaking these praises as a prayer, "Lord, I thank You for . . ." Each day, as we think of ten new things to be grateful for, God will bring more and more blessings to mind, and in the process, our heart will change, and we will see God's goodness in a fresh new way, even through our tears. Frank lost his wife to breast cancer years ago, and it was through this simple habit that he learned to sing the praises of God once more.

Pray daily for the baptism of the Holy Spirit! Since it is the Holy Spirit that leads us into truth and makes it possible for Jesus to abide in us, we should earnestly seek this gift each day.

Again Ellen White writes,

> If all were willing, all would be filled with the Spirit. Wherever the need of the Holy Spirit is a matter little thought of, there is seen spiritual drought, spiritual darkness, spiritual declension and death. Whenever minor matters occupy the attention, the divine power which is necessary for the growth and prosperity of the church, and which would bring all other blessings in its train, is lacking, though offered in infinite plenitude.
>
> Since this is the means by which we are to receive power, why do we not hunger and thirst for the gift of the Spirit? Why do we not talk of it, pray for it, and preach concerning it? The Lord is more willing to give the Holy Spirit to those who serve Him than parents are to give good gifts to their children. For the daily baptism of the Spirit every worker should offer his petition to God.[9]

Memorize Bible promises. I can't tell you how many times a memorized passage of Scripture has come to my mind to give me encouragement or direction in time of need. I'm so thankful that my mother began teaching me to memorize Scripture from my earliest years. Many of those childhood verses remain with me to this day.

However, even if you didn't learn Bible promises as a child, it's not too late to begin! You may say, "I don't have the mind to memorize!" That's no excuse. I have a friend whose mind was damaged due to a lifestyle of heavy drug use, but when he gave his heart to Jesus, he slowly began memorizing little bits of Scripture. The more he memorized, the more he could memorize, and gradually his mind was fully restored. Today, my friend Rich, who has memorized more than a thousand Scripture passages, works as a pastor. In fact, you would have no idea of his past because his mind is bright and he is radiant with the love of God.

The Bible says, "Your word I have hidden in my heart, that I might not sin against You" (Psalm 119:11). The more God's Word is in your heart and mind, the more He can bring it to your memory in your time of need.

In *The Great Controversy*, we are told, "Temptations often appear irresistible because, through the neglect of prayer and the study of the Bible, the tempted one cannot readily remember God's promises and meet Satan with the Scripture weapons. But angels are round about those who are willing to be taught in divine things; and in the time of great necessity they will bring to their remembrance the very truths which are needed."[10]

For practical tools and tips on how to grow your Scripture memory skills, I encourage you to visit FAST Missions at www.fastmissions.com.

Pray the Word, and pray through until breakthrough! We should especially pray earnestly, even wrestle in prayer, for victory over sin, for strength to stand strong for Jesus, for the salvation of our loved ones, and for areas where our faith is weak.

Remember, God always honors His Word. Make His promises personal—for whatever your struggle, temptation, or need. And don't pray the promises just during spiritual crisis. Be intentional! Pray in preparation, with a decided heart, so that when the crisis or temptation comes, you are already prepared to meet it.

If you haven't yet read my book *Daring to Ask for More: Divine Keys to Answered Prayer,* I suggest you get a copy, because I cover the topic of wrestling prayer in much more depth there.

Act in faith, trusting that Jesus hears you! Often, we don't immediately see or feel the results of our prayers, but we need to act and live in faith, anyway. Let's talk faith, live the faith, act in faith, read stories of faith, and surround ourselves with people who encourage our faith. "Of one thing I am perfectly sure," Elisabeth Elliot writes, "God's story never ends in ashes."[11] It will end with victory.*

Guard the avenues of your soul as you go through your day! Let's not forget it is the little foxes that spoil the vineyard (Song of Solomon 2:15). It is the small spiritual compromises and breaches we allow in our life that eventually bring our spiritual downfall. So guard your heart, guard your thoughts, guard your eyes, your ears, your lips, and your footsteps. "Do not grieve the Holy Spirit of God, by whom you were sealed for the day of redemption" (Ephesians 4:30).

Listen to the following gem from the devotional, *The Faith I Live By*,

Every Christian must stand on guard continually, watching every avenue of the soul where Satan might find access. He must pray for divine help and at the same time resolutely resist every inclination to sin. By courage, by faith, by persevering toil, he can conquer. But let him remember that to gain the victory Christ must abide in him and he in Christ. . . . It is only by personal union with Christ, by communion with Him daily, hourly, that we can bear the fruits of the Holy Spirit.

All who have a sense of their deep soul poverty, who feel that they have nothing good in themselves, may find righteousness and strength by looking unto Jesus.[12]

Learn to abide! As Christians, it seems we constantly struggle to stay in an abiding experience with Jesus. Part of this problem, I believe, is because we tend to focus more on doing the right works, and receiving the right gifts, rather than receiving the *Giver Himself.* This is why it is so important that we learn to fight the battle where it is, and not where it is not!

In the book *The Desire of Ages*, we are told,

God desires to manifest through you the holiness, the benevolence, the compassion, of His own character. Yet the Saviour does not bid the disciples labor to bear fruit. He tells them to abide in Him. "If ye abide in Me," He says, "and My words abide in you, ye shall ask what ye will, and it shall be done unto you." It is through the word that Christ abides in His followers . . . The life of Christ in you produces the same fruits as in Him. Living in Christ, adhering to

---

* For some inspirational reading suggestions, to grow your faith and walk with God, see the Book Recommendations in the back of this book on page 243.

Christ, supported by Christ, drawing nourishment from Christ, you bear fruit after the similitude of Christ.[13]

Jesus modeled what it means to walk with God in an abiding relationship, while He lived on earth. The power He received from the heavenly Father for daily victory is also at our disposal as we abide in Him, through His Spirit. "All that Christ received from God we too may have. Then ask and receive. . . . claim for yourself all that God has promised."[14]

I love these words on the abiding experience from Harriet Beecher Stowe and Hudson Taylor:

"How does the branch bear fruit? Not by incessant effort for sunshine and air; not by vain struggles for those vivifying influences which give beauty to the blossom, and verdure to the leaf: it simply abides in the vine, in silent and undisturbed union, and blossoms and fruit appear as of spontaneous growth.

"How then shall a Christian bear fruit? By efforts and struggles to obtain that which is freely given . . . ? No: there must be a full concentration of the thoughts and affections on Christ; a complete surrender of the whole being to Him; a constant looking to Him for grace . . . [by learning to abide like an] infant borne in the arms of its mother. Christ reminds them of every duty in its time and place, reproves them for every error, counsels them in every difficulty, excites them to every needful activity. In spiritual as in temporal matters they take no thought for the morrow; for they know that Christ will be as accessible tomorrow as today, and that time imposes no barrier on His love. Their hope and trust rest solely on what He is willing and able to do for them; on nothing that they suppose themselves able and willing to do for Him. . . ."

Such is the "exchanged life," the abiding, fruitful life, *the life that is Christ*, which should be the possession of every believer.[15]

The beauty of the abiding life is, "If [we] abide in Him, the fact that [we] receive a rich gift today insures the reception of a richer gift tomorrow."[16]

As we continue our journey through the distractions and trials of life, let's close our ears to the enemy's alluring music and spend time at Jesus' feet, learning to abide and learning to sing Heaven's sweeter song. For it truly is *the most beautiful song*!

Daring to Live by Every Word—Going Deeper!
Fullness of Joy at Jesus' Feet: Psalm 16:11

Perhaps you are trapped in difficult life circumstances, and it's hard to learn Heaven's sweeter song. Perhaps you are struggling to get through another day, and you wonder if God hears your prayers or can provide for your needs? Have you ever thought about what it takes each day to feed all the birds of the air? It requires so much food that we can hardly comprehend it! Perhaps that's why, as I've heard it said, "Birds don't worry. They sing."[17] Now, if God daily feeds all the birds of the world, don't you think He can take care of you and me?

Let's open our Bibles as we consider the following "going deeper" questions:

- Psalm 16:11—What is it that gives us the fullness of joy?
- Ephesians 1:23; 3:19; 4:13; Colossians 2:9, 10—Based on these passages, if there's greater "fullness in Jesus" available, how do we receive this?
- 2 Chronicles 5:13, 14—What happens when we sing praises to God?
- 2 Chronicles 20:22—What lessons can we learn from this story?
- John 15:1–17—What does it mean to abide in Christ? What happens when we don't bear fruit? Has God been doing some pruning in your life?
- Matthew 6:25–33—What lessons on faith can we learn from nature?
- Psalm 27:6—How can we worship God with hearts of praise?
- Job 35:10—What does it mean that He "gives songs in the night"?
- Sing or reflect on the song, "Blessed Assurance," hymn no. 462.

It's not easy to sing songs in the night seasons of life, but did you know that when we sing, our voices of praise unite with the angels in heaven? If we are going to sing in heaven, why don't we ask God to teach us how to sing here!

Time to dig deep into God's Word, get on our knees, and allow the Holy Spirit to take this message deeper into our hearts!

Chapter 8

Finding Hidden Treasure

Experiencing the Living Word

> *Your words were found, and I ate them, and Your word
> was to me the joy and rejoicing of my heart.*
> —Jeremiah 15:16

D ear Jesus, could You please send me a Bible!" was the desperate plea of one half-starved boy from a poor village in the Henan Province. But this was Communist China, and there were no Bibles to be found where he lived, and those who were caught in possession of one would be tortured, if not killed. However, so deep was the longing this young boy had for the Word of God that he began to fast, weep, and plead with God to send him a Bible. His family thought he was losing his mind, but he did not give up. Miraculously, one hundred days later, God answered his prayer.

While this young boy had only a third-grade education and could barely read simple Chinese, he used a dictionary and painstakingly looked up one Chinese character at a time, treasuring every word. Every day, whenever he had opportunity or a break from his work in the fields, he would secretly steal away to read his Bible. The Bible was such a sacred treasure to him that at night he slept with it upon his chest.

Finally, after he'd read through the whole Bible, he went back to the New Testament and started to memorize one chapter a day. After twenty-eight days, he had memorized the entire Gospel of Matthew. Next, he began to memorize the book of Acts.

It was while memorizing Acts that God showed him that He wanted to use him, like the apostles, to win souls for the kingdom.

This young boy, now known as Brother Yun, from the book *The Heavenly Man*, went on to preach and testify of the gospel of Christ to many starving souls in China. In fact, he made such an impact that the police began constantly tracking him. He was arrested more than thirty times, but he often escaped. However, during one of his lengthier imprisonments, Brother Yun fasted from food and water for a period of seventy-four days. While it is considered medically impossible for someone to survive that long without water, God miraculously sustained him. Despite much opposition and constant danger, Brother Yun's labor's continued once he was released. Many house churches were started, many miracles witnessed, and thousands came to know Jesus.

Finally, the authorities, determining to put an end once and for all to Brother Yun's ministry, captured him and locked him up in a maximum-security prison in Zhengzhou. To ensure that he would never escape again, his legs were beaten until he was permanently crippled. However, not six weeks later, Brother Yun walked out of that prison, just like Peter in the book of Acts. Doors and gates that were always bolted and locked opened silently and Brother Yun passed by guards as if he was invisible. No one had ever, in the history of this prison, successfully escaped. It was not until Brother Yun was safely outside the last big prison gate that he realized what God had done. He was walking on completely healed legs.[1]

When I read testimonies like that of Brother Yun, I often ask myself, "Do I recognize the treasure I've been given in the Word of God?"

The Waldensian Bible

A couple of summers ago, I had the privilege of traveling with a group from Weimar College through Europe, retracing the steps of the leaders of the Protestant Reformation. We started in Rome, visiting the Vatican, as well as the ancient Roman Colosseum, where many Christians were martyred.

We even saw the Mamertine Prison, where Peter and Paul were held captive before their deaths, and we stopped by Chiesa Gesu, the church of Ignatius Loyola, founder of the Jesuits, whose chief task was to wipe out the Protestant faith. If you don't think the great controversy is real, just take a trip to Rome, and you will see the history for yourself.

The pagan symbolism and the spiritual pomp seen, even today, throughout Rome and the Vatican was overwhelming for me—I can't imagine how it might have been hundreds of years ago. It was with great relief and joy in my heart that we left the city behind and traveled north to Torre Pellice, Italy, where we got to spend a few days learning about the history of Waldenses in the valleys of the Piedmont. What a peaceful contrast to the hustle and bustle of the city.

However, while the Italian mountains breathed refreshment to my weary soul, history tells the sobering story that many Waldenses died atrocious deaths in these mountains simply because they dared to live and preach the Word of God.

As my friends and I hiked up one of these mountains on Sabbath afternoon, we stopped many times to peer into old Waldensian homes built of crude stones, which had been built by hand. Some of these homes have stood for nearly five hundred years. Throughout our hike that afternoon, I often asked myself, "If I had lived five hundred years ago, would I have been willing to live in a crude rock home on a dangerous mountainside, or even been willing to die rather than give up God's Holy Word?"

While in Torre Pellice, our guide, a pure-blooded Waldensian named Esteban Janavel, whose ancestors used to be leaders in the Waldenses' movement, shared about the history of his people and their fight to live by the Word of God. Esteban showed us the College of the Barbs, where young students would learn Scripture and then be sent out as missionaries, many never to return because they were captured and killed. He told us sobering stories of Waldenses dying for their faith in caves, on mountainsides, and in the cold of winter, being forced to live as outcasts and wanderers—all because they wanted to obey the Holy Scriptures. He even told the story of his own family Bible that had been miraculously preserved and passed down through the generations for almost five hundred years.

As the story goes, troops sent in to extinguish the heretics had found the small mountain village where Esteban's Waldensian ancestors lived, and all the Bibles were being collected and burned. However, one brave Waldensian man threw the family Bible over a cliff to escape the fire. He was immediately killed. Fifty years later, when the remaining Waldensian family members finally crept back to the mountainside to rebuild, they discovered their Bible, on the edge of the mountain buried in the brush, but still very much intact. It was a complete miracle that God had preserved their family Bible all those years.

As our group looked at this old Waldensian Bible and listened to Esteban's family story, many of us cried. In a small way, it was a symbol to me of how God has so beautifully preserved His Word throughout the ages.

As history shows us, except with the Waldenses, the Bible was largely lost sight of for many centuries as it was locked up in languages that only the learned could understand. During the Dark Ages, the common person could not read the Scriptures for himself. But thankfully, God had a plan to break the chains that had kept His Word hidden in darkness for so many centuries. And now, because of the blood and sacrifice of many martyrs, we have free access to this sacred book.

The forgotten treasure

Today, the Bible is the most widely published of all books ever written.[2] Although it continues to be the number one selling book every year, and it is more accessible then it has ever been throughout history, it seems we are suffering from a famine for the Word of God—a famine in our homes, in our hearts, and in our land. While the Bible may be on our bookshelves, on our phones, iPads, computers, and digital devices, it seems we've lost our holy awe and love for this amazing gift.

Inspiration tells us, "The Bible is God's voice speaking to us, just as surely as though we could hear it with our ears. If we realized this, with what awe we would open God's word and with what earnestness we would search its precepts! The reading and contemplation of the Scriptures would be regarded as an audience with the Infinite One."[3]

Our attitude toward the Bible reflects our attitude toward Jesus. God wants us to regard the Bible as precious because it leads us to Him! So how should we treat God's Holy Word?

The Bible tells us we are to tremble before the Word of God (Isaiah 66:2, 5). We are to receive it with all readiness and search it daily (Acts 17:11). We are to receive it because it is, in truth, the Word of God

(1 Thessalonians 2:13). We are to receive it gladly (Acts 2:41). We are to keep it, follow it, bend to it, revere it (1 John 2:5). We are to treat it as precious (1 Samuel 3:1). It is to reside on our tongues (2 Samuel 23:2). We are to be always mindful of the Word and abide in its reality (1 Chronicles 16:8). We are to praise the Word and trust it (Psalm 56:4, 10). We are to allow the Word to try our souls and purify our hearts (Psalm 105:19). We are to hide the Word in our hearts, cherish it in our innermost being, protect it as our most sacred possession (Psalm 119:11). We are to publish the Word and testify of it (Psalm 68:11). We are to delight in it and never forget it (Psalm 119:16). We are to be quickened by its power, its grace, its majesty (Psalm 119:50). We are to allow it to be our strength (Psalm 119:28). It is to be our measuring tool for truth, and we are to trust it implicitly (Isaiah 8:20; Psalm 119:42). We are to hope in the Word (Psalm 119:81). We are to love the Word and delight in its purity (Psalm 119:140). We are to meditate on it (Psalm 119:148). We are to let it be the joy and rejoicing of our hearts (Jeremiah 15:16). It is to be our sustenance, the food of our soul, the life of our very being (Matthew 4:4).[4]

In the book *Steps to Christ,* we read: "There is nothing more calculated to strengthen the intellect than the study of the Scriptures. No other book is so potent to elevate the thoughts, to give vigor to the faculties, as the broad, ennobling truths of the Bible. If God's word were studied as it should be, men would have a breadth of mind, a nobility of character, and a stability of purpose rarely seen in these times."[5]

In years past, Seventh-day Adventists were always known as being the "people of the Book." But can we still boast of that reputation today? Do we know how to dig deeply in God's Word or even how to give a Bible study? Are we daily growing in our understanding of the deep truths of heaven? Or have we grown careless with our Treasure? Have we lost the awe for the words that introduce us to the Author of life?

Perhaps you aren't sure how to read the Bible, or you feel that things are a bit dry. You want to go deeper, but you aren't sure where to start. Let me put some hope in your heart. If you open your Bible and ask the Holy Spirit to teach you, He will help you! That's God's promise. You don't have to be a Bible scholar to find gold in God's Word. You just need a hungry heart! As I've heard it said, "There is no better way to learn to read the Bible than just to start reading the Bible."

However, as you open your Bible, let me share a few practical suggestions that have made a big difference in my study. This will not be a comprehensive overview, but these brief tips[6] are worth their weight in gold. In fact, I believe that if you follow these suggestions, you will soon be thriving in your study of God's Word, not just surviving.*

Experiencing God's Word

As Ezra prepared his heart to seek the Lord (Ezra 7:10), so we should prepare our hearts as well. No matter our education, our age, or our experience in ministry, we don't have the intellectual discernment, let alone the intellectual capacity, to grasp the deep truths of Scripture without the power of the Holy Spirit, for spiritual things are spiritually discerned (1 Corinthians 2:13, 14). That's why we must stay humble!

How can we grow closer to Jesus if we don't keep a humble, teachable spirit and if we don't recognize our own frailty and desperate need for divine wisdom and instruction? James 4:6 tells us, "God resists the proud, but gives grace to the humble." Truly, "there is nothing so offensive to God or so dangerous to the human soul as pride and self-sufficiency. Of all sins it is the most hopeless, the most incurable."[7] However, we are promised, "To those who in humility of heart seek for divine guidance, angels of God draw near."[8]

As you begin your Bible study, pray for Holy Spirit wisdom. Then read the Bible passage several times, letting it soak in. As you read, circle and highlight keywords, themes, or phrases, and highlight promises and words of encouragement that you find. Meditate on the passage and verses that speak to you, and allow the Scripture to interpret itself.

I love Proverbs 15:6, 15, which tells us, "In the house of the righteous there is much treasure. . . . But he who is of a merry heart has a continual feast." Jesus is our Treasure, and He is our continual feast! However, only those who diligently search will find the hidden jewels.

Remember, Bible study is not just a scholastic exercise. It's about learning, listening, and savoring sweet moments with our Lord and Savior. So pause throughout your study to pray and listen to what the Holy Spirit might want to tell you.

Next, ask probing questions like What is the message of this passage?

---

* These study tips I have summarized on a bookmark called *Experiencing God's Word* that you can download from https://www.revivalandreformation.org.

What is the context surrounding the passage? What is God saying *to me* in this passage? What commands, instructions, and life principles are found here? What changes should I ask God to make in my life to align with this scripture? What can I learn about God's character in this passage? How does this passage lead me to Jesus? How do I see the great controversy played out? (And don't forget the "who, what, when, where, why, and how" questions.)

There are many beautiful themes woven throughout the individual passages and Bible books. Two major underlying themes run throughout Scripture as a whole—Jesus Christ and the great controversy between God and Satan. Stay on the lookout for both these themes.

Learn to linger! Just as we take time to chew and enjoy our food, so God's Word should be prayerfully contemplated, lingered upon, and enjoyed in an unhurried manner so that the Holy Spirit can speak to our hearts. This is not just about learning new knowledge. It's more about building an intimate relationship with our Savior.

In the book *As Light Lingers: Basking in the Word of God*, author Nina Atcheson teaches us what it means to linger in the Word of God. Not only does she bring the principles of Bible study to vibrant life in everyday situations, teaching us how to dig deeper and savor the words of Scripture, she also gives excellent pointers on how to engage your children in daily devotions. If you hunger for a deeper experience, or if you want to teach your children to fall in love with the Word, then this book is a worthwhile investment.[9]

To help deepen my spiritual understanding and help myself linger, I often practice six additional habits during my Bible reading to enrich my study time. I will outline these briefly in the following two paragraphs.

While I usually study with one specific Bible translation, I have found it helpful to (1) compare different Bible translations as this often adds some additional clarity and perspective to the passages I'm reading. I also love looking up (2) cross-references and parallel passages, (3) reading what different scholars write in commentaries, as well as discovering (4) what keywords mean in the original Greek and Hebrew. In times past, this meant lugging around multiple books, concordances, and commentaries, but now with advancing technology, it is so easy. You can do this all very quickly with the *E-Sword* app (or other apps) on your smartphone.

Another resource I use heavily is the (5) Ellen G. White app, as I search for words, themes, or topics. There is so much gold in the words of Inspiration—the more you read, the more you will discover. I especially enjoy reading what the (6) *Seventh-day Adventist Bible Commentary* (also within the EGW app) has to say about the specific passage I'm studying. If you own a smartphone, and you haven't become familiar with these helpful Bible study applications, I encourage you to get acquainted. While our smartphones can become tools of distraction in our Bible study and time with God, they can also be incredible tools for good. Use them for good!

Be a careful, diligent Bible student! With every wind of doctrine running rampant, and with spiritual deceptions threatening us on every side, we can't be lazy, and we can't be haphazard in our Bible study, nor can we rely on others to do our study for us. We need to learn for ourselves what it means to be diligent Bible students. We need to compare Scripture with Scripture, like the Bereans, seeking a deeper understanding of what we believe and why (Acts 17:11).

Did you know that Satan is an excellent Bible student? He studies so he can learn how to keep us from recognizing the truths found in God's Word. That's right!

Ellen White writes, "[Satan] is a diligent student of the Bible and is much better acquainted with the prophecies than many religious teachers. He knows that it is for his interest to keep well informed in the revealed purposes of God, that he may defeat the plans of the Infinite."[10]

Keep in mind to get the full breadth of Scripture; the Bible must be studied as a whole, not just in part. We often tend to enjoy sticking with our favorite books or chapters of the Bible and reading them again and again, which is fine, but we should also routinely make time to read through the whole Bible from cover to cover.

We also need to guard against building a single doctrine on a single verse (Isaiah 28:10) or being quick to interpret Scripture according to our private interpretation or preconceived ideas (2 Peter 1:20). It is important that we let the author's words speak for themselves. That's why the Bible should be "its own expositor."[11]

As we evaluate what is happening around us, let us strive to measure everything by the "it is written" standard. As the Bible says, "To the law and to the testimony! If they do not speak according to this word, it is because there is no light in them" (Isaiah 8:20). When man's ideas, man's doctrine, man's commands, man's desires, or even man's culture conflict with God's Word, we must stand with the Holy Scriptures.

And if we think we are above being spiritually deceived, remember the Bible warns us in 2 Timothy 4:3, 4, and in Matthew 24:24 that even "the brightest among us" are going to be in danger of being deceived. That's why we need to take 1 Corinthians 10:12 to heart: "Therefore let him who thinks he stands take heed lest he fall." In fact, inspiration tells us, "So closely will the counterfeit resemble the true that it will be impossible to distinguish between them except by the Holy Scriptures. By their testimony every statement and every miracle must be tested."[12]

As we reflect on what it means to be good Bible students, I'm reminded of the encouragement one respected theologian gives—to always approach Scripture with intellectual carefulness, intellectual fair-mindedness, intellectual honesty, and intellectual humility.[13] This approach will make all the difference in the world!

Keep a journal and record your findings. Just as the children of Israel took up stones while crossing the Jordan to remember what God had done (Joshua 4:6, 7), so we should routinely collect "remembrance stones" to remind ourselves of what God has taught us along our own journey.

If you haven't been in the practice of journaling, I encourage you to give it a try. Two journals that I have found to be exceptionally helpful in recent years are the following:

1. The *Give Me Jesus* Journal, by Gretchen Saffles: This journal follows a beautiful outline with space for writing a daily gratitude, space to put aside your distractions, a nice page for Bible study notes, and then space for you to write what you've learned about God, how your reading applies to your life, and then a space to record a short prayer in response to your reading. Gretchen has coined the phrase "Word before World,"and if we all followed this motto, how different our lives might be. You can purchase her journal online at https://wellwateredwomen.com.

2. The *Longing for God: A Prayer and Bible Journal,* by Frank M. Hasel: This journal is unique because it is specifically designed to help you read through the entire Bible in one year. Each day it has an assigned daily Bible reading, which includes passages from both the Old Testament and the New Testament or Psalms. It includes a small space for you to journal key thoughts from your daily reading, as well as a corresponding space to

record a daily prayer. Also included are twelve short chapters throughout the journal (one per month) with tips on how to grow your prayer life. If you'd like to read the Bible through in a year or enrich your devotional experience, I recommend this resource, which can be purchased on Amazon or at your local Adventist Book Center.

And last but not least, share what you've learned! We should always be ready and looking for opportunities to share with others what God has taught us (1 Peter 3:15), whether that's with a friend, a coworker, or even a complete stranger. It might make all the difference in their world.

I'm reminded of an experience my friend and mentor in the ministry told me not too long ago. Jerry Page, who works as a secretary for the General Conference Ministerial Association, shared how years back when he was working as a conference president, he had been struggling with a staff member that was gossiping and spreading rumors. Jerry had spoken to the man (who we will call Bob) about the issue previously, but it seemed as though the problem was continuing. So Jerry set up an appointment to meet with Bob the next Tuesday. Jerry intended to go over a long list of what Bob was doing wrong, watch him grow embarrassed, and then make it clear that his behavior must change.

However, Tuesday morning, as Jerry was having his quiet time with the Lord, God convicted him through the Word that he (Jerry) needed to look at himself first. "A fool's wrath is known at once, but a prudent man covers shame. . . . There is one who speaks like the piercings of a sword, but the tongue of the wise promotes health" (Proverbs 12:16, 18), he read.

With remorse Jerry realized, *I may be right about the facts, but I am wrong in spirit. I often do my worst sinning when I am right!* And so he began to pray that God would change his heart and make him like Jesus and show him how to restore Bob gently (Galatians 6:1).

Later that day, as he met with Bob, Jerry began by asking, "Bob, would you pray for me about something? Sometimes I talk negatively about people behind their backs, and I want to be more like Jesus." Then Jerry gently shared his concerns, and Bob understood. Instead of getting into a heated confrontation, the two men ended up on their knees with tears in their eyes, as they prayed for one another.

As providence would have it, not many hours later, a pastor called Jerry on the phone, irate about how his elders were gossiping and saying negative things about him. He told Jerry he was going to sit them down the next day and set them straight. However, having just experienced the grace and teaching of God in his own difficult situation, Jerry was able to share his experience from that day, calm the pastor down, and help him take a more gentle, biblical approach.

Isn't that often what happens when God teaches us a lesson? He will bring situations into our lives where we can pass on what we've learned to help others, and what a difference it makes!

When we spend time in God's Word, it will be like a fire in our bones that we cannot contain (Jeremiah 20:9). And that is God's plan! He feeds us living bread so we can share with others the goodness of His mercy and love.

Sweeter than honey

As I close this chapter, I'm reminded of an experience my friend Nina Atcheson shares in her book *As Light Lingers: Basking in the Word of God.*

Nina, who lives in Australia, was gifted one day with a slab of honeycomb from a friend. She and her family had never tried honeycomb before, and they weren't exactly sure how to eat it. But once they figured the process out, they were pleasantly surprised by how good it tasted. As a result of that gift, honeycomb became Nina's favorite dessert. When I visited the Atcheson home in Australia, not long after, Nina gave me some honeycomb to taste as well. She was right. It was wonderful! And addicting. I wanted more![14]

And so, as we reflect on the sweet experience of eating raw honeycomb, we can grasp a deeper understanding of how passionately David loved the Word of God when he wrote: "How sweet are Your words to my taste, sweeter than honey to my mouth! Through Your precepts I get understanding" (Psalm 119:103, 104).

"As our physical life is sustained by food, so our spiritual life is sustained by the Word of God. And every soul is to receive life from God's Word for himself. As we must eat for ourselves in order to receive nourishment, so we must receive the Word for ourselves."[15]

Job wrote, "I have treasured the words of His mouth more than my necessary food" (Job 23:12). Is this our attitude toward God's Word? Let's not take this treasure for granted any longer. Let's taste and see that He is good!

Daring to Live by Every Word—Going Deeper!
Experiencing the Living Word: Jeremiah 15:16

Time to open our Treasure Chest and dig for gold! Consider the following Bible passages as you reflect on these going deeper questions:

- Jeremiah 15:16—How can we worship God through the study of His Word?
- Think about the times (maybe even today) when God's Word has brought joy to your heart. Share that experience with someone. If you haven't experienced this joy recently, how could you experience it again?
- Matthew 6:21—Where is your treasure, and where is your heart?
- 2 Peter 1:21; 2 Timothy 3:16—Where did God's Word come from?
- 2 Timothy 2:15; John 5:39; John 15:3; John 17:17—What do these passages teach us about the importance of diligent study?
- Psalm 119—As you read this psalm, write down all the times the "Word" is mentioned, and the blessing associated. (This chapter is packed!)
- Deuteronomy 8:1–10—What is God's promise for the future! Could we receive this blessing even now?
- Sing or reflect on the song, "Give Me the Bible," hymn no. 272.

While finding cross-references in Bible study is exciting, may we never forget the power of the Cross! While looking up a bunch of chain-references, let us never lose sight of Jesus, who gave all His blood that our chains might be broken and we might be set free.[16]

"You should search the Bible; for it tells you of Jesus. As you read the Bible, you will see the matchless charms of Jesus. You will fall in love with the Man of Calvary, and at every step you can say to the world, 'His ways are ways of pleasantness, and all His paths are peace.' "[17]

The Bible is a treasure map—and Jesus is our greatest Treasure!

Time to dig deep into God's Word, get on our knees, and allow the Holy Spirit to take this message deeper into our hearts!

Chapter 9

Praying the Promises

Gaining Strength for the Everyday Journey

> *"If you abide in Me, and My words abide in you,*
> *you will ask what you desire, and it shall be done for you."*
> —John 15:7

Todd sat motionless in the living room as he stared out the window of his tiny apartment. It seemed as if all color had suddenly drained out of his life. His father had just phoned sharing that his mom had breast cancer. "We don't know yet what is going to happen, but just pray, son!" his father had told him with quivering voice. *"You know how to pray."*

Todd hadn't moved since he'd received the phone call. He hadn't cried either. Still reeling in shock, he struggled to take everything in. Then his dad's final words pierced his heart again. *"You know how to pray."*

Todd was a seminary student preparing for the ministry. He was active with the youth at his local church and had already graduated from a well-known Christian university. He'd been raised in a good home by Christian parents. Yet the shocking realization hit him like ice water: *I really don't know how to pray.*

A couple of days later, still struggling to take it all in, Todd called an old friend, his former Bible professor, asking if he could come for a visit. His professor, Dr. Warren, warmly welcomed him to come. So not long after, he drove to the man's office.

Dr. Warren was kind and gentle, and his Christianity was the kind that made you feel safe, for he had a calm peace about him. In former years he had been a great influence in Todd's life, so it was only natural for Todd to turn to him for help now.

Dr. Warren welcomed Todd warmly into his office. "Todd, I'm happy you called. Thanks for coming to visit," Dr. Warren said as he offered Todd a seat.

"Thanks for taking the time," Todd replied with a smile. The two men sat down.

After they exchanged some small talk, Dr. Warren asked, "So what's on your mind?" Todd swallowed hard, and then shared the circumstances that had led up to his visit.

"Here's the hard truth, Dr. Warren! I don't know how to pray. Of course, I pray every day, several times a day. But really, beyond 'God, bless the food and thanks and please give us a great youth night,' I don't know how to pray."

"I understand what you are saying. I've been where you are," said Dr. Warren thoughtfully. He paused. "It's hard to believe, but people can write books on theology and Bible commentaries and scholarly articles—but still not have any idea how to pray."

"But Dr. Warren! You know how to pray. I've heard you pray. You are one of the godliest men I know. Something must have changed for you!"

"You are right!" Dr. Warren nodded. "Something did change. And it can change for you too. I think you have a very common problem, a problem that is wide spread throughout the church. It's called APD—arrested prayer development. That means you are suffering from the interruption of a healthy, growing prayer life. What you need is the Scripture prescription."

Todd began taking notes as Dr. Warren continued, "The Bible is God's prescription for APD. The way to break through in your prayer life is to pray Scripture. Read Ephesians 6:17, 18. Take the sword of the Spirit, the Word of God, and, 'praying always with all prayer and supplication in the Spirit,' pray! What God has brought together we should not separate. The Bible and prayer go together. Pray the Word."[1]

Todd listened intently as Dr. Warren continued to share how all through history people's lives have been revolutionized when they began the discipline of praying Scripture. Dr. Warren talked of Martin Luther, George Müller, and Hudson Taylor.

With a sparkle in his eyes, Dr. Warren shared how Hudson Taylor's children would often wake up in the middle of the night to see their father reading the Bible and praying by candlelight. Then he shared how George Müller had struggled to keep his mind focused in his prayer time until he started praying with his Bible open before him. Müller would read, then pray, read, then pray. Müller discovered that when he allowed the Bible to set his prayer agenda, he ended up praying for many more things beyond what he would normally have prayed for: prayers of confession, prayers of adoration, prayers for the outcast, bold prayers of faith, and more.

Finally, Dr. Warren concluded, "What changed these men and their prayer life is what has also changed mine—praying Scripture."

As Dr. Warren and Todd continued to talk together, Dr. Warren laid out a few prayer principles. These principles are not only the keys that Todd needed that day, but they are keys we need as well.

- Keep things simple!
- Choose a book or passage of the Bible.
- Read a few verses each day.
- Reflect on what you've read, taking notes on key points.
- Then say, "Lord, how should I pray?"
- Read the verses again, letting them sink into your heart.
- Then *pray* the passage in your own words, making it personal.
- At first it may seem awkward, but the more you follow the read-reflect-pray method, the deeper your prayer life will go.[2]

Todd followed Dr. Warren's advice, and a few months later, when they talked again, he was a different man. "Praying the Word has completely changed my life!" He told Dr. Warren enthusiastically. "Thank you so much!"

Todd's mom wasn't healed, at least not immediately. She was still receiving treatment when Todd shared this testimony, but Todd was at peace as he had found the strength he needed. Most important, he had finally learned how to pray.[3]

Praying the promises changed my life!

When people ask me what is the biggest thing that has positively impacted my own spiritual life and my walk with God, it doesn't take long for me to answer. It is learning to pray the Word! My experience is different than Todd's but not any less transformational.

While I grew up with special Bible promises that I called my own, it wasn't until my adult years that praying the Word really became a vital part of my prayer life. Now, I can hardly pray without thinking of Scripture promises to claim with my prayers.

At first, I made a notebook of Bible promises—promises for a deeper walk, for cleansing of heart, for more of the Holy Spirit, for victory over sin, and so on. I just prayed over these promises during my morning devotions. Then I started putting my prayer requests on little cards on a key ring that I could easily carry with me through the day. On one side of the card I wrote specific prayer requests, and on the other side I wrote appropriate Bible promises to claim as I prayed. This collection of prayer cards became such an encouragement that I started praying the promises multiple times during the day.

The amazing thing was that when I truly started claiming the "it is written" promises from Scripture in my daily prayer life, not only did my walk with God go deeper, but I saw Him working in new ways with those around me. Suddenly, new doors in ministry began to open, and unexpected opportunities to witness for Him were put before me.

There are many testimonies I could share. However, one very special experience of growing practical faith occurred back when I was writing my first book, *Daring to Ask for More: Divine Keys for Answered Prayer*.

About the time I began to write the book on prayer, the income I had been depending on for ministry was cut off. Now with no money to pay my bills, I asked myself, "Should I look for a job for a few months until I've saved up enough money to take time off for writing, or should I move forward by faith and start writing, trusting that God will provide for my financial needs?"

Not long after, I came upon the passage of Matthew 6:31–33:

"Therefore take no thought, saying, What shall we eat? or, What shall we drink? or, Wherewithal shall we be clothed? (For after all these things do the Gentiles seek:) for your heavenly Father knoweth that ye have need of all these things. But seek ye first the kingdom of God, and his righteousness; and all these things shall be added unto you" (KJV).

As I thought about this passage, I realized that "take no thought" really means, don't stress, and don't worry.

With amazement I also realized that Satan has taken the very things God said not to worry about and made them our *primary obsessions*. It's not only about putting food on our tables—food has become our obsession! It's not only about getting water to drink—we are now addicted to caffeine, alcohol, and every kind of sugar-filled soda. And don't even get me started about the fashion industry, and the consuming materialism that has followed. So here we go, day after day, focusing on the "take no thought incidentals" while the eternal mission that we should be thinking about, we ignore.

"OK, God," I prayed one day. "I'm not going to worry about these incidentals anymore. I'm not going to worry about paying the bills, or about buying food for my table. I'm going to trust that You will be my daily provider. I know You've asked me to write this book, so I'm going to move forward by faith on the promises of Your Word!"

While I had seen God provide for my needs countless times over the years, this was probably the biggest step of faith yet, because I literally had no income, and I felt as though I was walking off a cliff financially. To make matters worse, no one knew the predicament that I was in. But I knew God was asking me to trust Him completely, and I felt impressed that I shouldn't tell anyone, not even my family or closest friends. As I prayed, God assured me that He knew, and He would provide.

I began to write as I daily reminded the Lord, "You said 'take no thought,' so I'm holding You to Your Word." I think God loves it when we hold Him to His Word.

Inspiration tells us, "The honor of His throne is staked for the fulfillment of His word unto us."[4] In another place we read, "Bear your whole weight on the promises of God. Believe it is your privilege to believe."[5]

As I moved forward claiming the promises from the Bible, my faith grew.

Not long after, complete strangers wrote me a letter, sharing that they'd been convicted to start supporting me as their "home missionary." They included a sizable check in their letter. Soon, other funds started coming in from various random places. I couldn't believe it. Just when I had a bill to pay, God would provide exactly the amount I needed. It was only after six months that I confided in awe to my parents and closest friends that I no longer had a regular income, but God had been paying my bills and supplying my daily needs each month. I couldn't contain my joy. Truly, He was proving His Word.

It's been a few years since this experience, and finances are still limited as I live on a part-time salary. But God is continuing to prove His Word true in my life as I daily seek to honor Him.

However, more thrilling than seeing God provide my daily bread and take care of my financial needs is seeing Him change hearts, restore marriages, and turn lives around. The biggest miracle is what He's been doing in my own heart. God has honored His Word time and time again in my life.

Why should we pray the Word?

First and foremost we should learn to pray God's Word because His Word reveals His will (1 John 5:14, 15). If we want to know God's will, and if we want to see God answer our prayers, we need to pray prayers that align with His will as revealed in His Word. When we know God's will (for wisdom and direction, for deliverance from sin and spiritual compromise, for salvation, for provision for our daily needs, for the gospel to go forward, etc.), we can stand boldly upon His Word when we pray, not because we are worthy but because we have an Advocate in heaven who is already interceding on our behalf. His prayers make our prayers acceptable (see Hebrews 4:14–16; Romans 8:26). We can also pray confidently upon God's Word because His Word is already settled in heaven (Psalm 119:89). He cannot lie (Numbers 23:19), and His Word does not return unto Him void (Isaiah 55:11).

Learning to pray Scripture does not have to be complicated, whether you pray over entire passages and chapters in the Bible, as Todd learned to do, or whether you pray the promises over specific prayer requests as I love to do. These are both powerful ways to saturate your mind with the Word of God and grow in faith as you pray His will. It doesn't matter whether you know a lot of Bible promises. The point is, open your Bible and pray! This is especially meaningful when coupled with your daily Bible reading. As I've often said, our Bible study and prayer life should go hand in hand.

In the chapter "Asking to Give" in *Christ Object Lessons*, we are told, "God stands back of every promise He has made. With your Bible in your hands say, I have done as Thou hast said. I present Thy promise, 'Ask, and it shall be given you; seek, and ye shall find; knock, and it shall be opened unto you.' "[6] (Take time to read this full chapter if you can!)

As we spend time in God's Word, we will discover that it is both our offensive and defensive weapon against the attacks of the enemy. That's why we are told, "Above all, [take] the shield of faith with which you will be able to quench all the fiery darts of the wicked one. And take the helmet of salvation, and the sword of the Spirit, which is the word of God" (Ephesians 6:16, 17).

Faith quenches the darts of discouragement and fear. Instead of cowering when the spiritual attacks come, we can stand strong. But "in order to strengthen faith [our shield], we must often bring it in contact with the Word."[7]

Perhaps you are struggling with many temptations? You are trying to overcome, but you keep falling. Remember that God's Word is your only safety! And He promises to give victory! Cling to Him! "Now unto him that is able to keep you from falling, and to present you faultless before the presence of his glory with exceeding joy" (Jude 1:24, KJV).

If only I'd memorized more Scripture
I will never forget the incredible story of Richard and Sabina Wurmbrand, founders of The Voice of the Martyrs, a nonprofit organization whose mission is to defend the human rights of persecuted Christians.

During World War II, with the Nazi occupation of Romania, life became a living nightmare for Jews. Although devout Christians, both Richard and Sabina were Jewish. As a result, Sabina's parents, two sisters, and one brother were killed in Nazi concentration camps. However, Richard and Sabina managed to avoid arrest and spent their time rescuing Jewish children. But greater trials were to come.

Toward the end of World War II, Communists seized control of Romania and took over all the churches—wanting to use them as propaganda tools for their own purposes. Richard and Sabina now turned their attention to developing an "underground" ministry to the enslaved Romanian Christians.

One day, during a great Communist convention in 1948 that they were required to attend, the couple sat watching pastor after pastor get up and praise the new government and leadership. Both Sabina and Richard were infuriated.

Finally, Sabina whispered to her husband, "Will you not wash this shame from the face of Jesus?"

Richard responded, "If I speak up, you will lose a husband."

"I don't need a coward for a husband!" Sabina replied.

Richard did get up and speak for the glory of God that day, and what he said made such a stir that the angry leaders immediately severed the wires to the microphone as his message was being broadcast all over Romania.

Not long after, Richard was arrested. He would end up spending fourteen years in Communist prisons, three of those years in solitary confinement, suffering unimaginable torture at the hands of his captors. It was the Scriptures that he had learned that gave him comfort amid the horrors of prison life. It was his relationship with Jesus that gave him strength to hold on.

Sabina was eventually arrested herself, as well, having to leave her young son to fend for himself on the streets. She spent three years in a Communist Romanian labor camp, where she and hundreds of other women had to deal with unimaginable hardship. It was especially difficult for Sabina to see the women suffering who had no foundation or relationship with God. "They were like empty tin cans, tossed to and fro. They had nothing to hold on to," she wrote in the after years. Sabina's comfort during those dark days was the Bible promises she had memorized.

Despite her own pain, Sabina sought to minister to these women, and many came to her side for comfort, asking her to recite the scriptures she knew. "Oh, if only I'd memorized more of the Bible," she cried. That was her biggest regret, as she would share after her release. However, the promises that she had memorized enabled her to stay strong.

In 1964, she and her husband and son were finally reunited. Their faith-testing experience became the foundation for a ministry that would eventually touch the lives of millions.[8]

The reality is, if we want to be prepared for the future trials to come, we must learn to depend upon God's Word today. It's time to soak up God's Word, memorize the promises, and pray!

Daring to Live by Every Word—Going Deeper!
Praying the Promises: John 15:7

How can we worship God through prayer? Could it be by learning to pray His Word in simple childlike faith? In *The Ministry of Healing*, we read, "Grasp His promises like leaves from the tree of life."[9]

The following are a few of my favorites Bible promises for various needs. What Bible promises can you add to this list?

- The Holy Spirit—Luke 11:13; Ephesians 1:13
- Salvation—Romans 10:13; 5:8; Ephesians 1:4
- Forgiveness—1 John 1:9; Psalm 103:12; Isaiah 1:18
- A new heart—Ezekiel 36:26; Deuteronomy 30:6; Philippians 2:13
- Wisdom—James 1:5; 1 Corinthians 1:3; Ephesians 1:17
- Guidance—Psalm 32:8; Proverbs 3:5, 6; Isaiah 30:21
- Strength—Isaiah 40:29–31; Ephesians 3:16; 2 Corinthians 12:9
- Help in trials—Psalm 50:15; 2 Chronicles 20:12; Isaiah 41:10
- Help in temptation—Ephesians 6:10–17; 1 Corinthians 10:13
- Deliverance—Psalm 34:6, 7, 19; Luke 18:7, 8; Romans 7:24
- Physical needs—Philippians 4:19; Matthew 6:31–33; Psalm 4:3
- Physical food—Isaiah 33:16; Psalms 34:8; 37:25
- Spiritual needs—Psalm 81:10; Matthew 5:6; Jeremiah 15:16
- Spiritual fruit—Psalm 1:3; John 15:4; 2 Chronicles 16:9
- Souls saved—Psalm 2:8; Joshua 1:3; 2 Peter 3:9; Joel 2
- Endurance—Matthew 24:13; 2 Timothy 2:3; Hebrews 10:35
- Peace—John 14:27; Isaiah 26:3; Psalm 46; Psalm 119:165
- Revival—Psalm 85:6; 138:7; Ezekiel 37:5; Ephesians 5:14

As you think about the message of this chapter, I encourage you to sing or reflect on the song, "Standing on the Promises," hymn no. 518.

However, if you can, stand up and sing the song as if you really mean it. In fact, you might consider memorizing the words to this and the other hymns I've been sharing throughout this book. You never know when you might need them and have no hymnal available.

Also, to help yourself go deeper, consider downloading my "Prayer and Promise" card collection. To help people learn to pray the Word, I've put together a collection of one hundred cards covering the topics of marriage, children, ministry, spiritual growth, overcoming breaches, the Holy Spirit, and more. These can all be downloaded for free at www.revivalandreformation.org. Just search for "Praying the Word."

For those who would prefer not to carry around rings of cards, or sheets of paper, there are several excellent educational applications that can be used on smartphones for memorizing Scripture, or making your own prayer and promise cards. My favorite phone app to use is *Flash-cards*, by NKO Ventures, LLC. Some additional helpful apps to use for scripture memorization are *Bible Memory* or *e-Sword MEM*.

Remember, "prayer and faith will do what no power on earth can accomplish,"[10] but if we want to grow our faith, we must daily feed upon God's Word (Romans 10:17).

Time to dig deep into God's Word, get on our knees, and allow the Holy Spirit to take this message deeper into our heart!

Chapter 10

Daring to Live by Every Word

Life Lessons From Our Savior

> *But He answered and said, "It is written, 'Man shall not live by bread alone, but by every word that proceeds from the mouth of God.'"*
> —Matthew 4:4

Thomas Jefferson, the author of the American Declaration of Independence, claimed to be a follower of the teachings of Jesus Christ. The problem was, he didn't always like what he read in those teachings. He also "didn't always agree with how the Bible was interpreted by Biblical sources, including the writers of the four Gospels, whom he considered to be untrustworthy correspondents. So Jefferson created his own gospel by taking a sharp instrument, perhaps a penknife, to existing copies of the New Testament and pasting up his own account of Christ's philosophy."[1] In essence, he created his own Bible!

The *Jefferson Bible* is an example of "Scripture by subtraction." It's where people keep what they like and throw out what they don't like. Jefferson saw no problem doing this, and many Christians don't have a problem doing this today either. However, what a dangerous way to approach Scripture!

Because God's Word is divinely inspired, it is not like a mere human piece of literature that we can tamper with or adjust to suit our purposes. We don't change or twist it to meet our culture or the political correctness of contemporary times. If there's a conflict with culture or with our lifestyle, the Bible wins. It is the deciding rule and standard for all beliefs (Isaiah 8:20). We don't push it aside for higher criticism, for our own personal theories, or even for a church's traditions or interpretations. Why? Because it came by inspiration of God, and God does not change (see 2 Peter 1:20, 21; Malachi 3:6).

What does it mean to live by every Word? you may be asking. In essence, it means that we measure our life against the standard of God's Word. Then we pray, "Lord, change me! Show me how to align my life with Your Word!" Of course, this doesn't just happen in our own strength. We need divine power combined with human effort. But God will send the Holy Spirit to help us if we earnestly seek Him.

Sadly, Thomas Jefferson is not the only one who has claimed to be a follower of Jesus but who wanted to follow the Bible according to his own dictates. Eric Ludy, in the following appeal, shares how this grave crisis is facing modern-day Christianity:

You look at the Word of God, and then you look at modern Christianity. Do you see a discrepancy? Some of us don't want to see the discrepancy. . . . And so we come up with elaborate doctrinal excuses for why we are where we are now, and why we are largely impotent as a church, and why our prayers seem to hit a tin roof. [However], the Word of God is timeless and eternal. It defines what Christianity is meant to be. Our God is not altered. Our God is not evolving. He does not change; He does not lie. There is no shadow of turning in Him. He is rock-like. Our God has not moved. It is us that have moved. We have moved, and we've lost sight of the Rock.[2]

As we seek to regain our footing on the Rock and gain strength for our daily spiritual battles, perhaps it would be helpful to remind ourselves how Jesus fought His spiritual battles.

Life lessons from our Savior
After being baptized by John the Baptist, Jesus was ready for ministry—

well, almost. The Bible tells us, "Then Jesus was led up by the Spirit into the wilderness to be tempted by the devil. And when He had fasted forty days and forty nights, afterward He was hungry" (Matthew 4:1, 2).

While we don't know about the temptations during those forty days, we do know that at the end of the struggle, when Jesus was at His weakest point, Satan thought it would be a great time for one last battle. And isn't this the way he attacks us today as well? He knows that when we are hungry (physically, spiritually, and emotionally), we are at our weakest point and most likely to give in to temptation.

"If You are the Son of God, command that these stones be made bread" (Matthew 4:3), Satan taunted.

This temptation was not just meant to make Jesus doubt who He was as the Son of God, but it was also to force Jesus to depend upon His own strength. After all, His Father hadn't provided any bread for the past forty days. Wasn't it only right that Jesus, who had the power, should start taking care of His own needs now?

Thankfully, Jesus didn't fall for the temptation. As one author nicely puts it, "Jesus would rather be fed with the smallest crust of His Father's Word than with an entire landscape of fresh bread from anywhere else."[3]

Is this our desire as well? Are we so captivated by our love for the Lord that we'd rather starve from man-made bread (lust of the flesh, lust of the world, and pride of life) than be separated from God's presence?

Although physically weak, Jesus responded to Satan's temptation with heavenly dignity, "It is written, 'Man shall not live by bread alone, but by every word that proceeds from the mouth of God'" (Matthew 4:4).

While Satan was rebuked, he was not discouraged. Thinking that another strategy might be more effective, Satan then took Jesus to the top of the temple in Jerusalem. It's almost as if he were thinking to himself: *OK, if You really believe that you can live by every Word of God, then let me see You prove it. In fact, prove it publicly so all the world will see.*

Once again, Satan spoke, "If You are the Son of God, throw Yourself down. For it is written: 'He shall give His angels charge over you,' and, 'In their hands, they shall bear you up, Lest you dash your foot against a stone'" (Matthew 4:6).

Author Ken Gire describes why this temptation might have been very appealing to Jesus in His weakened state: "The temple was the center of religious activity for Israel. The jump would be seen by all the key leaders. And the rescue would convince them that Jesus was indeed the Son of God. In a single act, [Jesus] could win over every skeptic and avoid years of conflict with the religious establishment."[4]

But Jesus knew that this was not His Father's way. God is not about showing off His power but about quietly convicting hearts of truth. He does not seek to operate by fireworks but by the fire of the Holy Spirit moving upon hearts. His way is not the way of shortcuts but the way of righteousness.

Jesus replied again, "It is written again, 'You shall not tempt the LORD your God' " (Matthew 4:7).

Ruffled, but not ready to give up, Satan takes Jesus to an even higher place—an exceedingly high mountain overlooking the kingdoms of the world.

As the rightful ruler over the earth, since Adam's fall in the Garden of Eden, Satan has control of these kingdoms—the kingdoms that Jesus has come to reclaim. But now Satan offers one more easy way out, a way past all the suffering and pain of Calvary. "These kingdoms can all belong to You, Jesus," Satan offers with a sly smile, "if You will only bow down for just a moment, and worship me."[5]

But Jesus knew the devil's tricks, and He had already counted the cost. Not for a moment would He think of betraying His Father or the children of the world who could only be bought back by His perfect sacrifice of obedience.

"Away with you, Satan!" Jesus spoke with determination. "For it is written, 'You shall worship the LORD your God, and Him only you shall serve' " (Matthew 4:10).[6]

The power that gave Jesus the strength to stand against Satan in the wilderness is the same power we have access to today. "In Christ, divinity and humanity were combined. Divinity was not degraded to humanity; divinity held its place, but humanity by being united to divinity withstood the fiercest test of temptation in the wilderness. . . . [Jesus] withstood the temptation, *through the power that man may command*. He laid hold on the throne of God, and there is not a man or woman who may not have access to the same help through faith in God. . . . Christ came to reveal the source of His power, that man might never rely on his unaided human capabilities."[7]

Satan could not stand against "It is written" then, and neither can he stand against the Word today.

Inspiration tells us, "Christ resisted the temptations of the enemy with the only weapon that the soldier of the cross of Christ can successfully use—'It is written.' Where? In the Old and New Testaments. With these words we are to defend ourselves and warn others, holding forth to them the word of life."[8]

The revival in Oradea

For more than twenty years, during the days of the Cold War between the United States and the Soviet Union, the people of Romania suffered great hardship. They were forced to live under the iron-fisted rule of one of the most corrupt leaders of the twentieth century, the Communist dictator Nicolae Ceausescu. Life was difficult for all, but Christians especially suffered under Ceausescu's harsh regime as they endured much harassment, persecution, and many even torture, imprisonment, and death.

One Christian who suffered from the Communist harassment was a pastor who I will call Stefan. In 1969, the government took away Pastor Stefan's preaching license, and he was left on the streets. Without a way to support his family, Stefan resorted to gluing paper shopping bags together so they could buy food to eat. Despite their impoverished living conditions, Pastor Stefan never lost his heart for pastoring. Each day while he worked, he prayed that God would give him the opportunity to serve again. He also prayed earnestly for revival—not just for the Communist persecutors, but especially for the Romanian church members themselves.

Four years later, miraculously, Pastor Stefan's preaching license was reinstated, and he was once again assigned to the ministry, this time to a large church in Oradea.

From the beginning of his time at this new church, Pastor Stefan emphasized prayer and revival, and he appealed to the church members themselves to repent. He was not content to deal in generalities, but with humble earnestness, and without apology, he showed church members how the Word of God is to be the standard in every area of our lives.

Many in today's day and age would not have been comfortable with Pastor Stefan's approach. How dare he confront people about specific sins and address unholy attitudes and behaviors! Shouldn't that be left to personal conscience? Perhaps. Yet the Romanian church members took Pastor Stefan's appeals to heart—and they repented. And what happened as a result? God sent revival!

After almost six months of earnest prayer and putting away sin within the church, God's Spirit began to be poured out. Despite this being a time that profession of faith meant persecution and hardship, and for some even martyrdom, many people, even those who had formerly ridiculed the Christians of Oradea, began coming of their own accord to the church, and baptisms began taking place. In previous years, the large congregation of five hundred was lucky if they might baptize ten individuals in a year, but from June to December in 1974, the church in Oradea baptized more than 250 new converts. By the end of four years, Pastor Stefan's church had doubled in size.

As the story goes, the revival could not be contained in just this single church, but continued to spread, affecting the entire Christian community of Romania. In fact, it is believed by many that this revival fire and emphasis on prayer and living by the Word is what lead to the eventual overthrow of the Ceausescu regime some fifteen years later.[9]

As I reflect on this story, I can't help thinking of these words from Inspiration: "A revival of true godliness among us is the greatest and most urgent of all our needs. To seek this should be our first work. The time has come for a thorough reformation to take place. When this reformation begins, the spirit of prayer will actuate every believer, and will banish from the church the spirit of discord and strife."[10]

Remember, the world is watching all those who profess to be Christians, and they mock our attempts at revival. They mock our profession of following Christ that bears little Christlikeness in life. Meanwhile, we keep praying that they, the mockers, will repent. What if it is *we the Christians* who need to repent?

As one author writes, "The church has been waiting for the world to get right with God. When will we realize that the world is waiting for the church to get right with God?"[11]

Commenting about the great revival in Oradea, Nancy DeMoss

Wolgemuth, in her book *Holiness*, writes, "In many of our churches, we're knocking ourselves out trying to be 'relevant' so we can attract new members. We don't want to appear to be different, extreme, or too spiritual, for fear of turning off unbelievers. By contrast, once the church in Oradea was willing to be different from the world, the very unbelievers who had once ridiculed them were irresistibly drawn to Christ. We have accommodated to the world rather than calling the world to accommodate to Christ. When will we recognize that the world is not impressed with a religious version of itself?"[12]

It's interesting that when we look across the spectrum of the Christian community today, we see an increased focus on revival gatherings, prayer breakfasts, prayer marches, peace gatherings, and events dedicated to "spiritual awakening." Many, even within secular society, are beginning to recognize that we need God's intervention, and we need help! But while I see a semblance of repenting going on, I see a disturbing lack of people who are willing to make radical changes to their everyday lifestyle. What part of "take up the cross and follow Jesus" (see Matthew 16:24) are we missing? What part of "be doers of the word, and not hearers only" (James 1:22) do we not understand?

Reflecting on this disturbing lack in modern-day Christianity, Mrs. Wolgemuth comments further, "The fact is, if people are not changing their lifestyle, they're not repenting. And if we're not repenting, then all our singing and praising and praying and producing are useless—perhaps worse than useless, because all the noise and activity may deceive us into thinking that we're OK and that we are actually experiencing revival,"[13] when we are not!

It's time we experience a genuine revival that brings change from the inside out. It's time we stop looking at our church as a customer service organization to please and entertain sinners and look at it as the evangelistic saving network that it was intended to be, here to save souls.

While God is calling us to a higher standard, He's not asking us for anything more than He has given us resources to do. "He 'hath blessed us with all spiritual blessings in heavenly places in Christ.' It would not satisfy the heart of the infinite One to give those who love His Son a lesser blessing than He gives His Son."[14]

In the remainder of this book, we will be delving into even more specific principles of practical godliness in everyday Christian living. I encourage you to keep your seat belt fastened and keep your Bible open as we move forward, daring to live by every Word.

Daring to Live by Every Word—Going Deeper!
Life Lessons From Our Savior: Matthew 4:4

To take the message of this chapter deeper, I encourage you to read chapter 27 in *The Great Controversy*, titled "Modern Revivals."[15] As you do this, ask yourself, "What is the difference between a true revival and a false revival? How do we see these differences at work in the churches of today?"

Now let's look at four areas of our life as we ask ourselves, "How does God's Word revive and reform my own life? How can we worship God by daring to live by every Word?"

Our Daily Decisions and Life Decisions: Are these based on biblical principles or our own feelings and desires? (See Matthew 4:4; Proverbs 3:5, 6; 14:12; 11:14.)

We are told, "So utterly was Christ emptied of self that He made no plans for Himself. He accepted God's plans for Him, and day by day the Father unfolded His plans. So should we depend upon God, that our lives may be the simple outworking of His will."[16]

Our Attitudes: What are our thoughts and the motive of our actions? Are we looking at life through the lens of God's Word, or through our own human mind-set? (See Philippians 2:5; 2 Corinthians 10:5; Philippians 4:8; Psalms 19:14; 119:165; Isaiah 55:8, 9.)

It is one thing to treat the Bible as a book of good moral instruction, to be heeded so far as is consistent with the spirit of the times and our position in the world; it is another thing to regard it as it really is—the word of the living God, the word that is our life, the word that is to mold our actions, our words, and our thoughts. To hold God's word as anything less than this is to reject it. And this rejection by those who profess to believe it, is foremost among the causes of skepticism and infidelity in the youth.[17]

Our Lifestyle: Does our lifestyle (from how we spend our money to what we do for fun, to what we eat and how we spend our time) glorify God or is it more about glorifying self? (See 1 Corinthians 10:31; 6:19, 20; Romans 13:14.)

"Those who decide to do nothing in any line that will displease God, will know, after presenting their case before Him, just what course to pursue. And they will receive not only wisdom, but strength. Power for obedience, for service, will be imparted to them, as Christ has promised."[18]

Our Life Vision and Goals: Do these reflect heavenly goals or earthly goals? (See Matthew 6:33; Hebrews 11:16; 2 Corinthians 5:18.)

If our decisions/attitudes/lifestyles/goals do not align with "It is written" in Scripture, are we willing to make some changes? If so, how will we go about making these changes? (*Hint: Refer back to chapter 5 if you are not sure.*)

As you finish this chapter, take some time to sing or reflect on the song, "All the Way." It's number 516 in the *Seventh-day Adventist Hymnal.* Let us pray that God will help us go all the way with Him. Let us pray that we can truly learn to live by the "It is written" of His Holy Word!

Time to dig deep into God's Word, get on our knees, and allow the Holy Spirit to take this message deeper into our hearts!

Part 3

THE WORD THAT TRANSFORMS

Chapter 11

Jesus, Make Yourself at Home!

Handing Over All the Keys

"Behold, I stand at the door and knock. If anyone hears My voice and opens the door, I will come in to him and dine with him, and he with Me."

—Revelation 3:20

I'll never forget the day my friends and I had just finished leading an hour of united prayer at a large youth conference when someone brought us an expensive jeweled watch that had been left on one of the chairs. At first, we thought someone had forgotten the watch by accident, but then we found a note that had been left with the watch. The note was written in neat handwriting and read, "This watch has not been forgotten but is being surrendered. I knew better, and I should never have bought it. It has become an idol to me. There have been many layers in my heart between me and God, but now there is one layer less. Praise the Lord (Ezekiel 36:26)."

Naturally, we desire to touch and hold the things of the world in our hands. We desire to dress like the world, act like the world, and adapt to the world's standard of living. But the Bible tells us if we love the things of the world (in other words, if the things of the world absorb our primary focus and affections), we do not love God (1 John 2:3–6). In fact, those who are friends with the world are actually enemies of God (James 4:4).

The Bible also tells us, "Do not lay up for yourselves treasures on earth, where moth and rust destroy and where thieves break in and steal; but lay up for yourselves treasures in heaven, where neither moth nor rust destroys and where thieves do not break in and steal. For where your treasure is, there your heart will be also" (Matthew 6:19–21).

In Colossians 3:1–3, we read, "If ye then be risen with Christ, seek those things which are above, where Christ sitteth on the right hand of God. Set your affection on things above, not on things on the earth. For ye are dead, and your life is hid with Christ in God" (KJV).

Imagine with me that Jesus is knocking on the door of your home. In fact, you don't have to imagine, because the Bible tells us that He really is (Revelation 3:20). Of course, most of us have no problem inviting Jesus into the *living room* of our lives. Here we are on our best behavior and life is usually nice and tidy because things are in their proper place.

"Make Yourself at home!" we cheerfully tell Jesus as we motion to a comfortable chair. "My Bible is on the table, in case You want to read. Now, You relax here while I go do my own thing." Then we turn and go to some private room and close the door.

However, Jesus doesn't knock on the door of our home simply to stay in the living room. And so He begins to roam around the house, knocking on different doors, opening drawers, and looking in different rooms.

"You mean, You want in my kitchen and my office? You want in my bedroom too?" we groan as we reluctantly open the doors.

"Oh, Jesus, don't look in my closet! And please don't go down to the basement? It's such a mess."

"You said to make Yourself at home," Jesus responds. "Did you really mean it?"

Jesus is asking us to open the door of our life and invite Him inside, in *very real* and *tangible* ways. If we want the Holy Spirit's full blessing, this means we surrender every room in our life and heart to Him. We invite Him inside and say, "Jesus, this house is Yours! This life is Yours!

Make Yourself at home! I give You everything that goes in my food pantry and on my table, everything I put in my closet or hang on my wall, every dollar in my savings account, every internet hour, every Sabbath evening, everything I read on social media, everything I watch on my computer or television,[1] everything I listen to on the radio, every item on my agenda, every meeting, every task in ministry, every plan for my future, every relationship, every hope, every dream, every secret. Jesus, You can have my all!"

As blood from the heart flows through all our organs and tissues giving vitalizing life and oxygen to every area of our bodies, so true love for Jesus in the heart will impact every corner and every area of our lives and homes—not just figuratively, but in very real, practical, everyday sort of ways.

We are told, "God cannot reveal Himself till those who profess to be Christians are doers of His Word in their private lives, till there is oneness with Christ."[2]

While it may be easy to keep the living room looking respectable, if things that cause spiritual compromise live in the kitchen, the bedroom, or the closet, does the house really belong to God?

Remember, "Those who feel the constraining love of God, do not ask how little may be given to meet the requirements of God; they do not ask for the lowest standard but aim at perfect conformity to the will of their Redeemer."[3]

A home and life patterned after God's Word

A few years ago, my family and friends got together to help build me a small cabin, a small oasis, on our family property where I could rest and work in between my travels in ministry. What a precious gift and blessing this has been.

However, let me tell you how my cabin was built—not only was each part of the process a gift and miracle, but it was also built through much prayer. In fact, from the very beginning, even as the foundation of my new home was being laid, I was determined that this place was going to be dedicated to God, and so I prayed. As the floor, then the rafters and walls began to take shape, I prayed more.

Not only did I pray over this little building, but I also wrote Bible verses all throughout the walls and rafters, as I dedicated all the rooms of my home to Jesus. By the time my cabin was completed, more than 280 Scripture references were hidden within its small wooden frame.

Perhaps this might seem a bit extreme, but to this very day, guests who stay in my cabin often comment that they can feel the Holy Spirit in this little building, and I believe they are right. But He's not here simply because there are Bible verses written in my walls. He's here because I've chosen to give my heart, and all the rooms of my home and life, to Him.

Of course, I still fall short of God's perfect standard, and I often do things that grieve the heart of God; but as I keep running to the Cross and confessing my sin, I rest in the assurance that Jesus' perfect life covers mine.

You have a home as well! Have you dedicated all the rooms of your home to Jesus?

While your home may not be a cabin in the Ozarks of Arkansas, it's the framework and structure of the life in which you live. Some of us may have homes that are large and elaborate with lots of extra rooms, and some of us may have homes that are quite small and simple. It doesn't matter! Each home, each life, has similar functions. They are the places where we eat, sleep, love, work, study, socialize, play, and pray. Sometimes our homes are even the places where we hide our secret baggage.

As we ask Jesus to come and make Himself at home in our lives, let's take a few moments to talk about practical daily life as our home (both physically and spiritually) relates to the Word of God.

Prayerfully consider the following thoughts, and if possible, take time to look up the scriptures that I reference. You might even want to turn this section into a weeklong Bible study, looking at one theme per day.

The Foundation and Building: Is your physical home built on a solid foundation? How about your spiritual home? What are the foundational principles that guide you and hold you fast through the storms of life? What are the protective walls that guard your heart? What kind of roof helps your home be a haven where the Holy Spirit can dwell? (1 Timothy 6:19; Psalm 127:1; 1 Corinthians 3:11; Matthew 7:24, 25; Psalm 91:1; Isaiah 8:20; Psalm 16:8; Proverbs 29:18).

The Door: If you want to stay safe physically in today's world, you need doors that lock and keep out evil—the same spiritually. Just as nothing will be allowed into heaven that defiles, we need God to help us establish doors and boundaries in our life that lock out spiritual compromise and sin. We don't want to allow any spiritual breaches where the enemy can sneak in.

However, the Bible also tells us that we need to have an open door of love for the needy and that when people enter our homes, not only should they enjoy Christian fellowship, but they should see examples of a life lived according to the Word of God. Keep in mind that not everyone who comes through our doors will embrace the same biblical standards that we uphold. That's OK! We are to use our homes as a witness, even to the lost (Revelation 21:27; Deuteronomy 11:18–21; Matthew 5:14–16; Deuteronomy 28:6; Matthew 19:14; Isaiah 43:10).

I remember a story I heard recently about a mom whose daughter had chosen an alternative lifestyle. While the Christian mother stood unwaveringly for biblical truth, when her daughter came home, with girlfriend in tow, she loved them both. Her love, along with the power of the Holy Spirit, eventually melted the heart of both her daughter and the partner—and both girls ended up giving their lives to Jesus as a result. How different things probably would have turned out if the mom had taken a hard stance and said, "Since you've chosen this lifestyle, you are no longer allowed to visit your home!"

Remember, while we can't support anything that goes against God's Word, we are to continue to love all for whom Jesus died. Thankfully, God didn't wait until we had stopped sinning to invite us to His home. Even while we were yet sinners, the invitation was given from the cross (Romans 5:8; 1 John 4:8, 16).

The Living Room: This is usually the center of social activity and fellowship in our home and heart. This is where we relax and hang out during downtime. This is also where we entertain guests. How is this space being used in your home? Would you be comfortable inviting Jesus as a personal guest during your relaxed, downtime, to watch what you watch, to be part of your living room conversations? Is this space used merely for personal pleasures or is the living room of your life a place where you bring people together to pray and study God's Word, and to encourage others in the faith? (Proverbs 29:18; John 4:34, 35; Hebrews 10:24, 25; James 5:16; 1 Peter 3:15; Matthew 6:33; Ephesians 4:32; 5:4; Psalms 37:3–5; 115:1).

The Kitchen: "Oh, now we are getting a bit personal," I can hear you thinking. "Are you really going to tell us that Jesus wants in our kitchens too?" Yes! Absolutely! The Bible tells us, "Therefore, whether you eat or drink, or whatever you do, do all to the glory of God" (1 Corinthians 10:31).

Since the battle over appetite is so significant, I will focus on this subject a little more in-depth later on in this book. But can we all agree that we desperately need the Holy Spirit to change our appetites, not just for the food we put on our plate but for the food we put in our mind, what we feast upon in our thoughts, and for what we enjoy consuming for entertainment? Craving that which destroys comes naturally. That's why "over and over again the battle [against appetite] must be fought"[4] (Daniel 1:8; Proverbs 23:2; John 6:27; Psalm 101:3; Philippians 4:8).

The Bedroom: This is your private space. Only those closest to you are allowed into this room. This is the place where you rest, pray, and perhaps spend your most intimate heart-to-heart moments with family, and with God. But what else happens behind these closed doors? Does this private space honor God in every way, or would you be ashamed if the world could see some of the things that happen in this room? (Hebrews 13:4; Mark 6:31; 1:35; Isaiah 26:9; Matthew 10:27; Psalm 51:10–12; Ephesians 5:22–33).

John Kitcher writes, "The life you live in private determines the ministry you can have in public."[5]

But it's not just about what happens behind the privacy of a closed door. What is even more significant is about what happens in the privacy of your mind. What thoughts and motives prompt your actions? What are the things you fantasize and dream about at night? What things do you think about but never dare to say?

Ellen White reminds us, "God's law looks into the secrets of the heart. Every act is judged by the motives that prompt it. Only that which is in accord with the principles of God's law will stand in the judgment."[6]

The Closet and Storage Space: Not only does God care about the physical clothes we put on our body, He also cares about the emotional things we store in our private closet and storage space. Are you using your personal closet to store unforgiveness, bitterness, or resentment against others? Are you saving baggage from the past that Jesus is asking you to give to Him? Or are you using your closet to pray for those who have wounded you and for those who need salvation? Let's pray that even in our personal closets, God would be glorified (Isaiah 1:16–18; Romans 13:14; 1 Timothy 2:9; Isaiah 61:10; Matthew 6:6; Psalm 5:3).

There are more living spaces I have probably failed to mention, but I think you get the idea. While we might not physically write God's Word on the doorposts of our home, His Word should influence every area of our practical daily life, from what books we put on our shelves, to what we bring home from the grocery store, to what choices we make for family entertainment, to what motives prompt our actions, and even to what we choose to wear. This may seem a bit extreme to some, but it's not extreme for those who are preparing for a heavenly home (Hebrews 11:10) and for those who long to be part of the 144,000.

Revelation 14:4, 5 tells us, "These are the ones who follow the Lamb wherever He goes. These were redeemed from among men, being firstfruits to God and to the Lamb. And in their mouth was found no deceit, for they are without fault before the throne of God."

"O that you would search your hearts as with a lighted candle," writes Ellen White, "and discover and break the finest thread that binds you to worldly habits, which divert the mind from God!"[7]

Amy Carmichael once wrote the following, as she challenged Christians to give Jesus their all. Her appeal is timeless!

We must look upon the world, with all its delights and all its attractions, with suspicion and reserve. We are called to a higher Kingdom; we are touched with a divine Spirit. It is not that He forbids us this or that comfort or indulgence; it is not that He is stern, demanding us to follow a narrow path. But we who love our Lord and whose affections are set on Heavenly things voluntarily and gladly lay aside the things that charm and ravish the world, that, for our part, our hearts may be ravished with the things of Heaven and that our whole being may be poured forth in constant and unreserved devotion in the service of the Lord who died to save us.[8]

Each day Jesus is asking for the keys to our mind and heart, the keys to our home, and the keys to every area of our life. However, He only asks so that He can give us something greater in return. Give me the keys to your heart, He tells us, "and I will give you the keys of the kingdom of heaven" (Matthew 16:19).

As we close this chapter, I have one question—who holds the keys to your home and heart?

Daring to Live by Every Word—Going Deeper!
Handing Over All the Keys: Revelation 3:20

As you reflect on this chapter, what rooms in your home (life) are you reluctant to allow Jesus to enter? What is causing you to hold back the keys? Are you afraid that what He asks of you might be more than you can bear? What changes do you need to make so that Jesus will be completely welcome in your daily life?

Ellen White writes, "If the heart has been renewed by the Spirit of God, the life will bear witness to the fact. . . . A change will be seen in the character, the habits, the pursuits."[9]

It's time to ask the question, "How can we love and worship God more fully in our private home life?" If you ask this question in sincerity, the Holy Spirit will show you.

I encourage you to go back through this chapter with your Bible and look up each reference mentioned in the section titled "A home and life patterned after God's Word." What additional scriptures come to mind?

Here are some more heart-to-heart questions:[10]

- Does God stand as the head of my home? (Colossians 3:18–21)
- Have I truly put on the "new self" as Ephesians 4:17–24 calls us to do?
- Am I sensitive to the voice of the Holy Spirit? (Ephesians 4:30)
- Are my thoughts and motives pure? (Proverbs 12:5)
- Does God's peace fill my heart? (Colossians 3:15; Psalm 37:37)
- Do I exhibit godly character and moral purity? (Ephesians 5:1, 3)
- Do I always speak the truth? (Colossians 3:9, 10; Ephesians 4:25)
- Am I keeping a guard over my tongue? (Ephesians 4:29; 5:4)

- Am I walking in forgiveness and love? (Colossians 3:12, 13)
- Am I avoiding all appearances of darkness? (1 Thessalonians 5:22; Ephesians 5:8, 11)
- Am I actively walking in the light? (Ephesians 5:8–10)
- Am I covered in the blood of Jesus or trusting in my own works? (Ephesians 2:8, 9)
- Am I so focused on obeying the letter of the law that I've forgotten the spirit of the law? (Romans 2:28, 29; 2 Corinthians 3:6)
- Sing or reflect on the song, "The Savior Is Waiting," hymn no. 289.

Jesus tells us in Matthew 7:21 that if we call Him Lord and profess to serve Him but do not obey His Father's will (which is revealed in obedience to His Word—see James 1:22), we cannot hope to enter heaven. However, Jesus then adds, "Many will say to me in that day, 'Lord, Lord, have we not prophesied in Your name, cast out demons in Your name, and done many wonders in Your name?' And then will I declare to them, '*I never knew you*: depart from Me, you who practice lawlessness!' " (Matthew 7:22, 23; emphasis added).

Remember, if we do all the good things the Bible tells us to do, but *still don't know Jesus personally*, what have we gained? Nothing! Dear Reader, do you know Jesus personally? Is He your friend? Do you walk with Him and talk with Him and cry to Him as you would a trusted friend? Do you honor His Word out of genuine love, or is your obedience out of obligation or because of the expectations of others?

Let's pray that the Holy Spirit will teach us to truly know and love Jesus as a best friend, the Friend who will be more than a passing guest, but an integral part of our daily life, an integral part of every room in our home.

Time to dig deep into God's Word, get on our knees, and allow the Holy Spirit to take this message deeper into our hearts!

Chapter 12

Following in His Footsteps

Virtuous Living in an Unvirtuous World

> *He who says he abides in Him ought himself
> also to walk just as He walked.*
>
> —1 John 2:6

In 1994, the country of Rwanda experienced a horrifying genocide, which left more than a million people dead. About 100,000 of these were Adventist members.

During the heat of the conflict, one tribe was seeking to exterminate the other tribe. The tribe being attacked rushed to the churches for safety, thinking that they would not be killed while there. In one of these churches, a group of Adventists huddled together.

The doors were locked, and everyone clung to each other, praying for safety. But soon there was a loud banging on the doors, and the vicious mob broke in. As the killers came into the church, one young man shouted, "Who is the leader of this group?" The Seventh-day Adventist pastor slowly stood up. "I am," he replied. The young man rushed toward him with a machete, killing the pastor instantly. Then the mob began to kill everyone in the church. Only a few escaped. It was a horrific massacre.

A couple of days later, after the killers had moved on, those who had survived came to collect the dead bodies to bury them in a mass grave. When they were picking up the bodies, they found one woman's heart was still beating. They rushed her to the hospital, hoping to save her life. Her fight for life was very intense, but she survived. She was in and out of the hospital for the next three years. Finally, she began to start life over. She was the wife of the pastor who was the first one killed in the massacre.

As Marie began a new life, she decided that she did not want her husband's death to be in vain. She also decided that she would not live in bitterness and hatred but instead offer forgiveness to those who had hurt her so deeply.

In the book of Romans, she read, " 'If your enemy is hungry, feed him; if he is thirsty, give him a drink; for in so doing you will heap coals of fire on his head.' Do not be overcome by evil, but overcome evil with good" (Romans 12:20, 21).

Discovering that some of the killers had been captured and were in a nearby prison, Marie went to see them and take them food. As time passed, she became the mother of that prison, regularly bringing the prisoners food and blankets. She also began studying the Bible with the prisoners.

One day, while ministering to the prisoners, a young man whom I will call Paul came and fell at her feet and began kissing her feet. "Madam, do you remember me?" he asked. Marie swallowed hard as she recognized his face. It was the man who had killed her husband. He had tried to kill her, as well.

"Madam, would you forgive me?" Paul asked with tears in his eyes. She picked Paul up off the floor and hugged him. "I have already forgiven you. I have decided in my heart that I will not hate you. I will not waste my years with bitterness or grudges. I just want to love and serve the Lord. I have forgiven you."

For the next six months, Marie studied the Bible with Paul. As a result, Paul made the decision to be baptized. On the day of his baptism, he stood up in front of the whole prison and confessed his sins. It was beautiful and moving. Marie was there!

After a few years, the government of Rwanda gave Paul amnesty, and he was released from prison. However, Paul's family, including his father and mother, had also been killed in the genocide. And he had nowhere to go. Walking to Marie's home after his release, he knocked on her door. "I'm alone and don't know where to go. What should I do?" he asked. She smiled. "I'm alone too! I will adopt you as my son, and together we will wait for Jesus to return. Then we will meet our loved ones again."[1]

In the book *Christ Object Lessons*, we read, "The last rays of merciful light, the last message of mercy to be given to the world, is a revelation of His character of love. The children of God are to manifest His glory. In their own life and character they are to reveal what the grace of God has done for them."[2]

Perhaps Marie's actions might seem to be an extreme example of modeling the love and grace of Jesus; however, I believe that this is *just the kind of Christianity* that God is calling each of us to embrace. It's unthinkable! It's radical! It's supernatural! And it's humanly impossible, except for the person who is filled with the Holy Spirit.

The upside down model for Christian living!

When we read about the life of Jesus in the Gospels, we discover that the discipleship model He laid out for us to follow is completely upside down and backward to how society would encourage us to live. It's completely backward to the typical worldly rules for success.

Let me share some examples:

- The world says that if you want success, always strive to be first. Jesus says that in His kingdom, the first shall be last (see Matthew 20:16).
- The world says to take care of yourself. Jesus says that it's all about taking care of the needs of others (see Matthew 20:28).
- The world says to seek to pamper yourself and live this life to the fullest. Jesus says that it's time to die to self and selfish pleasures and live for others (see Matthew 16:24).
- The world says to do good so everyone can see you, and you will earn respect. Jesus says that if our motive is to be seen by humans, we will have no reward in heaven. In fact, He says that what we do in secret and without attempting to gain attention is what counts most (see Matthew 6:1, 6).
- The world says to make friends with the rich and famous so you can get an edge. Jesus says to learn what it means to serve the least of

these, for these are the famous and great ones in His kingdom (see Matthew 25:45).

- The world says to lay up your treasures now, focusing on getting as much as you can now. But Jesus says that the temporal treasures you lay up now will rust and be destroyed. The only treasures that last are those you send to heaven (see Matthew 6:19, 20).

If you think these principles are extreme, they are merely the icing on the cake of Christian living. This next command is where the rubber meets the road. This is where true Christianity is really put on display for the glory of God.

- The world says, "Eye for eye and tooth for tooth" and "Love your neighbor but hate your enemies." But Jesus says to love your enemies. If you are slapped, turn the other cheek (see Matthew 5:38–44).

Let's look at this command more closely, as recorded in the biblical book of Luke.

"Bless those who curse you, and pray for those who spitefully use you. To him who strikes you on the one cheek, offer the other also. And from him who takes away your cloak, do not withhold your tunic either. Give to everyone who asks of you. And from him who takes away your goods do not ask them back. And just as you want men to do to you, you also do to them likewise.

"But if you love those who love you, what credit is that to you? For even sinners love those who love them. And if you do good to those who do good to you, what credit is that to you? For even sinners do the same. And if you lend to those from whom you hope to receive back, what credit is that to you? For even sinners lend to sinners to receive as much back. But love your enemies, do good, and lend, hoping for nothing in return; and your reward will be great, and you will be sons of the Most High. For He is kind to the unthankful and evil. Therefore be merciful, just as your Father also is merciful" (Luke 6:28–36).

Imagine how different our world would be if every Christian put these principles into everyday practice! Imagine how soon the Holy Spirit would be poured out, and the work would be finished if this were the way we modeled the love of Christ.

John 13:35 says, "By this all will know that you are My disciples, if you have love for one another."

Turning the other cheek

I will never forget the day I met Tom.[3] At the time, I was traveling with one of my best friends, Julia O'Carey, throughout Southeast Asia. We were interviewing dozens of Bible workers and church planters for ASAP Ministries.[4]

Tom was a Bible worker serving in a difficult region where sharing the gospel is not always easy, and many Christians are persecuted for their faith.

With the help of a translator, Tom told me his moving story.

Not long before, he and his wife had been in a motorcycle accident. The accident had occurred as they had been stopped beside the road when another cyclist came along and hit them from behind. Thankfully, no one was seriously injured, even though both motorcycles were damaged. The man who hit them was drunk. He was also the chief of a nearby village.

Although Tom didn't have much money, instead of getting angry over the accident, he asked the chief, "How shall we solve this problem?"

"You need to fix my motorcycle!" the chief rudely responded.

Without argument, Tom paid for the motorcycle repairs—but he didn't stop there. In addition, he visited the chief and started looking for ways to help him and his family, even offering to go out and plow his field. Tom did so many nice things for this chief and his family that people in that village could not help noticing.

"Our chief is a very rude man!" someone told Tom one day. "Why are you being so kind to him?"

"Because I love Jesus, and I want to share His love with others," Tom responded.

Not long after, some of the villagers asked Tom if he would teach them more about Jesus. By the time Tom shared his testimony with me, he was already conducting Bible studies with a number of the villagers, and a few were already preparing for baptism. The amazing miracle is that this village was in an area that Tom had tried unsuccessfully to share the gospel with previously. But now, through Tom's kindness to the chief, God had made a breakthrough.

Can you imagine how different things might be in our world and even in our church today if we went the extra mile and served with such selfless humility, even when we've been wronged?

In *The Ministry of Healing*, we read, "We cannot afford to let our spirits chafe over any real or supposed wrong done to ourselves. Self is the enemy that we most need to fear. . . . No other victory we can gain will be so precious as the victory gained over self. We should not allow our feelings to be easily wounded. We are to live, not to guard our feelings or our reputation, but to save souls."[5]

Virtuous living in an UnVirtuous world

In an age when being *unvirtuous* is normal; when it's considered OK to honk your horn in anger at those who get in your way, or to show your attitude to those that don't serve you fast enough; when it's standard practice to use social media to vent your frustrations about life, the church, or bad politics, or when it's considered *courageous* to speak up and use strong heated words to make a statement, God is calling His people to a higher standard. He's calling us to virtuous living, to virtuous loving, to virtuous speaking, and even to virtuous thinking.[6]

While some might think that strong, passionate words or actions show strength of character, the reality is that the person who is mastered by his passions is the weakest. "The highest evidence of nobility in a Christian is self-control."[7]

Proverbs 25:28 reminds us, "Whoever has no rule over his own spirit is like a city broken down, without walls." In Psalm 119:165 we read, "Great peace have they which love thy law: and nothing shall offend them" (KJV). In Proverbs 15:1, 2 we are told,

A soft answer turns away wrath,
But a harsh word stirs up anger.
The tongue of the wise uses knowledge rightly,
But the mouth of fools pours forth foolishness.

Amazed by what he saw happening in the world around him, the apostle James also wrote, "But no man can tame the tongue. It is an unruly evil, full of deadly poison. With it we bless our God and Father, and with it we curse men, who have been made in the similitude of God. Out of the same mouth proceed blessing and cursing. My brethren, these things ought not to be so" (James 3:8–10).

It's time we put away our earthly ways of thinking, speaking, and living. Jesus didn't fight His battles like we tend to fight battles today. Jesus humbled Himself even to death on the cross. He did this not just for you and me, but for the very ones who hurt us most. Remember this next time you are tempted to be bitter or to give someone a piece of your mind. When Jesus was wounded, He bled love and forgiveness. He's asking us to bleed love and forgiveness too.

Jesus was the Fruit of the Spirit *in person*! In Galatians 5:22, 23, we are told, "But the fruit of the Spirit is love, joy, peace, longsuffering, kindness, goodness, faithfulness, gentleness, self-control."

If Jesus is abiding within us, and we are abiding in Him, good fruit will come out! When we recognize this beautiful truth, our whole focus will change. Rather than praying to be more loving, we will pray that Love Himself will fill us (John 15:10). Rather than praying to forgive, we will pray that Forgiveness Himself will live in us (Luke 23:34). Rather than praying that God will make us more peaceful or joyful, we will pray that the God of peace and joy will dwell within us, through His Spirit (John 14:27; 15:11). Rather than praying to be more faithful or self-controlled, we will pray that the God of faithfulness and self-control will live within us (1 Thessalonians 5:24; Hebrews 10:23). Rather than praying to be more good or kind, we will pray that God who alone is good and kind will overtake us (Matthew 19:17). This is the essence of what it really means to be God's holy dwelling place (Ephesians 2:22).

Remember, *love* is the basis for all God's laws and commands, and love for God should be the compelling motive for our obedience to His Word. That's why, when Jesus was asked by religious leaders what the greatest commandment was, He replied, " 'You shall love the LORD your God with all your heart, with all your soul, and with all your mind.' This is the first and great commandment. And the second is like it: 'You shall love your neighbor as yourself.' On these two commandments hang all the Law and the Prophets" (Matthew 22:37–39).[8]

So what comes out when *you* are wounded and when *your* anger is stirred? As the saying goes, "Knocking over a glass doesn't determine the contents that will be spilled. It merely shows what was already inside the glass."

While virtuous living, loving, speaking, and thinking is God's desire for every Christian, I appreciate the words of caution that my friend Frank Hasel shares in his book *Living for God: Reclaiming the Joy of Christian Virtue*. He writes:

> When pursuing virtue, we must be careful not to focus only on isolated behaviors. By focusing on isolated behaviors, we are easily tempted to define who we are by what we *do*. We often boast about those areas in which we excel and are successful. While it's true that *what* we do is important, *why* we do it is even more important. Our deepest spiritual identity is not derived from what we do but from who we are and to whom we ultimately belong. Only as we realize who we are [in Christ], will we be able to live virtuously.[9]

Here, we come to the very heart of Christian living! Let's not allow Satan to rob us of our identity in Jesus. Let's not allow him to create division among us or to cripple our witness. Jesus has purchased us with His own blood. We are His! We are royal sons and daughters of the Most High God. Let's live like it! Jesus has shown through His own example how to live virtuously in an un-virtuous world. Because He conquered, we can conquer through His virtue and strength! "If we are determined not to be separated from the Source of our strength, Jesus will be just as determined to be at our right hand to help us."[10]

Of course, we can't love as Jesus loved or live as Jesus lived in our own human flesh. It's simply impossible. But Luke 18:27 reminds us, "The things which are impossible with men are possible with God." Truly, we can do all things *through Him*! So, let's stay on our knees at the foot of the cross as we ask Him to teach us what it means to abide in His love and how to share His love with those around us.

Daring to Live by Every Word—Going Deeper!
Virtuous Living: 1 John 2:6

As you allow this message to go deeper in your heart, consider the following passage from Scripture. "He who does not love does not know God, for God is love. . . . Beloved, if God so loved us, we also ought to love one another. . . . If we love one another, God abides in us, and His love has been perfected in us. By this we know that we abide in Him, and He in us, because He has given us of His Spirit" (1 John 4:8, 11–13).

I love the following thoughts from *Steps to Christ*:

[Jesus] exercised the greatest tact and thoughtful, kind attention in His relationships with the people. He was never rude, never needlessly spoke a severe word, never gave needless pain to a sensitive soul. He did not censure human weakness. He spoke the truth, but always in love. He denounced hypocrisy, unbelief, and iniquity; but tears were in His voice as He uttered His scathing rebukes. . . . His life was one of self-denial and thoughtful care for others. Every soul was precious in His eyes. While He ever bore Himself with divine dignity, He bowed with the tenderest regard to every member of the family of God. In all men He saw fallen souls whom it was His mission to save."[11]

It's time to open our Bibles and consider God's call to virtuous living, even in an un-virtuous world!

- 1 John 2:6; 4:16—How can we worship God by virtuous living in an unvirtuous world?
- 1 John 4:20, 21—Can we love God and hate someone at the same time?
- Matthew 5:28—Why are "thought sins" like lust so dangerous?
- Matthew 12:34—Why is it important that our hearts be in the right place?
- Philippians 2:5—What type of mind should we pray for?
- 2 Corinthians 10:4, 5—What kind of weapons should we fight with?

- Revelation 12:10—When tempted to publicly accuse others, ask yourself who was the original "accuser of our brethren"?
- John 17:21—Why it is important that we be *one* in the Lord?
- Matthew 11:29—How did Jesus display meekness and humility in His life?
- John 17:8—How did Jesus choose what words to speak?
- Luke 23:34—How did Jesus respond when taken to Calvary?
- 1 Peter 2:18–23—What can we learn from Jesus' example in suffering?
- Sing or reflect on the song, "Tis Love That Makes Us Happy," hymn no. 579.

To take this message even deeper, I encourage you to turn to Appendix 3 in the back of this book and read *The Sentinel at the Door* as well as some heart questions by Mark Finley.

If you are tempted to get discouraged with your many shortcomings, remember that, "The Lord God through Jesus Christ holds out His hand all the day long in invitation to the sinful and fallen. He will receive all. He welcomes all. It is His glory to pardon the chief of sinners."[12] We all fall short of the glory of God, but praise the Lord, we have a Savior!

Time to dig deep into God's Word, get on our knees, and allow the Holy Spirit to take this message deeper into our hearts!

Chapter 13

Where All True Ministry Begins

A Home Ruled by Love, Mercy, and Grace

And be kind to one another, tenderhearted, forgiving one another, even as God in Christ forgave you.
—Ephesians 4:32

One day my friend Janet Page and her husband Jerry got a phone call that their teenage son Zac had been suspended from school. Hardly believing the news, Janet hung up the phone in shock. *How could our son do such a thing? He knows better. We have taught him better than this*, she thought angrily. Then it was that she heard God speaking to her heart, "Instead of wondering why Zac has done what he has done, why don't you ask Me what you have done?"

"But I haven't done anything," Janet argued with God. However, as Janet opened her Bible and knelt to pray, God began showing Janet that it was actually certain behaviors in her own life over the years that had prompted Zac to act as he was acting now. Janet was devastated. Right then and there on her knees, with tears in her eyes, she repented, confessed her sin, and asked God for forgiveness. "Please change me, Lord. Help me not to be this way anymore," she cried.

Later that day, when Zac arrived home from school, he expected a harsh scolding from his mother. Instead, Janet shared with him what God had laid on her heart. "Zac," she said, "I have confessed this as sin to God, and I know He forgives me, but will you forgive me for being a bad example to you as your mother?"

Tears came to Zac's eyes, and his hardened spirit softened as God began healing the spiritual breach in his own heart.

Isaiah 49:25 tells us, "For I will contend with him who contends with you, and I will save your children." And God fulfilled this promise to Jerry and Janet.

Now years later, Zachary Page is a pastor who, along with his wife Leah, joyfully serves the Lord in ministry. In fact, he is not only passionate about seeing souls won to Jesus but also about helping people overcome spiritual breaches that hinder their walk with God.

Perhaps you are a parent and have children who are struggling in their walk with God. Perhaps sometimes you are tempted to despair, feeling your own shortcomings and wondering if your prayers will ever make a difference.

Augustine of Hippo, the fourth-century bishop whose writings have added much to the Christian faith, was a very influential philosopher and theologian in early church history. Yet, according to historical records, he was not always a Christian. So what led to his conversion? The answer is his praying mother! Listen to what Ellen White writes about Augustine's mother.

The mother of Augustine prayed for her son's conversion. She saw no evidence that the Spirit of God was impressing his heart, but she was not discouraged. She laid her finger upon the texts, presenting before God His own words, and pleaded as only a mother can. Her deep humiliation, her earnest importunities, her unwavering faith, prevailed, and the Lord gave her the desire of her heart. Today [God] is just as ready to listen to the petitions of His people. "His hand is not shortened that it cannot save, neither His ear heavy that it cannot hear;" [Isaiah 59:1] and if Christian parents seek Him earnestly, He will fill their mouths with arguments, and, for His name's sake, will work mightily in their behalf in the conversion of their children.[1]

So long as there is breath, there is hope! Never stop praying for your straying children or loved ones!

As the Bible shows, there were many struggles and conflicts within the families of our biblical ancestors. Even our Adventist pioneers had their marriage struggles, children struggles, and faith struggles. And yet God still worked, and God still used these imperfect people with their imperfect family relationships to bring glory and honor to His name.

The simple reality is that we are all broken people living in an imperfect, broken world, but God does not forsake us. But neither does He leave us where we are! Maybe that's why Ellen White once wrote, "If there is in the family one child who is unconscious of his sinful state, parents should not rest. Let the candle be lighted. Search the word of God, and by its light let everything in the home be diligently examined, to see why this child is lost. Let parents search their own hearts, examine their habits and practices. Children are the heritage of the Lord, and we are answerable to Him for our management of His property."[2]

While this might be a painful assignment—could this appeal be not only for the salvation of straying children but also for the deeper conversion of parents as well?

Learning to love as Jesus loves
The Bible tells us, in Romans 8:29, that God's purpose for our lives as believers is to conform us into the image of His Son. This means that Jesus' character of love must become our character. "We should study more earnestly the character of our Saviour. We should imitate the lovely Pattern that God has given us. We should dwell upon the matchless charms of Jesus until there will be nothing satisfying in this perishing world. We should desire to reflect his image in kindness, in courtesy, in gentleness, and love, then 'when he shall appear, we shall be like him; for we shall see him as he is.' "[3]

When we look at the character of Jesus, we see that He was a beautiful picture of *unconditional love, mercy, and grace.* Of course, we worship and praise Him for these character traits, and we often preach about them from the pulpit. The ironic thing is that when He asks us to turn around and exhibit these character virtues to others, we hold back, because after all—these others, well . . . they really don't deserve such love! But are any of us deserving?

If you live with family, or if you have a difficult roommate, or if you happen to be married to an imperfect person, consider the following:

- How would we ever learn unconditional love like Jesus if we were living with someone who always met all the conditions for our love?
- How would we ever learn mercy, patience, longsuffering, and compassion if we were living with someone who never failed us, who was never difficult to live with, who never sinned against us, who was never slow to acknowledge their wrongs or ask for forgiveness?
- How would we learn to pour out grace on someone who does not deserve it if we were living with someone who was *always deserving of that grace*?[4]

Are we most like Jesus when our husband, wife, children, roommates, or family members are meeting all our needs, and we really don't have to sacrifice much at all? Or are we most like Jesus on the hard days, when grace is needed, when mercy is needed, when unconditional love is needed? Did you know that God actually intended that different personalities live and associate together to help us in our sanctification journey?

"Marked diversities of disposition and character frequently exist in the same family, for it is in the order of God that persons of varied temperament should associate together. When this is the case, each member of the household should sacredly regard the feelings and respect the rights of the others. By this means mutual consideration and forbearance will be cultivated, prejudices will be softened, and rough points of character smoothed. Harmony may be secured, and the blending of the varied temperaments may be a benefit to each!"[5]

If you are part of the human family, more than likely, you live with people who are very different than you, people who wound you, disappoint you, and at times fall short of the conditions you expected them to fulfill. Perhaps God allows us to live with less-than-perfect people so that we can learn to give what God has given us! While we don't have this kind of unconditional love and grace to give from within ourselves, the good news is that "[Christ is] the inexhaustible source of grace."[6]

When prayer and fasting saved a marriage

One of my favorite testimonies of how God is restoring marriages in answer to prayer comes from South Africa. The testimony occurred a few years ago when my friend Raluca Ril received an email from a complete stranger. We will call this stranger Laura to protect her privacy.

Laura's email was essentially a desperate plea for help with her marriage. "I need someone to pray for me and advise me on what to do. My marriage has serious problems, which is leaving me emotionally broken. And because of that, I am struggling spiritually. I don't know who I am anymore, and my life is falling apart."

Raluca wrote Laura back, promising that she would be praying for her. She also sent Laura some resources, challenging her to set apart specific time to fast and pray for her marriage, and her walk with God.[7]

A month or so later, Laura emailed again. Her email, which she's given permission for us to share, went as follows:

Dear Raluca,

For six years, my husband and I have been struggling with many issues in our marriage. We tried getting counseling from our pastor. It didn't work. We went for marital counseling. It didn't work. Marriage seminars didn't work. Nothing was working. From outside, our marriage looked perfect. People would tell us how wonderful we are. But inside, we both knew that we were not connected. Our love had faded away.

To make a long story short, as my marriage was falling apart, so was my relationship with God, and I was becoming more and more depressed. After I received your encouragement to fast and pray, I told my husband to pray for me because I was going to start twenty-one days of prayer and fasting. Guess what? Even though he'd been skeptical about the idea when I mentioned it in the beginning, without any hesitation, he told me, "I am doing it with you!"

That was my first miracle! You see, before we got married, we used to pray together, but after our wedding, everything faded away. So the fact that he was willing to do this with me was a dream come true for me.

And so we began. During the twenty-one days of prayer, my

greatest request was, "Lord, change my life and change my heart. I want to fall in love with Jesus again." I knew very well that if I didn't have the love of Jesus in my heart, the love of my husband could never fill my heart.

The Bible says in Psalm 34:8, "Taste and see that the Lord is good."

Dear Raluca, God is so good and so merciful; God has healed my marriage and brought peace and happiness back into our home. My husband is crazy in love with me again, more than you can imagine. But the greatest miracle God did is the work He did in my spiritual life. I fell in love with the Word of God again, and I love being in His presence. If I wrote about everything that has happened, it would take forever. Just know that I am not the same woman who wrote you that first message a little over a month ago! Jesus came to my heart, and this time He has come to stay.

Much love, Laura

The situation Laura found herself in with her marriage—disconnected with love faded away—is one far too many Christian couples are in today. But as Laura and her husband discovered, "Unless the Lord builds the house, they labor in vain who build it" (Psalm 127:1).

Ellen White writes,

The cause of division and discord in families and in the church is separation from Christ. To come near to Christ is to come near to one another. The secret of true unity in the church and in the family is not diplomacy, not management, not a superhuman effort to overcome difficulties—though there will be much of this to do—but union with Christ. Picture a large circle, from the edge of which are many lines all running to the center. The nearer these lines approach the center, the nearer they are to one another. Thus it is in the Christian life. The closer we come to Christ, the nearer we shall be to one another. God is glorified as His people unite in harmonious action.[8]

Last I heard of Laura, she and her husband were happily serving the Lord together, praising God for His miracle in their lives. And this is what God intended. Inspiration tells us, "The wife, united with her husband in the fear of God, is to be a strength and power in the church."[9]

Homes ruled by love, mercy, and grace
If you are the only Christian in a challenging relationship, trying to turn things around can be extremely difficult. In fact, the last thing you may want to give your partner is love, mercy, or grace. However, remember you are not alone. God is with you, and even in these challenging situations, God can still work miracles (see 1 Peter 3:1; 1 Corinthians 7:12–16). And through your unselfish life, even in the midst of difficulty, you can demonstrate the reality of the gospel.

> The badge of Christianity is not an outward sign, not the wearing of a cross or a crown, but it is that which reveals the union of man with God. By the power of His grace manifested in the transformation of character, the world is to be convinced that God has sent His Son as its Redeemer. No other influence that can surround the human soul has such power as the influence of an unselfish life. The strongest argument in favor of the gospel is a loving and lovable Christian. To live such a life, to exert such an influence, costs at every step effort, self-sacrifice, discipline. It is because they do not understand this that many are so easily discouraged in the Christian life.[10]

I think of my dear friends Pastor Rick and Cindy Mercer, who I often call upon when in need of encouragement or prayer. In their early marriage, Rick was consumed with alcohol, drugs, lusts, and more, and Rick and Cindy fought constantly. Cindy was so discouraged that she decided she was going to leave, but then she felt God telling her, "If you leave, you won't have a testimony! I want you to pray and fast for your husband." The impression Cindy had from God was strong. So, in a final desperate attempt to save their collapsing marriage, Cindy began earnestly praying and fasting for Rick.

Despite Rick's hurtful and verbally abusive behavior, rather than continuing to fight with him and getting angry, as she had done for many months, Cindy started patiently loving her husband and demonstrating kindness even though Rick was undeserving. Sometimes that meant cooking meals for him even when he would come home drunk in the middle of the night. This got Rick's attention. Something was different in his wife, and he wanted to know what it was. Eventually, Cindy's love and prayers and the power of the Holy Spirit won out, and Rick gave his life to Jesus. Now Rick is a Seventh-day Adventist pastor, and together he and Cindy joyfully serve the Lord in ministry. Their full testimony is printed in Cindy's new book, *Pray Big: God Can Do So Much More.*

As I've heard it said, "No marriage can survive without the words 'I'm sorry.' No 'I'm sorry' can survive without a change in behavior."[11]

However, the simple truth of the matter is that we can't force anyone to say I'm sorry. We can't change the home we came from, nor can we change our past or even the person we have chosen to marry, but there is one person, with God's help, you and I can change, and that person is ourselves—it's *me.*

I wonder what would happen in our homes, and with those closest, if we stopped playing the "blame game" and just said, "You know what, it's me! I have not had the right attitude. I have not lived as Jesus would have me live. I've been a horrible example of a Christian. I'm sorry."

I'm not talking about putting on a show of false humility and beating ourselves up so family members feel sorry for us or feel pressured to respond. We can't be the Holy Spirit to anyone—God alone must convict hearts. What I'm talking about is genuine, no-strings-attached, repentance to God, and to those whom our actions have wounded.

Ellen White writes, "If pride and selfishness were laid aside, five minutes would remove most difficulties. Angels have been grieved and God displeased by the hours which have been spent in justifying self."[12]

Home is where the rubber of Christianity really meets the road, and where all true ministry begins. Through the power of the Holy Spirit, let's strive to make our homes a little heaven on earth. With God's help, we can do this! We are encouraged, "You can make home so pleasant and cheerful that it will be the most attractive place on earth."[13]

Yes, so attractive that even the angels will love to linger there!

> **Daring to Live by Every Word—Going Deeper!**
> Homes Ruled by Love and Grace: Ephesians 4:32

In *Christian Service,* a book dedicated to the ministry of others, Ellen White writes, "The first great business of your life is to be a missionary at home. . . . Our work for Christ is to begin with the family, in the home. . . . There is no missionary field more important than this."[14]

As we pray and ask God how we can serve and love those nearest more effectively, let's consider the following Bible passages and questions:

- Psalm 138:6—How can we love and worship God by how we serve in the home?
- 1 Peter 3:7—Does how we treat our loved ones actually affect our prayers?
- Ephesians 4:32—How does genuine kindness display itself?
- 1 Corinthians 13—What can we learn about true love from this passage?
- 1 Corinthians 13:4–8—What are some of the ways that Jesus demonstrated this love in His own life?
- Matthew 5:23, 24—Why should we be willing to take the first step in reconciliation? How did Jesus demonstrate taking the first step?
- Mark 11:25, 26—Why is it important that we forgive?
- Mark 10:27—What if we find it impossible to forgive? What should we do?
- Philippians 2:5–8—How did Jesus model true servanthood?
- Psalm 119:165—How do we avoid being so easily offended?
- Proverbs 15:1—How should we respond when spoken to harshly?
- Matthew 27:14—How did Jesus display an attitude of inner peace?
- Sing or reflect on the song, "Love at Home," hymn no. 652.

The simple reality is that human love fails, but Jesus never fails.

"Every human resource and dependence will fail. The cisterns will be emptied, the pools become dry; but our Redeemer is an inexhaustible fountain. We may drink, and drink again, and ever find a fresh supply. He in whom Christ dwells has within himself the fountain of blessing,—'a well of water springing up into everlasting life.' From this source he may draw strength and grace sufficient for all his needs."[15]

If you are struggling in difficult relationships or situations, I encourage you to read "That We May Be One" in Appendix 4 at the end of this book, where Jerry and Janet Page share 7 Principles for Building Better Relationships. These practical and heart-warming tips have already been a big blessing to many.

Time to dig deep into God's Word, get on our knees, and allow the Holy Spirit to take this message deeper into our hearts!

Chapter 14

Opening the Windows of Heaven

Gaining a Heart for the Eternal

> *Prove me now herewith, saith the LORD of hosts, if I will not open you the windows of heaven, and pour you out a blessing, that there shall not be room enough to receive it.*
> —Malachi 3:10, KJV

During a recent visit to Tanzania, my friend Duane McKey, who is president of Adventist World Radio (AWR), met a man named Abraham, who is a wealthy Maasai cattle owner. Abraham shared a remarkable testimony.[1]

About a year earlier, Abraham had attended a series of evangelistic meetings and had decided to be baptized. Although he did not know how to read or write, when he discovered the new AWR station in Tanzania, he was overjoyed and began to listen regularly to the different programs.

As Abraham listened, he learned many new things about what it means to be a faithful Christian—from how to live a more healthy life, to the importance of returning an honest tithe.

Abraham owned more than one thousand head of cattle and large herds of sheep and goats throughout Tanzania and Kenya. So he decided it was time that he was faithful to God in his tithe. In order to accomplish his plan of giving, he placed his cattle in large pens and counted them as they walked through a narrow chute. He would count out cows one through nine for himself, and then the tenth cow he set aside as a tithe for God. As Abraham continued to do this, his friends and acquaintances were amazed.

In the Maasai culture, people's wealth is measured in cattle. One doesn't just give away his cows! As Abraham's friends watched him repeatedly go through the numbering process with more and more of his cattle, they began to laugh at him and make fun of him, telling him he was crazy and foolish for doing such a thing.

But nine months later, the laughter stopped when forty of Abraham's cows gave birth to twins! In addition to this miracle, many of his goats and sheep birthed triplets. It was obvious that God was blessing Brother Abraham just as He blessed Jacob in Bible times.

Abraham and his Maasai friends were learning that with God, nine-tenths always goes much further than keeping the whole amount to oneself. But Abraham didn't want to keep the blessings for himself.

Abraham was so thankful for how God was blessing him that he decided to start giving a double tithe. Now he counted out eight cows for himself and the ninth and tenth cows he gave to God. And God blessed Abraham even more. But there is more to the story, for God's blessing always comes with ripple effects.

On open ranges, such as those found in Kenya and Tanzania, thieves often steal cattle. But something interesting started happening in Abraham's situation. Whenever any of his livestock were stolen, the animals always found their way back home. They inevitably returned to Abraham's herd as if unseen hands were guiding them. Because of this, potential thieves began to be afraid to steal Abraham's cows.

Recently, the president of the Tanzania Union Mission of Seventh-day Adventists, Dr. Godwin Lekundayo, told Duane McKey that many of those who had mocked and made fun of Abraham now "want in" on the same blessings he has been receiving. They told the local Adventist pastors that they want to tithe like Abraham is doing. "But you aren't members of the Adventist Church," the pastors responded with surprise. "We don't care! We want God's blessings, so we want to pay tithe on our cows and goats and sheep."

The Maasai are traditionally reluctant to convert to Christianity, but because of Abraham's ongoing testimony, more than thirty-five Maasai have already been baptized, and even more are now listening to Adventist World Radio. What a testimony!

Saving to give!

In Malachi 3:8–10, we read, "Will a man rob God? Yet ye have robbed me. But ye say, Wherein have we robbed thee? In tithes and offerings. Ye are cursed with a curse: for ye have robbed me, even this whole nation. Bring ye all the tithes into the storehouse, that there may be meat in mine house, and prove me now herewith, saith the LORD of hosts, if I will not open you the windows of heaven, and pour you out a blessing, that there shall not be room enough to receive it" (KJV).

Like our Maasai brother, Abraham, have you ever taken God up on this challenge? Of course, being a good steward is much more than faithfully paying our tithes and offerings. Being a good steward impacts every area of our living and spending habits.

Many credit Martin Luther with saying, "People go through three conversions: The conversion of their head, their heart, and then their pocketbook. Unfortunately, not all at the same time."

All-too-easily, wealth can become an idol in our lives. Perhaps that's why we are told, "For the love of money is a root of all kinds of evil, for which some have strayed from the faith in their greediness, and pierced themselves through with many sorrows" (1 Timothy 6:10).

The desire to make "just a little more money," so we can buy something "just a little nicer," seems to be the driving force for the majority of the world today. Of course, if you can't make it, you can always borrow it. Thanks to the increasing availability of loans and credit cards, even the poor can now enjoy living above their means as they sink deeper and deeper in debt. But is this part of God's plan? Not according to Scripture! (See Deuteronomy 15:6, Proverbs 22:7.)

While it's obvious that our unhealthy spending habits are putting us in dangerous financial waters, could there be more eternal consequences at stake? What about the possibility of going spiritually bankrupt, because of our misaligned financial priorities?

When sharing the parable of the sower, Jesus warned, "The cares of this world, [and] the deceitfulness of riches" (Mark 4:19) will choke our ability to grow in the Word and bear fruit for God's glory. That's why we should "take heed and beware of covetousness, for one's life does not consist in the abundance of the things he possesses" (Luke 12:15).

My friends Alistair and Deborah Huong inspire me as they've made sacrificial living and giving a part of their everyday life. Incidentally, Al works for a small Christian non-profit organization,[2] and Deb is a stay-at-home-mom, so they don't make a large income to start with, yet they have managed to save 55 percent or more of their gross income in recent years while contributing at least 25 percent regularly to the church and other charitable causes. They live on the remaining 20 percent. While their lifestyle may be simpler than the average American, they still enjoy a very satisfying and comfortable life without debt, while still having all they need.

"Why do Alistair and Deborah choose to live on so little when they could live on more?" you may be asking. It's because of three specific reasons: so they can give more to God's work, so that they can serve others more, and so they can learn to be more content.

In their personal finance blog,[3] which they've developed to help others learn how to be more frugal money managers, Alistair writes a bit about why they've chosen a more simple approach to life.

When we live a simpler life, we don't need as much stuff. When we don't need as much stuff, we don't have to buy as much stuff. When we don't buy as much stuff, we learn to appreciate more what we have. We also become less irritable, less greedy, and less stressed out. No fighting our way through crowds on Black Friday morning, no worrying about how to pay the next credit card bill, no stress about people scratching our brand new car. One of the strangest things is that by needing less and spending less, we actually feel wealthier!

Satisfaction is no longer measured by how much money we have, but rather by how little of it we need. Fulfillment won't come when we have a million dollars, but rather when we recognize that we wouldn't want to spend it even if we had it!

. . . How we use money is really a barometer of our character. A life centered less on self and more on others and God is the only genuinely fulfilled life. It places a check on our human tendency towards greed and it helps us be more generous.[4]

Speaking of learning to live economically, Ellen White writes, "Christ sanctions no lavish or careless use of means. [Jesus'] lesson in economy, 'Gather up the fragments that remain, that nothing be lost,' is for all His followers. (John 6:12.) He who realizes that his money is a talent from God will use it economically, and will feel it a duty to save that he may give."[5]

As my mentor, Brian Holland, told me recently, "The best way to feel rich is to give to those in greater need than yourself. The best way to feel poor is to walk through an expensive department store."

So are you feeling more rich or poor these days? How are your spending habits? How are your giving habits? What captures your attention and heart focus?

Developing a heart for the eternal

In Matthew 19:16–22, the Bible tells the story of a rich young ruler who came to Jesus asking what was needed for him to inherit eternal life. When you first read this story, it seems that this wealthy young ruler, who held notable positions of responsibility, might be a bit proud and arrogant, and just wanting to get a piece of the pie that everyone is enjoying from Jesus. But in the words of Inspiration we discover a different picture.

> [The rich young ruler] saw the love that Christ manifested toward the children brought to Him; he saw how tenderly He received them, and took them up in His arms, and his heart kindled with love for the Saviour. He felt a desire to be His disciple. He was so deeply moved that as Christ was going on His way, he ran after Him, and kneeling at His feet, asked with sincerity and earnestness the question so important to his soul and to the soul of every human being, "Good Master, what shall I do that I may inherit eternal life?"[6]

We are told that Jesus looked into the face of this young man as if searching his innermost soul. He loved the man, and He longed to give him the full assurance of salvation. Finally, Jesus spoke, "Why do you call Me good? No one is good but One, that is, God. But if you want to enter into life, keep the commandments" (Matthew 19:17).

"I've kept all the commandments even from my youth," the young man replied.

Of course, Jesus already knew that the man was a model tithe-paying, Sabbath-keeping, commandment-keeping Jew. He was probably doing better than most of the people in his synagogue. However, Jesus also knew that "if [the young ruler] had a correct understanding of the cross, he would have realized that he could never *do* anything to earn eternal life. The cross tells us we must stop doing and start surrendering so that the One who [alone] is good can work in us that which is good."[7]

But Jesus pushed the man further. "If you want to be perfect, go, sell what you have and give to the poor, and you will have treasure in heaven; and come, follow Me" (Matthew 19:21).

Jesus, as always, saw the heart of the issue, and so when Jesus asked the young ruler to sell all that he had and give to the poor, Jesus was not actually seeking the young ruler's possessions or money, but rather his heart. No doubt, the young man was already giving money to the poor. But Jesus wanted complete control of every area of the man's life, and that the rich young ruler was not ready to give.

In *The Desire of Ages*, Ellen White writes, "Christ gave this man a test. He called upon him to choose between the heavenly treasure and worldly greatness. The heavenly treasure was assured him if he would follow Christ. But self must yield; his will must be given into Christ's control. The very holiness of God was offered to the young ruler. He had the privilege of becoming a son of God, and a coheir with Christ to the heavenly treasure. But he must take up the cross, and follow the Saviour in the path of self-denial."[8]

Sadly the rich young ruler failed his test. Let us not follow His example. Let's not wait to give. Inspiration tells us, "By all that has given us advantage over another,—be it education and refinement, nobility of character, Christian training, religious experience,—we are in debt to those less favored; and, so far as lies in our power, we are to minister unto them. If we are strong, we are to stay up the hands of the weak."[9]

The Bible tells us, "For where your treasure is, there your heart will be also" (Luke 12:34). So where is your treasure today?

Daring to Live by Every Word—Going Deeper!
Opening the Windows of Heaven: Malachi 3:10

"God so loved that He gave," the Bible tells us. He gives with loving, sacrificial benevolence. Giving is a foundational part of His character. When we pay our tithe and give generously to others, we are becoming more like Him. And that's beautiful!

Look up the following scriptures that tell how we love and worship the Lord, even in our giving. Then take some time to think about how these biblical attitudes could become a bigger part of your own life.

- We are to give willingly (Exodus 35:5, 21, 22; 1 Chronicles 29:6).
- We are to give cheerfully and joyfully (2 Corinthians 9:6–11; 2 Chronicles 24:10).
- We are to give generously (2 Chronicles 31:5; 1 Timothy 6:17–19).
- We are to give extravagantly (John 12:1–8; Mark 12:41–44).
- We are to give systematically (Deuteronomy 14:22; Proverbs 3:9, 10).
- We are to give reverently (Matthew 2:11; Deuteronomy 14:23; Malachi 1:6–9).
- We are to give proportionally (1 Corinthians 16:2; Deuteronomy 16:17).
- We are to give faithfully (Nehemiah 10:35–39; 2 Chronicles 31:4–8).
- We are to give expectantly (Malachi 3:8–10; Luke 6:38).
- We are to give eternally (Matthew 6:19, 20; Mark 10:21).

As you reflect on these passages, I encourage you to sing or reflect on the song, "Give of Your Best to the Master," hymn no. 572.

In *Christ Object Lessons*, we read,

Our money has not been given us that we might honor and glorify ourselves. As faithful stewards we are to use it for the honor and glory of God. Some think that only a portion of their means is the Lord's. When they have set apart a portion for religious and charitable purposes, they regard the remainder as their own, to be used as they see fit. But in this they mistake. All we possess is the Lord's, and we are accountable to Him for the use we make of it. In the use of every penny, it will be seen whether we love God supremely and our neighbor as ourselves.[10]

If you struggle in the area of money management, or if you would like some practical principles to help you in everyday spending and living, read "Biblical Tips for Managing Your Resources" in Appendix 5.

Time to dig deep into God's Word, get on our knees, and allow the Holy Spirit to take this message deeper into our hearts!

Chapter 15

Conformed to Transformed

Redeeming the Time

> *See then that you walk circumspectly, not as fools but as wise, redeeming the time, because the days are evil.*
> —Ephesians 5:15, 16

My friend Gem Castor exudes joy and enthusiasm like few people I've ever met. In fact, he overflows with such warmth and friendliness that once you make his acquaintance, you will probably never forget him.

What is the source of Gem's unending joy and enthusiasm, you might ask? It's Jesus! Gem has fallen in love with Jesus, and his greatest desire in life is to help others learn to have a closer walk with God. However, there was a time when things were much different.

Gem grew up in the Philippines, and while he was raised in an Adventist home and was even active in youth ministries, for many years, it was more lip service than heart service. Gem didn't really know God personally, nor did he understand what it means to really pray. And speaking of addictions, there was one addiction that completely consumed him, and that was his addiction to media, entertainment, and movies.

Gem would spend hours watching the latest movies. In fact, it was not unusual for him to stay up all night to complete an eighteen-episode series. Sometimes he would even spend up to twenty-four hours a day, putting in one DVD after another into the player. Gem was so caught up in his love for this kind of entertainment that he would often rush home from work so that he could turn on the television or DVD player. All his spare time and his spare change went to buy new movies. In fact, this activity was more important than friends, than God, and even normal life activities. In short, Gem was addicted, but he's not the only one who has struggled with this addiction!

Scott Ritsema, leader of *Belt of Truth Ministries*,* often speaks on the overpowering effects of media on the brain. Most households contain at least one television—with many having two or more. What was once a luxury is now considered a normal commodity. And according to a recent American Time Use Survey, the average person in the US watches nearly four hours of television per day. That amounts to around sixty-one days out of a year, just spent on television. Not surprisingly, children and toddlers are getting in the same amount of viewing time, and it is estimated that by the age of six the average child will have spent more time watching TV than he will spend speaking to his parents in his entire lifetime.[1]

Unfortunately, Americans are not the only ones struggling with this all-consuming addiction. Even in remote jungle villages, high on a mountainside, you can often find a small television surrounded by a large crowd of onlookers, all eagerly soaking up every word and picture.

Don't misunderstand me. I believe that the television and digital media have a tremendous capacity for good if used rightly, and they have obviously helped increase our outreach effectiveness in monumental ways. Where would we be without networks such as Hope Channel, 3ABN, or Amazing Facts TV? They and many others like them are reaching millions in concrete jungles and many other places that would yet be left unreached. Unfortunately, Satan has taken the opportunity to use the alluring magic of the silver screen to take many captives for his own kingdom—and what success he's been achieving. Thankfully in Gem's case, he was not successful at keeping his captive bound.

Things began to change dramatically for Gem after he attended a

---

* For more information visit: https://beltoftruthministries.org/.

youth conference and was convicted to surrender his heart completely to the Lord. Not long after, he ended up spending hours praying in a prayer room where our united prayer team was leading. Up until this point, Gem had never experienced the beautiful power of united prayer, nor had he felt so clearly the presence of the Holy Spirit. As a result, his decision to consecrate himself fully to God was sealed.

After this, Gem and a small group of friends decided to have a big bonfire to burn all the idols in their lives that had been keeping them from a walk with God (see Acts 19:19). For Gem, this meant destroying and burning more than 1,500 movies and DVDs that he had collected over the years! What a liberating experience this was. Interestingly, not long after their bonfire, Gem and his friends discovered that more than 150 young people in other locations around the region had also come under the same conviction that very weekend and had also surrendered their addictions to God in their own bonfires. As a result of this collective Holy Spirit–inspired movement, a small revival began to break out.

In fact, what Gem discovered was that the moment he and his friends removed the spiritual idols from their lives, the Bible began to come alive in a whole new way, and the Spirit of Prophecy became so desirable that they would read it, along with their Bibles, every spare moment they could. They no longer found their enjoyment in talking about fashions, movies, sports, or entertainment, as they had previously, but instead, they desired more than anything to study the Bible and share with each other what they had learned. Soon this group of young people could hardly wait for each Sabbath to arrive so they could study and fellowship together.

Gem's personal time with Jesus also continued to grow. As he spent time each morning in prayer and Bible study, he soon discovered that one hour in the morning was not near enough time to quench his deep spiritual thirst. Following the promptings of the Holy Spirit, Gem began getting up an hour earlier. After another few weeks, this time was not long enough either, and so he got up even earlier. Soon he was spending almost three hours every morning studying his Bible and praying.

Over time, as Gem continued to grow in his relationship with God, he was convicted to walk away from his work as a professional photographer to follow God's call into full-time ministry. Some thought he was crazy, because they didn't know how he would pay his bills, but God rewarded Gem's steps of faith.

Today Gem, inspired by the life of George Müller,[2] continues to live completely by faith, trusting God with his daily needs and looking to God for direction in his travels. As a result, God has opened ministry opportunities for Gem all over the world, and many have been drawn closer to Jesus.

In the book *Christ Object Lessons*, Ellen White writes, "Our time belongs to God. Every moment is His, and we are under the most solemn obligation to improve it to His glory. Of no talent He has given will He require a more strict account than of our time. The value of time is beyond computation."[3]

I don't know about you, but I shudder to think of how I've wasted the *talent of time* throughout the years, especially as we consider how short our time is here on earth.

Ellen White continues,

Christ regarded every moment as precious, and it is thus that we should regard it. Life is too short to be trifled away. We have but a few days of probation in which to prepare for eternity. We have no time to waste, no time to devote to selfish pleasure, no time for the indulgence of sin. It is now that we are to form characters for the future, immortal life. It is now that we are to prepare for the searching judgment. . . . We are admonished to redeem the time. But time squandered can never be recovered. We cannot call back even one moment. The only way in which we can redeem our time is by making the most of that which remains, by being co-workers with God in His great plan of redemption.[4]

Thankfully, although we are all guilty of squandering our gift of time, there is a way to redeem the time, and that's the path that Gem has chosen—wholehearted service to God.

The great distraction dilemma

So how do we make the most of our time today, especially while living in a world full of so many distractions? Of course, when Ellen White penned the words above, Christians were not dealing with the same number of distractions that we face now. One hundred years ago, there was no such thing as television, movies, computers, internet surfing, online shopping, video gaming, smartphones, tablets, texting, or social media. Back then, *games* were what children played outside after school, and *into-the-net* was where the kids tried to kick the ball. *Social chats* were held face-to-face in person. *Tweeting* was for the birds, *posts* were part of a fence, and *texts* actually required ink and paper. But life has changed![5]

Perhaps you are old enough to remember what life was like before the advent of computers and cell phones. It was during my senior year of high school, back in the early 1990's, that I got my first big box-like Macintosh computer. The thing was a monster, but I was so excited! (These computers can only be found in a museum now, which makes me feel very old.) A few years later, I got my first cell phone. It was a simple flip phone. Oh, what joy! No more hunting down pay phones or searching for quarters when I needed to make a call on the road. However, about ten years ago, I got my first smartphone, and life has never been the same since.

Today, I can't go anywhere without my phone. My iPhone is my computer, my schedule manager, my Google search engine, my in-box for chats and emails, my GPS map, my camera, my movie maker, my calculator, my flight tracker, my exercise log, my alarm clock, my E-Sword study Bible, my diary, my hymn book, my lesson quarterly, my library, my shopping assistant, my bank and credit card manager, my entertainment system, my music collection, my social media connection, and a hundred things more. But despite all the smartphone advantages, I don't feel smarter, nor do I feel as though it's helped me save much time. In fact, on the contrary, I think it's the most distracting device I've ever owned, and sometimes for my own health and spiritual sanity, I have to turn it off and walk away.

Not surprisingly, research is showing a disturbing correlation between high digital usage and decreased ability to focus and concentrate, decreased ability to learn and retain information, decreased ability to think abstractly or solve problems, and decreased ability to engage with others, to empathize, and to be relationally intimate. If this isn't concerning enough, there's also evidence of increased depression, anxiety, and aggressive tendencies with those who spend significant time on their digital devices.[6]

While God is calling us to love Him with heart, body, mind, and soul, while He's calling us to learn to dig deeper in His Word and spend significant time in prayer, so we can fight for the salvation of souls, it seems we have grown content to feed on endless trivialities. In fact, we feel entitled to indulge day after day, scrolling mindlessly through hundreds of curiosities that grab our attention but add no lasting benefit to our lives. These meaningless habits are stealing the best of our years, which we will discover at the end of life we have wasted "not in sweet sins, but in a dreary flickering of the mind over it knows not what and knows not why, in the gratification of curiosities so feeble that [we are] only half aware of them."[7]

Some have likened "scrolling" to the new smoking, and I think they are correct. As one author writes, we are no longer able to "simply worship God in admiration or pray to Him without a compulsive fidgeting for our phones."[8] We have become so addicted to scrolling the virtual world that we have become oblivious to the real world and to the real spiritual battles going on daily all around us. In fact, we are quickly becoming people with spiritual ADD.[9] We can't sit still. And the more distracted we become with our devices, the more displaced we become spiritually.

However, God's Word tells us that we are not our own and that we have been bought with a price. This means that we are to glorify and worship God with everything that we do—that includes our fingers, our ears, our eyes, our mouth, and everything else!

If we understand the great controversy, as seen throughout God's Word, we will realize that we do not have time to waste—we only have time to redeem. So what are we doing with our time?

Ellen White writes soberly, "The masses professing to be Christians have been satisfied to be spiritual dwarfs. They have no disposition to make it their object to seek first the kingdom of God and His righteousness; hence godliness is a hidden mystery to them, they cannot understand it. They know not Christ by experimental knowledge."[10]

She goes on to say that could these people who are "satisfied with their dwarfed, crippled condition in divine things be suddenly transported to heaven and for an instant witness the high, the holy state of perfection that ever abides there,"[11] they would not be able to handle the glory. They could not endure the inexpressible bliss. They could not participate in the heavenly songs. Why? Because "their probation was lengthened for years that they might learn the language of heaven, that they might become 'partakers of the divine nature, having escaped the corruption that is in the world through lust.' "[12] But they did not take advantage of *their time*. They frittered the years away in selfish pursuits, in mindless pleasures. They did not commit their minds and hearts to God unreservedly.

"One of the great uses of Twitter and Facebook [and all other social media and digital distractions] will be to prove at the Last Day that prayerlessness was not from lack of time."[13] In other words, God gave us all the time we needed, but how did we spend our moments?

Taking a digital detox

Breaking an addiction is never easy. But with our smartphones and computers, it is especially difficult because we can't just throw these things in the trash and walk away. The simple reality is, our phones, our computers, and many other digital devices that we regularly use are here to stay. So the question is not necessarily how do we get rid of them, but how do we keep appropriate boundaries in place that allow us to use them constructively, instead of them overtaking and using us?

To help gain a fresh focus in your life, perhaps you might consider doing some digital detoxing and fasting. As I've heard it said, "A diet changes the way you look, but a fast changes the way you see." Another author writes, "By abstaining from what consumes and nourishes me on a daily basis, I signal that I, as a human being, do not live by bread alone nor by my online connection [or by my phone alone], but by 'every word that comes from the mouth of God' (Matthew 4:4)."[14] And isn't that our whole goal?

To help in this journey, I'd like to share some practical suggestions that I've taken and modified from Tony Reinke's book *12 Ways Your Phone Is Changing You*.[15] While the following suggestions will apply in many areas, we will focus specifically on the use of the smartphone, for this is one of our top distractions.

- Number one, turn off all nonessential push notifications on your phone. You simply do not need to get alerts for everything that happens on all your applications or accounts.

- Delete expired, nonessential, and time-wasting applications.[16]
- At night, store your cell phone outside of your bedroom.
- Use an alarm clock, not your phone alarm, to keep your phone out of your hands early in the morning.
- Guard your morning devotions and evening sleeping patterns by using phone settings to mute all notifications, between one hour before bedtime and when you can reasonably expect to finish your devotions in the morning. (For example, you might mute notifications from 9:00 P.M. to 7:00 A.M.)
- Before going to bed, read a book, instead of browsing online.
- In the morning, after you've had your time with God, prayerfully plan your agenda for the day before you look at the messages on your phone or computer. This way, God can help you determine your agenda, rather than you being controlled by the messages and emails you've received.
- Recognize that much of what you respond to quickly in emails and text messages can wait until later. Remember that you have a smartphone for your convenience, not the convenience of others.
- Even if you need to read your emails on your phone, use strategic times throughout the day to answer your emails from your computer, rather than responding from your phone.
- While at work, work for an hour or two at a time with your phone completely turned off. You will be much more productive.
- When you do get online, especially on social media apps, be intentional and make time limits for yourself so you don't lose track of time.
- Use self-restricting apps, if needed, which will help limit your smartphone functions and the amount of time that you spend mindlessly browsing.
- Consider making your social media accounts witnessing platforms, not just a place to share your trivial personal pursuits. (Not that it's wrong to share personal things, but stay intentional in what you share. You never know who is watching.)
- Ask yourself, When posting on social media, does this glorify God, does it help draw someone closer to Jesus, is it edifying, is it a blessing, or is it just bragging about me?
- Invite your family members and close friends to give you feedback

on your digital habits and to help you be aware of excessive phone absorption.

- When eating or spending quality time with family or friends, leave your phone out of sight and on silent mode, so you're not distracted.
- While at church, consider leaving your phone in the car or turn it off completely. You wouldn't be looking at your phone if you were in the presence of an earthly dignitary or king, so why allow it to distract you while you're in church worshiping your heavenly King.
- Consider taking strategic times in your life to detox and recalibrate your priorities digitally. That might mean stepping away from social media for days at a time, or taking a digital fast each Sabbath (where you keep your phone completely off for the entire day). It also might mean going on a phone fast for an entire week, several times a year.[17]

As my friend Derek Morris often likes to say, "We fast from the world so we can feast on Jesus." As we learn to disconnect and disentangle ourselves from our digital devices, we will find a fresh spiritual focus and new perspective in our walk with God. And this new focus makes all the difference in the world!

Before we close this chapter, I want to briefly mention one of the biggest spiritual distractions coming through our phones, televisions, and media devices, a distraction that is rotting out the spiritual foundation of our homes, our church, and that of many hearts. It is the allurement of unbridled sexual lust. It is the viewing of pornography.

Unfortunately, statistics reveal that the number of men within the church viewing pornography virtually mirrors the national average.[18] And men are not the only ones struggling. Women are getting sucked into the industry as well. And we wonder why there is such spiritual impotence in the church today, why there is such a shortage of strong godly leaders? I believe it's because many are being spiritually gutted from the inside out through this deadly disease. Thankfully though, even in this area, there is hope for deliverance.

New eyes, new heart!

A couple of years ago, a young man (somewhere in his upper thirties) attended a Bible conference that I was helping organize. As we later discovered, this man didn't come just for Bible training. He came for spiritual victory. You see, he was a married man, and yet he had been controlled for years by his addictions to pornography and sexual lusts. After the conference began, he came to the prayer room and began praying earnestly (on his own) that God would give him spiritual victory in this area of his life. For three days, he came to the prayer room and wrestled alone for hours with God. On the third day, God gave him the spiritual breakthrough that he'd been looking for, and he knew that he had been set free of his sexual addiction. However, at this point, none of us knew what had been going on; not that is, until another miracle occurred.

You see, this young man also had a physical vision problem. He could not see without his glasses. However, the next day, after receiving the spiritual breakthrough, he was walking to one of our meetings and discovered that he wasn't wearing his glasses, and he could see perfectly. Yes, just as God had given him a new heart and spiritual eyesight, so God had healed his physical eyesight. As a result, his glasses went into the trash, and he went home a new man, victorious in Jesus.

This is an incredible testimony to me of God's power in answer to prayer and how He longs to do for us amazingly abundantly above all that we ask or think (Ephesians 3:20). Remember, no addiction, no spiritual bondage, no digital device, no secret affair or worldly lover is too big for God to deal with. He is waiting to give us balance, to give us victory, to transform us and make us new creatures in Him—if we will give Him control!

Daring to Live by Every Word—Going Deeper!
Redeeming the Time: Ephesians 5:15, 16

As we reflect on the message of this chapter, let's ask ourselves: how can we love and worship God more fully with our time? How can we love and worship God authentically in those secret private places where no one sees but Him? Perhaps it might seem a bit extreme to think men and women should walk in moral purity when we are obviously wired with deep sexual attractions. Perhaps it might seem extreme to worry about what we listen to and watch during our down time. But we must remember that God is calling us out of the wilderness of spiritual mediocrity. He's calling us to be spiritual giants. This means we must surrender our private world to Him!

The Bible tells us the following:

- We are called to be pure (Matthew 5:8).
- We are called to be dead to sin (Romans 6:10–12).
- We are called to redeem the time (Ephesians 5:15, 16).
- We are called to be holy living sacrifices (Romans 12:1).
- We are called to be slaves of righteousness (Romans 6:19).
- We are called to be pictures of supernatural love (Luke 6:27–31).
- We are called to take every thought captive to Christ (2 Corinthians 10:5).
- We are called to holy conversation with no corrupt words (1 Peter 1:15; Ephesians 4:29).
- We are called to daily deny self, pick up our cross, and follow Jesus (Matthew 16:24).

If the call seems impossible, don't be discouraged. Ellen White tells us, "God has called His people to glory and virtue. . . . [but] it is the glory of God to give His virtue to His children."[19]

As you pray about the message of this chapter, I encourage you to sing or reflect on the song, "Take Time to Be Holy," hymn no. 500. Jesus is just waiting for your time!

If you need help overcoming spiritual breaches in your own life, I encourage you to read my book *Daring to Ask for More.* You can also download the document "Removing the Spiritual Breaches" from www.revivalandreformation.org. This document contains Five Steps to Freedom, which will be especially helpful.

Remember, "Repentance includes sorrow for sin and a turning away from it. We shall not renounce sin unless we see its sinfulness; until we turn away from it in heart, there will be no real change in the life."[20]

Time to dig deep into God's Word, get on our knees, and allow the Holy Spirit to take this message deeper into our hearts!

Chapter 16

Entertainment Center Versus Holy Temple

Living for the Glory of God

> *Therefore, whether you eat or drink, or whatever you do,
> do all to the glory of God.*
> —1 Corinthians 10:31

Have you ever struggled with some habit that you knew was not good for you, but you still kept doing it because no matter how hard you tried, you just couldn't stop? A few years ago, Doug Batchelor shared about one such struggle. His "cold confession," as he called it, was a thirty-plus-year addiction to ice cream.[1]

Doug's ice cream addiction started as a child and continued throughout his tumultuous youth. When allowed, he would eat plates of ice cream at a time. He could never get enough of the stuff. And amazingly, he never gained weight or got sick, but he did have other struggles. As time went on, Doug got into more and more trouble. His dad didn't know what to do with him, and neither did his mom.

Eventually, Doug chose to leave home and move into a cave way up in the mountains above Palm Springs, California. During this time, Doug didn't have much money, but when he did manage to collect a little change panhandling on street corners, instead of spending the money for normal food or life essentials, what did he buy? You guessed it! Ice cream!

However, while in the cave up in the mountains, Doug discovered an old Bible that someone had left behind. As he read God's Word for the first time, his heart slowly began to recognize that God had a purpose for his life.

You'll have to read the book *The Richest Caveman* to hear Doug's full amazing story. But as the Holy Spirit moved on his heart, Doug was convicted and gave his life to Jesus. As a result, he stopped smoking, stopped drinking, and he even became a vegetarian. Eventually, he moved back to civilization and began living a more normal life. In time, he was baptized, and slowly God began opening the doors for ministry. One day he was asked to become president of the well-known organization called Amazing Facts.

Fast-forward a few years, and Pastor Doug was preaching all over the world, and bringing thousands to Jesus. He even had his own television program and radio show. He would also talk enthusiastically about the benefits of the Adventist health message. He became vegan (almost) and drank rice milk instead of real milk. But . . . well, he still couldn't do without one thing, and that was a daily pint of his favorite ice cream.

In fact, his ice cream addiction became such an issue that sometimes he would purposefully avoid going to grocery stores where his church members worked because he didn't want them to see him buying ice cream. Other times while traveling, he would drive miles out of his way just to find his favorite brand of the sweet indulgence.[2]

But God was working on Pastor Doug, and slowly the conviction grew that not only was his daily ice cream habit unhealthy and extremely expensive, but for Doug, it had become a form of spiritual hypocrisy. So Doug would stop eating ice cream for a few days, and peace would fill his heart. Then he would be tempted and splurge some more; this back-and-forth struggle went on for years.

Sometimes, in exasperation, Doug would argue with the Lord. "This is just ice cream. I've overcome addictions in so many other areas. I don't drink. I don't smoke anymore . . . Lord, compared to what other people struggle with, this is a little thing!" (Have we ever used those same arguments?) But then God would remind Doug, "What controls you is your god. Will you be a slave to righteousness or ice cream?"

God convicted Pastor Doug that hypocrisy of any kind is very dangerous. And he realized that many, even in the church, are living a form of godliness, but they deny the power. Many profess to honor God with their mouth, but daily they defile His temple. Pastor Doug was convicted that he didn't want to be part of this group.

He also realized he could not claim to be sanctified through the truth of God's Word if his appetite continued to rule his life. Ellen White writes, "It is the indulgence of appetite and passion which makes the truth of none effect upon the heart. It is impossible for the spirit and power of the truth to sanctify a man, soul, body, and spirit, when he is controlled by appetite and passion."[3]

With this in mind, Pastor Doug continued to pray for deliverance from his ice-cream addiction. As he prayed, he often meditated on Romans 8:1, "There is therefore now no condemnation to those who are in Christ Jesus, who do not walk according to the flesh, but according to the Spirit."

God heard Pastor Doug's desperate prayer, just as He hears each prayer pleading for help and deliverance today. At long last, his addiction was finally broken. "One day, the desire for ice cream just left me," Pastor Doug later shared, as he reflected on how God set him free. "It's been years now. I'm not pulled anymore."

The battle is real!

Perhaps your struggle isn't about eating too much ice cream, but could it be for some other unhealthy lifestyle habit that is destructive to your body temple, and that hinders the sacred worship that God deserves? Gluttony and intemperance come in many forms. And we shouldn't fool ourselves into thinking these things don't matter to God. In fact, in God's eyes, when we engage in health-destroying habits, He considers it robbery—not just against Himself, but against all humanity.

The misuse of our physical powers shortens the period of time in which our lives can be used for the glory of God. And it unfits us to accomplish the work God has given us to do. By allowing ourselves to form *wrong habits*, by *keeping late hours*, by *gratifying appetite* at the expense of health, we lay the foundation for feebleness. By *neglecting physical exercise*, by *overworking mind or body*, we unbalance the nervous system. *Those who thus shorten their lives and unfit themselves for service by disregarding nature's laws, are guilty of robbery toward God.* And they are robbing their fellow men also. The opportunity of blessing others, the very work for which God sent them into the world, has by their own course of action been cut short. . . . The Lord holds us guilty when by our injurious habits we thus deprive the world of good.[4]

What a strong rebuke, especially for those of us in full-time ministry. In fact, I'm ashamed to admit that I have often justified long work hours, late nights, and skipping exercise because of my work responsibilities with the thought, *Well, it's for God that I'm doing this.* But when I recently read the statement above, it really made me re-think my workaholic tendencies, and forced me to ask myself, "Am I living a balanced lifestyle that truly guards the temple God has given me?"

Let's be honest. We all want to be ready for Jesus when He comes in the future, but woe to the person who tries to tell us how to take care of our body temple now. Yes, we want to learn how to deny ourselves and take up the cross, but we are also squirming inside, because we think, *Just don't touch my dessert plate. Just don't try to take away my cheese, or my meat, or my morning coffee, or tell me how much I should exercise.*

Now in case you are getting worried, I'm not going to make a long list of what we should or should not be eating, or how much we should be sleeping or exercising. I will leave the work of personal conviction up to the Holy Spirit. However, we all know where our weak points are, and it's time we start listening to what the Holy Spirit is trying to tell us. It's time we listen and obey!

"Oh, but if only this were not such a struggle!" we say with a deep sigh. I understand. Obedience is not always easy—sometimes it is the most difficult thing we have to do. And even when we try our hardest, we still fail.

I will never forget the time I actually struggled for five whole days over a specific sugary treat that I had brought home from an overseas trip. I'd been praying that God would give me victory over my love affair with sugar, and I knew this treat wasn't healthy. But I didn't want to throw it out. Daily the Holy Spirit was convicting me to throw it away, and daily I kept resisting with all sorts of rationalizations.

Finally, in a moment of weakness, I just told myself, "I'm tired of the struggle. If I just eat the treat, I won't be tempted anymore! It's as simple as that." And so I ate my temptation. You may laugh because you've done the same, but is there any lasting pleasure when we disobey what God is asking us to do?

Now, don't misunderstand me. I'm not saying that it's wrong to have a piece of dessert or an occasional treat. Nor am I trying to set a rigid standard. But in my own life, I have discovered that after I give into an indulgence (food or otherwise) that God has *specifically asked me to resist*, the thought will often immediately enter my mind, "Well, I've already eaten this; I guess I might as well eat *that* as well! I've already done this; I might as well do *that* as well!"

Isn't it interesting how the enemy works? He gets us to compromise just a little, and then he tells us, "Just a little more isn't going to make any difference now. You can always start over fresh tomorrow . . . but right now, just enjoy it, *just one more time, just one more bite*."

You are probably smiling as I share these testimonies because you've experienced the same struggles. So given this is a normal part of our daily life, you may be wondering, "Melody, what is the big deal?"

The big deal is our physical bodies weren't built to be entertainment centers for our desires, appetites, and lusts. Our body was designed to be a living temple, for the dwelling of the Holy Spirit. That's why the Bible tells us, "Do you not know that your body is the temple of the Holy Spirit who is in you, whom you have from God, and you are not your own? For you were bought at a price [the price of the precious blood of Jesus]; therefore glorify God in your body and in your spirit, which are God's" (1 Corinthians 6:19, 20).

We have been called to be holy and set apart for a specific purpose, to bring God glory. So this brings us back to our most important question—who has our heart? If God has our heart, wouldn't it make logical sense that He would also have our taste buds and appetite?

Our body, God's temple!
The Bible tells us in Exodus 25:8 that God loved Israel so much that in their journey through the wilderness from Egypt to Canaan, He gave

them the highest honor—the gift of His actual presence. He said, "Build Me a sanctuary so I can come live with you."[5]

And so today God is giving us the same call. "Build Me a sanctuary so I can come live with you!"

However, just as God had detailed instructions for how Israel was to care for the earthly sanctuary, in the same way, God has detailed instructions about how we should take care of our body sanctuary. This includes what we watch (Psalm 101:3), what we listen to (Deuteronomy 13:3), what we think about (Philippians 4:8), what we wear (1 Timothy 2:9), and it even includes what we eat (1 Corinthians 10:31). That's why we are told soberly, "Put a knife to your throat if you are a man given to appetite" (Proverbs 23:2).

Why such drastic measures? Because what we put in our stomachs affects the health of our bodies and minds, which in turn affects our ability to hear and respond to the voice of the Holy Spirit. This, in turn, affects our ability to achieve spiritual victory in every area of life.

Ellen White soberly writes, "The controlling power of appetite will prove the ruin of thousands, when, if they had conquered on this point, they would have had moral power to gain the victory over every other temptation of Satan."[6]

This passage is especially significant when we realize the sobering reality that we are currently living in the antitypical day of atonement when we need to be searching our hearts, making sure there is nothing between God and us, because Jesus is looking over the record books of heaven.

Again, don't misunderstand me. "This isn't about righteousness by veggie burgers, or soy cheese, or green smoothies," as my friend Dr. Zeno likes to say. This isn't merely a game of forks over knives, nor is this a test of "who's more spiritual than who." No! This is about maintaining the best environment possible for growth of mind and advancement of spiritual thought so that we can be in tune with the Holy Spirit.

If ever there were a time that we needed to be turning our minds and hearts heavenward, it is now. If ever there were a time when we needed to be morally healthy and mentally clear-headed to avoid spiritual error, it is today. Most of all, we need a healthy mind and body if we desire to develop godly characters.

Perfection of character cannot be attained when the laws of nature are disregarded; for this is transgression of the law of God. His law is written by His own finger upon every nerve, every muscle, every fiber of our being, upon every faculty, which has been entrusted to man. These gifts are bestowed, not to be abused and corrupted, but to be used to His honor and glory in the uplifting of humanity. The relation that exists between mind and body is very intimate: when one is affected, the other is always more or less in sympathy. *It is impossible for men, while under the power of sinful, health-destroying habits, to appreciate sacred truths.* When the intellect is clouded, the moral powers are enfeebled, and sin does not look sinful. The most ennobling, grand, and glorious themes of God's Word seem but idle tales. Satan can then easily snatch away the good seed that has been sown in the heart; for the soul is in no condition to comprehend or understand its true value. *It is thus that selfish, health-destroying indulgences are counteracting the influence of the message which is to prepare a people for the great day of God.*[7]

If we desire to be prepared for Jesus' coming, we will take the call to honor God's temple seriously, in practical, everyday life. Ellen White writes that those who are looking for the soon coming of Jesus should be the *first* to take an active interest in diet and health reform.[8]

Diet and the everlasting gospel

For years, we as Seventh-day Adventists have been known for our healthy lifestyle and our extensive health institutions and lifestyle programs. A few years ago we were even listed in *National Geographic* as part of the "blue zones," which reflect those regions of the world where people live the longest.[9]

However, while most Adventists still embrace the health message, unfortunately, it's alarming to see how many have begun to feel that it's restrictive and legalistic to hold to such health standards today. As a result, many have started eating and living more and more like the world, and the diseases of the world are now fast becoming our own.

On the other hand, I find it interesting that healthy diet and lifestyle have become a huge fad for millions in secular society. In fact, vegan and raw food advocates have become especially popular in the New

Age and Eastern Mysticism culture, as people want to achieve optimal health for that body-mind-spirit connection. I sometimes wonder, *Are the children of darkness wiser than the children of light?* I wonder if God might be preparing many who still live in spiritual Babylon to have clarity of mind so they will awaken to the truth when the Loud Cry goes out.

It's interesting to note that Ellen White consistently linked the third angel's message with the health message. She spoke over and over again how the two work together as the hand with the body.[10]

Author Herbert Douglass writes, "Ellen White was specific and practical as she joined the spiritual with the physical and the mental. Placing health matters within the context of the three angel's messages of Revelation 14 raised the health issues from personal opinion to the level of spiritual commitment and character development."[11]

Douglass goes on to share how Ellen White directly linked a healthy lifestyle to self-development, heart reform, being prepared for the latter rain, and the journey of sanctification. A few of her powerful statements are as follows:

Our first duty toward God and our fellow beings is that of self-development. . . . We cannot afford to dwarf or cripple any function of the body or mind.[12]

Men will never be truly temperate until the grace of Christ is an abiding principle in the heart. . . . No mere restriction of your diet will cure your diseased appetite. . . . What Christ works within, will be worked out under the dictation of a converted intellect.[13]

God's people are not prepared for the loud cry of the third angel. . . . Lustful appetite makes slaves of men and women, and beclouds their intellects and stupefies their moral sensibilities to such a degree that the sacred, elevated truths of God's Word are not appreciated.[14]

A diseased body and disordered intellect, because of continual indulgence in hurtful lusts, make sanctification of the body and spirit impossible.[15]

Talk about some serious conviction! Shall we ignore these statements and continue to bury our heads in the sand, choosing to do as we please? Not if heaven is our goal! The health message is a vital part of the everlasting gospel of Revelation 14:6 because it is to help "fit a people for the coming of the Lord."[16]

In the book *The Ministry of Healing,* we are told, "We must individually answer to God for our habits and practices. Therefore the question with us [should not be], 'What is the world's practice?' but, 'How shall I as an individual treat the habitation that God has given me?' "[17]

Yes, the battle is daunting, and every day there are new temptations. But the good news is that whatever the temptation we face, Jesus can give us victory. "However strong the passion or appetite, we can gain the victory, because we may have divine strength to unite with our feeble efforts. Those who flee to Christ will have a stronghold in the day of temptation."[18]

Are we truly willing to give God our all? Even what we put on our dinner plate? If our heart belongs to Jesus, "[We] will come to regard obedience to the laws of health, not as a matter of sacrifice or self-denial, but as it really is, an inestimable privilege and blessing."[19]

Daring to Live by Every Word—Going Deeper!
Living for the Glory of God: 1 Corinthians 10:31

As we think about what it means to be God's "dwelling place," I want to encourage you to take some time to pray and ask God how He wants you to respond in very real and practical ways to the message of this chapter.

As you look at the following scriptures, what can you learn for your life today?

- 1 Corinthians 10:31—How can we love and worship God through our appetite choices? In what other ways might we bring glory to God?
- Daniel 1:8–21—How did Daniel and his three friends guard their bodies, and what difference did this make?

- Daniel 2–12—Do you think Daniel's initial commitment not to defile his body had any bearing on the remainder of his life and ministry for God?
- Genesis 1:29—What was God's original diet for humanity? What kind of diet do you think we will have in heaven?
- Listen to or sing the song "Live Out Thy Life Within Me," hymn no. 316.

If you need help incorporating healthy choices into your daily life, consider making NEWSTART[20] a lifestyle focus. This acronym stands for living a balanced life that includes proper *nutrition*, adequate *exercise, water, sunshine, temperance, air, rest,* and, most important, *trust in Divine Power.*

For additional pointers and encouragement in making NEWSTART practical, read "Practical Tips for Growing a Healthy Body," by Dr. Zeno Charles-Marcel. This can be found in Appendix 6 at the end of this book.

Let us remember, just as Jesus led the way in overcoming Satan in that wilderness of temptation, today He longs to give us the same victory. "Christ began the work of redemption just where the ruin began. His first test was on the same point where Adam failed. . . . His victory is an assurance that we too may come off victors in our conflicts with the enemy. But it is not our heavenly Father's purpose to save us without an effort on our part to cooperate with Christ. We must act our part, and divine power, uniting with our effort, will bring victory."[21]

Let's do our part, claiming the victory God has promised!

Time to dig deep into God's Word, get on our knees, and allow the Holy Spirit to take this message deeper into our hearts!

Part 4

THE WORD THAT EMPOWERS

Chapter 17

It's All About Worship

Moving Beyond the Adventist Cliché

> *"Fear God and give glory to Him, for the hour of His judgment has come; and worship Him who made heaven and earth, the sea and springs of water."*
>
> —Revelation 14:7

B ack in the early 1960s, only eight Adventists lived in Răteşti, a little village located to the northwest of Romania's capital of Bucharest. Unfortunately, amid a harsh Communist crackdown, many Adventists were being arrested and imprisoned.

So one morning a driver, with horse and oxcart, was assigned to take this small group of Adventists to the local jail. As the cart shook and swayed along the bumpy gravel road, the Adventists prisoners began to sing hymns and songs of praise. The driver listened, very surprised at the beautiful words about Jesus and His love.

About a week or so later, the same driver was called back to the same village to pick up the local Orthodox priest and take him to his church. While they were driving along on the same bumpy road, the cart struck a pothole en route to the church, and the priest immediately unleashed a torrent of blasphemies and curses.

The driver listened in shock. *Why is the priest cursing his God for a pothole in the road as he goes to church while the Adventists sang such beautiful songs of joy and praise to God while they were going to prison? This doesn't make sense*, he thought to himself.

The contrast between the two passenger groups left such a deep impression on the driver that he determined that he wanted to learn more about Seventh-day Adventists. And he did!

After a few months of study, this man decided to be baptized into the Adventist Church, and it was because of his influence that many more came to discover the biblical truths found in God's Word. In fact, my friend Elvis Dumitru, a Romanian pastor who now serves in Ontario, Canada, and his entire family came into the faith as a result of this driver's testimony. If only those Adventist Romanian prisoners had known that difficult day that their faithfulness in worship to God, even while on their way to prison, would later shape at least two generations of Seventh-day Adventists, wouldn't they have sung even more joyfully?[1]

So how do we worship God in our daily lives? And when do we worship God?

This morning, as I was out on my morning bike ride, I was enjoying the beauty of nature all around me. Several times I stopped to take pictures of flowers or to listen to the sweet songs of the birds in the trees. Even though I've enjoyed these blessings countless times before, they always fill my heart with fresh joy and wonder. And what happens in my heart? *Worship*. As I rode my bike this morning, I was worshiping. I was telling God, "Thank You for who You are, thank You for these blessings, and thank You for these evidences of Your love."

But worship is more than singing God's praises for our daily blessings. It's more than worshiping Him when we are having our morning devotions or when we are out enjoying the glories of creation. And worship is more than singing praise songs while we are on our way to prison. In fact, if we haven't been faithful in our *daily worship*, we won't be prepared to worship God when the hard times come! That's why it's so important that we learn to submit and sacrifice *self* to the authority of God's Word in every detail of nitty-gritty life today. In fact, this is actually the truest form of worship.

Even in the Old Testament, God made it clear that the true sacrifice that God demands is the sacrifice of self: "You do not delight in sacrifice, or I would bring it; you do not take pleasure in burnt offerings. My sacrifice, O God, is a broken spirit; a broken and contrite heart you, God, will not despise" (Psalm 51:16, 17, NIV).

You see, God cannot accept worship offered in a state of disobedience, even if its intent is the worship of the true God. Jesus reiterated this lesson in the Sermon on the Mount. "Not everyone who says to Me, 'Lord, Lord,' shall enter the kingdom of heaven, but he who does the will of My Father in heaven" (Matthew 7:21). It is adherence to God's will and not merely man's intent that distinguishes between worship that is deemed acceptable versus unacceptable to God.[2]

King Saul professed to worship God, but when God asked him to destroy the Amalekites and all they owned, he only partially obeyed. Then he justified his disobedience by telling the prophet Samuel, "Well, I saved the best of the sheep and cattle for sacrifices. They are for God!" What was Samuel's response? "Has the LORD as great delight in burnt offerings and sacrifices, as in obeying the voice of the LORD? Behold, *to obey* is better than sacrifice" (1 Samuel 15:22; emphasis added).

The message is clear: If we aren't living a lifestyle of obedience, we haven't really learned what it means to worship!

"Obedience is the test of discipleship," Ellen White writes. "It is the keeping of the commandments that proves the sincerity of our professions of love. When the doctrine we accept kills sin in the heart, purifies the soul from defilement, bears fruit unto holiness, we may know that it is the truth of God."[3]

As Seventh-day Adventists, our whole identity actually centers in worship, as emphasized in Revelation 14. In fact, it is in the beautiful three angels' messages that we find our rallying points! These are what set us apart as God's remnant church. They define who we are, why we are here, and what our mission is to the world. They also remind us that the key issue at the end of time is all about whom we will worship.

Moving beyond the Adventist cliché

I have to admit that although coming from nearly five generations of Seventh-day Adventists, for many years, whenever someone started to preach about the three angels' messages, while I nodded my head in agreement, my eyes usually began to glaze over and my thoughts began to drift elsewhere. This was because I never really understand the relevance of what was being shared or how it related to my everyday life. I'm afraid this has been the experience of far too many. It's almost like the phrase "three angels' messages" has become an old Adventist cliché. We know it's important to preach, but deep inside, we are asking ourselves, *Why does this really matter?*

Recently my friend David Steward, a pastor and evangelist, shared how he spoke with a large group of high school students at one of our prominent Adventist academies on the West Coast. During his talk, he passed out a sheet of paper asking the students the following questions:

- What is your mission on this earth?
- What is the mission of God's last-day church and people?
- Where is that mission found in the Bible?
- How would you summarize this mission?
- Would you be willing to die for this mission?
- What is the mark of the beast?
- How would you prove the mark of the beast from Scripture?[4]

Of course, all of David's questions centered around the three angels' messages from Revelation 14:6–12, the most prominent teaching of the Seventh-day Adventist Church. And yet *not one* of the nearly one hundred and twenty Seventh-day Adventist high school students in attendance that day could answer any of these questions with any reference to the three angels' messages.

To be fair to the young people involved, when I was in high school, I probably couldn't have answered these questions either. However, now that I recognize how foundational the three angels' messages are to our mission as a church, I have to ask, "Why aren't we teaching these messages more clearly to our young people?" The three angels' messages should be the core and backbone behind all of Adventist education. They also should be the motivating force behind everything that we do each day as Christians, for the central focus of the three angel's messages is about worship—who we worship, how we worship, and why.

Ellen White writes, "In a special sense Seventh-day Adventists have been set in the world as watchmen and light bearers. To them has been entrusted the last warning for a perishing world. On them is shining wonderful light from the word of God. They have been given a work of the most solemn import—the proclamation of the first, second, and third angels' messages. *There is no other work of so great importance. They are to allow nothing else to absorb their attention.*"[5]

It is time we take a brief look at these messages again and discover why they are so relevant to our lives today. Let's begin with the first angel's message.

Followers of the Lamb

As we open our Bibles to Revelation chapter 14, we find a picture of a Lamb (Jesus) standing on Mt. Zion along with 144,000. The Bible tells us, "These are the ones who were not defiled with women, for they are virgins. These are the ones who follow the Lamb wherever He goes. These were redeemed from among men, being first fruits to God and to the Lamb" (Revelation 14:4).

This verse provides a picture of a group of people who have a pure, undiluted faith. They haven't been influenced by the popular "What's most comfortable for me?" gospel. No! They are people of the Word, willing to do whatever the Bible says. Joyfully they lay down their all for the Lord. As a result, they get to follow the Lamb wherever He goes.

Referencing Revelation 14:4, Ellen White writes, "All who follow the Lamb in heaven must first have followed Him on earth, not fretfully or capriciously, but in trustful, loving, willing obedience, as the flock follows the shepherd."[6]

The first angel's message is found in Revelation 14:6, 7: "Then I saw another angel flying in the midst of heaven, having the everlasting gospel to preach to those who dwell on the earth—to every nation, tribe, tongue, and people—saying with a loud voice, 'Fear God and give glory to Him; for the hour of His judgment is come; and worship Him who made heaven and earth, the sea and springs of water.' "

As we look at this passage, we find three central themes: the everlasting gospel (which shows that we are saved by Jesus' work, not our own—see Romans 1:16), the judgment (which is a call to flee to the safety of Christ), and worship of the Creator (which reminds us exactly where we came from and how we got here). Since I've already focused on the significance of the gospel (Jesus' work on our behalf) in earlier chapters of this book, I'm only going to address the themes of the judgment and worship here.

As we look at the first angel's message, do you find it interesting that the message actually begins with the call to fear God? Time and time again throughout God's Word, one of the key identifiers of God's people has been that they "feared God." This means they had absolute loyalty to God and full surrender to His will. This also means that they have learned to take God and His Word seriously! Unfortunately, most people don't take God seriously these days. They live and act in certain ways based on their *fear of society* and what others think of them, not their *fear of God* or respect for His Word.

"The remarkable thing about fearing God," says Oswald Chambers, "is that when you fear God, you fear nothing else, whereas if you do not fear God you fear everything else."[7]

While "fearing God" starts with an inner attitude and commitment of the heart toward God, that attitude is to be carried out in everyday actions. And that's where the "give glory to God" comes in. It has to do with living a lifestyle that brings God glory.

The Bible tells us, "Do all to the glory of God" (1 Corinthians 10:31). Giving glory to God is not natural. Naturally, we want to give glory to self! But we are called to die to self that Jesus may live in and through us.

Can you begin to see why understanding the three angels' messages really does have a lot to do with how we worship in our everyday lives? God is calling us to a revival of genuine godliness that is all-encompassing. It's about coming out of spiritual Laodicea and learning to live a set-apart, Christ-centered life. It's a message that affects our entire lifestyle.

A new perspective of the judgment

Usually, when you talk about a "coming judgment," great fear and trepidation will come to hearts. This is natural, for if a judgment is taking place, it often means a law has been broken. In this case, it's not just any man-made law. It is God's law that has been broken, as summarized in the Ten Commandments of Exodus 20. The Bible tells us, "For all have sinned, and fall short of the glory of God" (Romans 3:23). That means we are guilty of breaking His law.

When we look closely at Revelation 14:7, the Bible tells us, "for the hour of *His judgment* has come." This means that God, not just His people, is on trial here. Satan has told everyone in heaven that sinful human beings can't be saved and that God is unjust in bringing us to heaven while he and his angels have been cast out. He's right in a way. It would be impossible if it were not for the fact that a perfect Substitute has taken our punishment and now stands in the judgment in our place. Satan and his angels did not repent when they had the opportunity. But when we repent, we are no longer under the condemnation of our sins. We are free in Jesus! As long as we are trusting in the blood of Jesus, God's name and honor are vindicated, and He has the right to bring us home! (John 5:24; Romans 6:22, 23).

So, in essence, the judgment is an urgent appeal for all to confess their sins and flee to the safety of Jesus while probation's door is still open. When we flee to the safety of Jesus, the judgment becomes good news, because the Judge is on our side. The Bible tells us, "For the LORD is our Judge, the LORD is our Lawgiver, the LORD is our King; He will save us" (Isaiah 33:22).

While the judgment is good news, because we have an Advocate in heaven interceding on our behalf (Hebrews 4:14–16; Daniel 7:22), we still cannot be presumptuous and careless. In fact, just as the Israelites during the Day of Atonement each year earnestly searched their hearts to make sure there was nothing between them and God, so we must be doing the same today.

As we stand in the time of heavenly judgment, let us fully surrender our hearts to the spotlight of God's Word, for we are told, "That He might sanctify and cleanse [us—the church] with the washing of water by the word, that He might present her to Himself a glorious church, not having spot or wrinkle or any such thing, but that she should be holy and without blemish" (Ephesians 5:26, 27).

Why the seventh day?
Before we move on, let's not forget the final appeal of the first angel's message. It is the call to "worship Him who made heaven and earth, the sea and springs of water" (Revelation 14:7). Interestingly, the only place that the Creator God is referred to in the Ten Commandments is in regard to the seventh-day Sabbath.

The Bible tells us, "Remember the Sabbath day, to keep it holy. Six days you shall labor, and do all your work, but the seventh day is the Sabbath of the LORD your God. In it you shall do no work: you, nor your son, nor your daughter, nor your male servant, nor your female servant, nor your cattle, nor your stranger who is within your gates. For in six days the LORD made the heavens and the earth, the sea, and all that is in them, and rested the seventh day. Therefore the LORD blessed the Sabbath day and hallowed it" (Exodus 20:8–11).

However, the Sabbath is not just a sign of who is responsible for our creation; it is also a sign of who is responsible for our redemption (see Deuteronomy 5:12–15). When we honor the Sabbath, we are showing that our allegiance is with the one true Creator God, and we are resting from all self-work (covered by the righteousness of Jesus), acknowledging that He is our Redeemer.

The irony is that Sunday worship is actually man's day and so represents righteousness by man's works. This is the enemy's primary goal—to get us to trust our own works rather than that of the works of Jesus (Revelation 13:18). However, on resurrection morning, rather than continuing His rest, Jesus rose from the dead to go and work on our behalf in heaven. It was not a holy day, but a workday. In the same way, the first day of each week represents our call to go and work on His behalf here. But before we work, we must first have rested and been covered by His robe of righteousness by keeping the Sabbath holy.

Now let's pause and think back to when we were children for a moment. Most of us remember playing the game Simon Says. According to the rules of the game, when Simon says something, everyone should obey. However, if someone *other* than Simon says to do something, don't pay attention. The point is trying to trick people into standing up or doing something, even when Simon didn't say to do it. Sooner or later, someone mistakenly follows an order, and everyone starts laughing as the leader of the game says, *"But Simon didn't say!"*

Here's the application: If it weren't for God's Word, it really wouldn't matter what day of the week that we chose to worship or if we worshiped at all. But the problem is, we are in a contest between God's Word (Simon) and Satan's word. In the very beginning of the world, at Creation, God said, "Keep the seventh day holy!" and ever since, Satan has been saying, "No, it doesn't matter what day you worship. Sunday is better, or Tuesday is better, or whatever day you want to worship is fine."

The first deception in the Garden of Eden was over the "Word" and the command of God. The last deception at the end of time is once again, over the "Word" and command of God. So whose word will we follow?

The times we are living in are serious ones. The first angel of Revelation 14 is crying out to God's people today, "Get ready, get ready, get ready. [You] will have to die a greater death to the world than [you] have ever yet died."[8]

We will talk more about the second and third angel's appeal in the next chapter, but for now, I'd like to close with a short story.

Do you have your Bibles?
One time a couple of Adventist Bible workers, who were working in a dangerous part of the world, were seized with guns and accused of being spies. "We are not spies!" they told their captors. "We are Adventist missionaries, simply here to share the love of Jesus."

One of the men holding a gun to their backs looked at them with new interest. "You say you are Adventist missionaries! Then I have a question for you. Come with me." He led them to a small building, where he sat them down. "Do you have your Bibles?" They quickly pulled out their Bibles. "Show me with your Bibles what the three angels' messages mean and why Adventists believe these messages are so significant!"

Immediately, the men opened the Word and began explaining Revelation 14 as their captor calmly listened. When they were finished, his face had relaxed, and he smiled. "I used to go to an Adventist school," he told them. "I knew if you were really Adventist missionaries, you would be able to explain the three angels' messages. If you couldn't show me these things in the Bible, we probably would have held you hostage or worse, but now, because I am certain you are not spies, we will set you free."[9]

Talk about being put on the spot! Are we ready to share God's Word? Are we ready to stand for truth, even if a gun were put to our back? Are we ready to sing God's praises, even if being hauled away in an oxcart to jail? "Believers . . . must be firmly founded upon the word of God, so that when the testing time shall come . . . they may be able to give a reason for the hope that is in them, with meekness and fear."[10]

The time to get ready and learn what we believe is now, not tomorrow!

Daring to Live by Every Word—Going Deeper!
It's All About Worship: Revelation 14:7

While we've been reminded in this chapter about the significance of the Sabbath, worship is not just an event that we attend each week. Worship is something that Christians should do each and every day. So how can we worship God more fully by obedience to His Word and by sharing the three angels' messages?

- Revelation 14:6—Is the everlasting gospel just for me? Or should it be shared?
- Revelation 14:7—How can we give God glory today?
- James 1:22—What action is God asking us to take?
- Ecclesiastes 12:14; Matthew 12:36, 37—What happens in the judgment?
- Exodus 32:33; Isaiah 43:25—What gets blotted out in these two passages?
- 1 John 2:1; Hebrews 7:25—What gives us hope in the day of judgment?
- Matthew 28:19, 20—What is our great commission? Is there something specific that we should teach people?
- Sing or reflect on the song, "Crown Him With Many Crowns," hymn no. 223.

To gain a deeper understanding of the Day of Atonement, and why we must confess and repent of our sins if we want Jesus to stand as our Intercessor, read the chapter "Facing Life's Record," in *The Great Controversy*. This chapter is very eye-opening and sobering.

As we awaken to the seriousness of the times in which we live, let's not keep the appeal of the three angels' messages to ourselves. This message is to go everywhere. Sometimes we think about reaching the "entire world," and we conveniently forget about our neighbor next door. Or we justify the good we are doing for our neighbor down the street, and we ignore the cry of distant lands.

Mark Finley tells the story of William Carey, who, before he became a well-known missionary, was a shoe cobbler in London, England. Carey would put heels and soles on shoes. However, hanging on the wall next to where he cobbled shoes was a big map of the world. When asked about this map one time, he replied, "I cobble shoes to pay expenses, but soul winning is my business!" Later he went on to become the "father of modern missions" and saw many souls brought to the Lord.

Let's show the people of the world who we worship and why they can worship Him too! Let's make soul winning our first business.

Time to dig deep into God's Word, get on our knees, and allow the Holy Spirit to take this message deeper into our hearts!

Chapter 18

Having the Faith of Jesus

Are We Ready to Take Our Stand?

> *Here is the patience of the saints; here are those who keep*
> *the commandments of God and the faith of Jesus.*
> —Revelation 14:12

Wisam was born into a powerful Muslim family in Nazareth, where his father was the chief and his uncle the imam, or Islamic religious leader. As a young man, Wisam was taught to hate Christians and their pork-eating and alcohol-drinking ways. So, one day, when he learned that his sister—who had gone to Austria to pursue her studies—had become a Christian, he was irate and immediately told his family.

A family tribal council was called, and when Wisam recounted what he had learned, his uncle immediately exclaimed, "You must go to Europe and find her and kill her!"

Before long, Wisam was on a flight to Europe, and then on a train to Austria. Not having his sister's address, he phoned her and said, "I have been sent by the tribe to kill you." Much to his surprise, his sister remained calm. "OK," she replied. "That's fine, but will you give me a year?"

As he had no choice since he didn't know where to find her, he agreed. She suggested he stay at Bogenhofen, one of our Seventh-day Adventist schools in Austria, and study German while he waited. What Wisam didn't know is that she had a boyfriend—and he was an Adventist pastor!

But as time passed, something began to change in Wisam. There grew in him a desire to know the Jesus, who raised the dead and forgave sins. One of the theology professors at the school befriended Wisam and offered to study the Bible with him.

This opened a whole new understanding for Wisam. All his life, he had been taught "an eye for an eye and a tooth for a tooth" religion—but this Jesus taught forgiveness. Soon, there was no holding back—Wisam gave his heart to Jesus and was baptized. When the year was up, instead of killing his sister, he was present at her wedding and gave her his blessing.

Wisam excitedly returned to Nazareth, eager to share his newfound faith with his family. However, when he arrived, he was received with suspicion, and his relatives called a tribal council. He was questioned about his loyalty to the Muslim faith, and the men asked, "Did you kill your sister?"

Instead of answering, Wisam asked them if they knew Jesus the Creator. He said, "Please tell me who this Jesus is that is mentioned in the Quran?"

This made his family very angry. His uncle, incensed at Wisam's insolence, shouted, "Stone him!"

The young men immediately picked up rocks and began to pelt Wisam until he fell to the ground. Wisam's father cried out to his other son, "Save your brother!" Wisam's brother immediately fell over Wisam's body, blocking the stones from hurting him more.

Wisam was immediately taken to the emergency room and, in a few days, was miraculously well enough to be released from the hospital. But after he recovered, the same thing happened again! This time, his father suggested he leave Israel if he wanted to stay alive. So Wisam returned to the Bogenhofen Seminary in Austria, where he studied theology.

Shortly after that, Wisam came to Southern Adventist University in Tennessee and eventually married Adri, a beautiful Adventist girl from South Africa.

They then moved to Europe and pastored several churches. But a few years ago, Wisam received a call to work as a pastor in the Israel

Field—in the Nazareth Adventist Church. His mother was thrilled and assured him his uncle was dead, and if Wisam returned, he would be safe. His family would protect him.

Wisam told his mother, "If I return, no one can stop me from preaching the truth."

She not only agreed but also offered him a special place in the family business.

Wisam and Adri have now been working in Nazareth for more than four years. But the story doesn't end here, because something happened recently that shook the entire local Arab community in Nazareth and showed how God continues to protect Wisam and guide his ministry.

A few months ago, two of Wisam's cousins, still angry because he became a Christian, rallied a mob and went early in the morning to Wisam's house to attack him. His cousins carried a large butcher knife, and when Wisam came out of the house, they rushed him, screaming, "We're going to kill you!"

Wisam's wife, Adri, was upstairs when she heard the commotion. She looked out the window and saw what was happening. Realizing that without a miracle, Wisam was about to be killed, she immediately fell on her knees and cried out to God.

As Adri prayed, Wisam faced his aggressors. But realizing that they would not be appeased, Wisam turned to leave. In that moment, his cousins charged, stabbing him in the back with enough force as to plunge the sharp knife deep into his body. But to their shock, the blade of the knife bent at a ninety-degree angle, as if Wisam had on a metal bullet-proof (or knife-proof) vest!

At this, his cousins dropped their weapon in confusion, unable to understand what had just happened. As they turned to run away, one of the cousins shouted over his shoulder, "Wisam, you will not know how or when or where, but we will kill you!"

Of course, Wisam's family encouraged him to fight back, but Wisam, who had remained uninjured, calmly replied, "There is no need to fight. God will fight for us."

Not long after, the two cousins who had threatened Wisam were riding their motorcycle, and coming around a corner they hit a truck head-on. One cousin was killed instantly. The other died a week later from his injuries, never regaining consciousness. Both his attackers were now gone!

As you can imagine, this caused a huge impact in the Muslim community there in Nazareth. Wisam's family is prominent in the city, and it was a well-known fact that his uncle's family had vowed to kill him for being a Christian. The Muslims are amazed not only for the miraculous way Wisam was delivered but also for his refusal to fight back and instead trust in Jesus.

As a result of God's miraculous intervention, Wisam is now so well respected by both Arabs and Jews, that he was recently asked to be board chair of the largest school in Nazareth. Wisam and Adri have also opened a center of influence in the heart of Nazareth. Wisam teaches English straight from the Bible, and there is now a long waiting list to attend his classes. He is also studying the Bible with several Muslim men, and Adri is working with the women in the community. Many Muslims are having dreams and seeing visions and are searching for answers that Wisam gladly shares.[1]

Just a few months ago, many precious souls from an Arab church were baptized in the Sea of Galilee as a direct result of Wisam's ministry. My friend Cami Oetman, host of *Adventist World Radio 360°*, has featured Wisam and Adri in several of Adventist World Radio's ministry spotlights. I encourage you to watch these inspiring videos online.[2]

As I reflect on Wisam's testimony, I am reminded that Jesus is coming soon, and as a result, He is waking up His church. He is calling them out of Babylon and out of the compromised religions of the world—and there are many. That's why the three angels' messages of Revelation 14 are so relevant for today. They are to be a wake-up call for God's people still in spiritual Babylon.

Time to leave spiritual Babylon!

In the last chapter, we talked about the first angel's appeal. Now let's pick up with the second angel's appeal. In Revelation 14:8, the Bible tells us, "And another angel followed, saying, 'Babylon is fallen, is fallen, that great city, because she has made all nations drink of the wine of the wrath of her fornication.' "

Pastor Randy Maxwell, in his inspiring book *Boot Camp for the Last Days: Living All Out for Jesus in the Judgment Hour of Earth's History*, shares how the initial city of Babylon, founded by Nimrod, a descendant of Noah, was built because of two chief sins:

- The first sin was *doubt of God's Word.* God had promised never to send another flood, but Nimrod and his followers said, "We don't believe God. We are going to build a tower that reaches up to heaven to save ourselves just in case He's lying."

- The second sin was *defiance of God's will.* God told Noah's decedents to spread out and repopulate the earth. Nimrod and his followers said, "We are sticking together. We aren't going anywhere."[3]

And so the stage was set. Ever since, "Babylon" has been in defiance of God's Word, in defiance of God's will, and ultimately in defiance of God's worship—for true worship cannot occur apart from true obedience and love.

However, when we read Revelation 14:8 and Revelation 18:4, 5, it's important to note that when John was writing the second and third angels' messages, *physical Babylon had already fallen.* So John is not calling God's people out of a literal location but out of a spiritual condition, a condition of spiritual adultery.

While Babylon represents a *network of counterfeit religious systems* that are leading multitudes to disregard the Ten Commandments of God, it's important to remember that the majority of God's children still live within this system. So we must guard against a "holier than thou" mentality and treat all, even those who disagree with our understanding of Scripture, with utmost love and respect.

Inspiration tells us, "Notwithstanding the spiritual darkness and alienation from God that exist in the churches which constitute Babylon, the great body of Christ's true followers are still to be found in their communion."[4]

Thankfully, Wisam escaped from his *Babylon*, and so will many others.

Don't take the mark!

The third angel's appeal is a warning to those who linger in Babylon, the counterfeit religious systems of the world. It's a plea to all God's people still in Babylon, "Don't take the mark. Don't worship the beast. Get out while you still can."

Revelation 14:9, 10 tells us, "If anyone worships the beast and his image, and receives his mark on his forehead or on his hand, he himself shall also drink of the wine of the wrath of God, which is poured out full strength into the cup of His indignation. He shall be tormented with fire and brimstone in the presence of the holy angels and in the presence of the Lamb.'"

It's important to recognize that if we want to escape the mark of the beast, outlined in the third angel's message, we must embrace the first and second angels' messages.

Ellen White writes, "By rejecting the two former messages, [professed Christians] have so darkened their understanding that they can see no light in the third angel's message, which shows the way into the most holy place. . . . [And so] they cannot be benefited by the intercession of Jesus there."[5]

No benefit by Jesus' intercession? Do we recognize the significance of this sobering statement? The third angel's message is actually "the most fearful threatening"[6] ever addressed to humankind: Think of what it means to be subject to the wrath of God poured out without mixture!

Remember, when you were a child and your parents wanted you to take some bitter medicine, they mixed it with something sweet, so it didn't taste so bad. While the wrath of God has been seen here and there throughout history, it's always been diluted with God's sweet mercy. But a time is coming when His wrath won't be held in restraint anymore. God's wrath is really His love in action. And for the good of the universe and even in mercy to the unrepentant sinner, God will finally annihilate all sin and those who hang on to it. Unless the blood and intercession of Jesus covers us, we will not be able to stand.[7]

So the million-dollar question then is—how do we avoid worshiping the beast, taking his mark, or giving reverence to the image of his name? The answer is simple: We make sure we are living by the standard of God's Word, and we obey no authority, no church, or no ruler that leads us to contradict the plain "thus saith the Lord."

The Bible tells us in Revelation 12 that the beast is a pagan religious power, so the image of the beast would be an entity that gives power or authority back to the beast. And taking the mark of the beast would be obeying a specific form of worship that the beast (this pagan religious power) requires.[8]

Is this sobering? Yes indeed! As God's people take a stand for biblical truth and honor of God's Ten Commandments, we are warned that great persecution will come, but we are to hold fast—because Jesus will be the final victor.

Revelation 12:17 tells us, "And the dragon was enraged with the woman, and he went to make war with the rest of her offspring, who keep the commandments of God, and have the testimony of Jesus Christ."

Clearly, we are in a battle much bigger than we can comprehend! And it's time we take our stand—not on the teachings or doctrines of man, but on the pure, undiluted authority of God and His Word.

Ellen White writes the following sobering statement—a warning for us all!

As the storm approaches, a large class who have professed faith in the third angel's message, *but have not been sanctified through obedience to the truth*, [will] abandon their position and join the ranks of the opposition. By uniting with the world and partaking of its spirit, they have come to view matters in nearly the same light; and when the test is brought, they are prepared to choose the easy, popular side. Men of talent and pleasing address, who once rejoiced in the truth, employ their powers to deceive and mislead souls. They become the most bitter enemies of their former brethren.[9]

What a sad day this will be! Let's make sure we stay on the right side of the battle. Let's make sure we keep studying God's Word and obeying the truth we discover. Then when He returns in the clouds of glory, our testimony will be, "Here is the patience of the saints: here are they that keep the commandments of God, and [have] the faith of Jesus" (Revelation 14:12).

Daring to Live by Every Word—Going Deeper!
Having the Faith of Jesus: Revelation 14:12

What we've covered in these pages is just a brief overview of the second and third angels' messages. There is so much more to be learned. I encourage you to study these truths out in a deeper way for yourself.[9] But as my friend Randy Maxwell likes to say, as you study Revelation, don't get so caught up in the horns and beasts and dates that you forget who your faith is in. It's in Jesus! And the same Jesus, who brought us this far, will carry us safely through the storm.

Time to open the Word as we reflect on the message of this chapter, and God's appeal to His last-day remnant people.

- Revelation 14:12—What does it mean to have the faith of Jesus?
- Revelation 12:17—How has Satan persecuted God's church through the years?
- Isaiah 10:20–22—What is a remnant?
- Isaiah 37:31, 32; Zephaniah 3:13—What characteristics do we find in God's remnant?
- Micah 4:6–8—What is God's promise to His remnant?
- Revelation 12:17—What are the identifying marks of the remnant?
- Revelation 19:10—What is the testimony of Jesus?
- Psalm 95:8—What should we be doing now to prepare for the coming crisis?
- Sing or reflect on the song, "Faith Is the Victory," hymn no. 608.

In the last days, we are told that a great shaking is going to come upon the church and upon all Christians. Will we stand through this great shaking?

Ellen White writes,

The greatest want of the world is the want of men—men who will not be bought or sold, men who in their inmost souls are true and honest, men who do not fear to call sin by its right name, men whose conscience is as true to duty as the needle to the pole, men who will stand for the right though the heavens fall.

But such a character is not the result of accident; it is not due to special favors or endowments of Providence. A noble character is the result of self-discipline, of the subjection of the lower to the higher nature—the surrender of self for the service of love to God and man.[10]

God is looking for men and women, boys and girls, teenagers as well as the elderly, who will love God more than life itself, who will stand strong though the heaven's fall, who will be willing to share their faith no matter the pain or cost. Will you be that person?[11]

Time to dig deep into God's Word, get on our knees, and allow the Holy Spirit to take this message deeper into our hearts!

Chapter 19

Set Apart for His Glory

Keeping Holy Things Holy

"Now sanctify yourselves, sanctify the house of the LORD God of your fathers, and carry out the rubbish from the holy place."
—2 Chronicles 29:5

Nickolai Panchuk was pastor of eleven Adventist house churches during difficult days of spiritual oppression in the Soviet Union. Again and again, the KGB harassed and imprisoned him, trying to get information about the other Adventist members in his congregations, but every time he refused to give them information.

Finally, the Russian KGB decided they'd had enough and shipped Nickolai off to a Siberian prison camp. Knowing that tough days were ahead, Nickolai prayed earnestly, "Please Lord, help me to keep courage and be faithful to You and to the church I love. And help me to be a witness to the guards."

The first Sabbath at the Siberian prison camp, Nickolai refused to work. He told the guards, "I must honor God and keep the Sabbath holy." As a result, he was beaten. The second Sabbath he refused to work, he was locked up in a box in the cowshed, a box so small that he couldn't stand up or lay down, but had to sit with legs up against his chest. He was left there for ten days with only water to drink. But his faith remained strong. He was determined he would not dishonor God's holy day.

Finally, at the end of ten days, he was taken out of the box, but his legs were so numb from the loss of circulation that he could hardly move. It took him two days before he could walk again. Gradually he regained his strength and went back to work, but then it was time for Sabbath again. Knowing that more time in the box was ahead, he prayed earnestly for strength and peace.

Sure enough, he was taken back to the box for another ten days. And so started a painful routine that would last for the next two years. Ten days in the box, two days recovering, two days working, and then back to the box he would go, all because he refused to dishonor the seventh-day Sabbath.

The only thing that sustained Nickolai during those long agonizing days was prayer, singing songs of worship, reciting Scripture, and the extra bread and water that one of the guards gave to him secretly. Through the long cold winters, and back into spring, summer, and fall, his torture continued, but he remained faithful to God.

Finally, when a higher-ranking colonel came to the prison camp for an inspection, the cruel treatment that Nickolai was receiving was discovered. The visiting colonel ordered that Nickolai be set free from the box. He then challenged Nickolai to a new job of gathering water for the camp. "If you can get all the water this camp needs for the week in six days instead of seven, you can have your Sabbaths off," he told Nickolai. Nickolai rejoiced at the opportunity to prove God's faithfulness.

Once he got his legs working again, he began his new job. But the ox that pulled the water cart was in no big hurry to make the daily trips, and for the first five days, no extra water was brought in from the creek. Nickolai began to despair. How would he ever be able to keep the Sabbath in peace if he couldn't get the extra water brought in?

However, on that first Friday, it was like a fire had been lit under that ox, and it raced back and forth the entire day, from the creek to the camp, dragging Nickolai behind. With a miracle of God, all the extra water was brought in, and Nickolai enjoyed his first Sabbath rest undisturbed.

This amazing phenomenon continued for the next seven years. For five days of the week, the ox would lazily move along, much to

Nickolai's frustration. But come Friday, it would take off as if in a race, and to God's glory, all the water would be brought in.

Ten long years after being taken to the Siberian prison camp, Pastor Nickolai was released and allowed to return home to his church and family. He had honored God faithfully every Sabbath of his imprisonment and had witnessed to many people of God's love. In fact, even after he left the prison camp, his witness remained, because the faithful ox worked hard six days of the week but refused to work on Sabbath.[1]

What an amazing story! Of course, we all admire testimonies like that of Pastor Nickolai. Our hearts swell with courage and resolve as we think, *If I ever face persecution for keeping the Sabbath, I will be faithful too.*

However, today, for the most part, we don't struggle over whether we will be imprisoned for keeping the Sabbath holy. Our biggest Sabbath struggles are over whether it's OK on Sabbath to go out to eat, attend a movie, take an extra shift at work, or let the kids play a soccer game in the afternoon. Conversations about business, politics, and secular subjects are the norm, and the activities we pursue are usually more for our own pleasure rather than God's. Even the way we worship at church has become more about us than about Him. One author sadly writes, "Reverence for the house of God has become almost extinct. Sacred things and places are not discerned; the holy and exalted are not appreciated."[2]

Of course, God never intended the Sabbath to be a day of drudgery, but a special set-apart day filled with delight and rejoicing in the Lord (Isaiah 58:13).[3] In fact, it is to be the sweetest, most blessed day of the whole week, a day when we spend time with God in deeper communion, when we reflect on His creative power through the beauties of nature, and when we love and minister to those around us.

But have we grown careless with how we honor God's holy day? Are we losing our reverence for this set-apart gift of time?

Hot potatoes here we come!

Speaking of Sabbath worship, there's probably few topics that create more discord among believers these days than that of music and worship styles. In fact, according to many, the music department in the church is often referred to as the war department, because, unfortunately, that's where some of the biggest church fights take place. So perhaps I should apologize in advance for the toes that I will probably step on here. But before you put this book down, give me a few minutes to share.

I want to begin by turning our eyes to a worship service that took place thousands of years ago outside the Garden of Eden.

Adam and Eve's sons, Cain and Abel, had built altars and come to worship the Lord. Abel brought a lamb for his sacrifice. Cain brought the fruit of the ground for his offering, the best of his sweat and labors. From outward appearances, both seemed like perfectly good offerings. However, only one offering was accepted. It was that of Abel's—because Abel showed by His offering that He trusted in the sacrifice of the coming Redeemer, not in his own righteous works.[4]

However, Cain's sacrifice was an outpouring of his selfish heart. Cain's "gift expressed no penitence for sin. He felt, as many now feel, that it would be an acknowledgment of weakness to follow the exact plan marked out by God, of trusting his salvation wholly to the atonement of the promised Saviour. He chose the course of self-dependence. He would come in his own merits."[5] And so by his deviation from God's plan, Cain changed the focus of worship from God to himself and to the work of his own hands.

Today when we worship, we give visible evidence of where we focus and in whom we put our trust. The way we worship also shows what we truly believe.

Not long ago, a pastor of one of the larger megachurches in the United States shared the secrets to his congregational growth. The key, he explained, is having a "seeker-sensitive" philosophy. This philosophy encourages everyone to "come as you are." How do he and his leadership team accomplish their goals? It is through music!

" 'Music sets the atmosphere of the church service, communicates doctrine through singing, and expresses our view of what God is like,' the pastor stated. 'The style of music you choose to use in your service may be the most influential factor in determining who your church reaches for Christ and whether or not your church grows.' "[6]

I believe this pastor is on to something. In the book, *Education*, we read,

"There are few means more effective for fixing [God's] words in the memory than repeating them in song. And such song has wonderful power. . . .

It is one of the most effective means of impressing the heart with spiritual truth."[7]

However, it might be good to ask, what kind of doctrine is this megachurch leader hoping to teach his followers? And what type of music does he feel best accomplishes his goals?

"We use the style of music the majority of people in our church listen to on the radio," the pastor shared. "They like bright, happy, cheerful music with a strong beat. Their ears are accustomed to music with a strong bass line and rhythm. And," he adds, "for the first time in history, there exists a universal music style that can be heard in every country of the world. It's called contemporary pop/rock."[8]

Keeping holy things, holy!

Now let's pause for a moment and turn to another story in the Bible.

Aaron's sons Nadab and Abihu were priests in Israel. However, one day, they took their censers, put common fire in them and added incense; and they offered unauthorized fire before the Lord, contrary to His command. "So fire went out from the LORD and devoured them, and they died before the LORD" (Leviticus 10:2).

This seems like a pretty harsh punishment, don't you think? Why did they have to die for this offense? It was because they had mixed the sacred with the common. In the experience of Nadab and Abihu, we are told, "God designed to teach the people that they must approach Him with reverence and awe, and in His own appointed manner. He cannot accept partial obedience."[9]

This is why it is so critical that worship to God be *exclusively* the domain of sacred associations, because "there is always danger, when the common is mingled with the sacred, that the common will be allowed to take the place of the sacred,"[10] and thus the Creator be replaced with the created (idolatry).

With this in mind, is using secular music styles an acceptable practice when it comes to God's sacred worship? Not according to Scripture (James 4:4). "Conformity to worldly customs converts the church to the world; it never converts the world to Christ."[11]

Now, I love good music! And God loves good music too! In fact, we are told, "Music is of heavenly origin."[12] Either by inspiration or endowment, true and proper music comes from God. It existed before the creation of this world (Job 38:4–7) and will exist in heaven after the redeemed leave this world (Revelation 5:9; 14:3). That's why "we should endeavor, in our songs of praise, to approach as nearly as possible to the harmony of the heavenly choirs."[13]

However, like most blessings of God, Satan offers a counterfeit. Remember, long before the earth was created, Satan (then Lucifer) actually directed the heavenly choir. If anyone knows the music of heaven, it is Satan. Wouldn't it seem logical then that he would do everything in his power to turn our ears and hearts away from heavenly music, to earthly sensual music? He knows if he can get us to embrace the music and worship practices of the world, we will have no taste for the holy praises of heaven, or for the sweet truths of God's Word.[14]

Former rock 'n roll performer Dan Lucarini, in his book *Why I Left the Contemporary Christian Music Movement*, points out that the key premise in much of the CCM industry is that music is amoral.[15] In fact, a growing number of Christians today feel that as long as the lyrics are acceptable, the music itself is not an issue so that anything can be used in the worship setting, and no one should judge another's style.

However, in centuries past, things were seen much differently. As Pastor Wolfgang Stefani writes, "Two and a half millennia ago, music was considered to be such a potent and influential force in society that leading philosophers and politicians advocated its control by the nation's constitution. This was the case in Athens and Sparta, city-states of ancient Greece."[16]

"Why all the fuss?" Stefani continues. "For the ancients, the problem was clear. They believed music affected the will, which in turn, influenced character and conduct."[17] Half a world away, in China, Confucius expressed a similar understanding. "If one should desire to know whether a kingdom is well-governed, if its morals are good or bad, the quality of its music will furnish the answer. . . . Character is the backbone of our human culture, and music is the flowering of character.[18]

If you look around at our culture today, there is no mistaking the intimate connection between music and morality. However, despite the evidence, emergent church leaders of today are promoting a false gospel that teaches that God accepts us just as we are, so it doesn't matter how we come, and it doesn't matter how we worship. The only thing that matters is our individual tastes and desires. While it's true that God does accept us as we are, the reality is that He does not allow us to *stay as we are*. Our tastes have been distorted by sin, and our desires are naturally corrupt. That's why God's goal is to *transform* us and *change* us.

When we look at the big picture, we must remember that God gave clear instructions to Israel as to the place and manner of His worship (Deuteronomy 12:1–28). Furthermore, He specifically warned against blending worship elements from the surrounding nations into the worship of Jehovah (Deuteronomy 12:30, 31). And He is just as concerned about our worship practices today. In fact, Ellen White tells us, "Because of the irreverence in attitude, dress, and deportment, and lack of a worshipful frame of mind, God has often turned [His] face away from those assembled for [His] worship."[19]

True worship is accomplished when we come to God in consecration of both heart and mind, in spirit and truth (John 4:23). Jesus reiterated this message when He equated vain worship with letting "go of the commands of God" (Mark 7:6–8).

If heaven is our goal, let's pray that God would help us run from worldly worship styles and ask what He most desires (James 4:4).

Biblical principles for worship

Before I close this chapter, you may be wondering, "How do I evaluate our worship service?" Or, if you are a music leader, you may be asking, "How can I be sure I'm bringing glory to God in my music?"

Let me share some basic principles of worship that might help things be clearer. Keep in mind, these are not to be used as a battering ram against others but are intended specifically for helping one make their own personal choices in regard to worship. (*If someone has not already walked through the previous chapters of consecration and surrender in this book, the principles shared here will likely not be very palatable.*)

Matthew 10:16 tells us, "Behold, I send you out as sheep in the midst of wolves. Therefore be wise as serpents and harmless as doves." We have to be wise and gentle with how we communicate with those we disagree with. Remember, our first responsibility is not to change the world or the church, but to ask God to change our own heart. So with this in mind, consider the following:

1. Worship as a whole should be conducted in an atmosphere of reverence and respect and should be organized (Hebrews 12:28, 29; 1 Corinthians 14:33).

2. Worship should be centered on God and His work, not on us (Matthew 4:10; Ephesians 2:8, 9).

3. Worship music should remain subservient to the Word and communicate the Word of God and present truth for today's world (Colossians 3:16).

4. Worship music should not usurp the time devoted to the preaching of God's Word. The church musician should also work with the direction of the ministers so that the music service supports rather than detracts from the message being given (2 Timothy 3:16).

5. Worship forms and theology should be consistent and should align with the biblical doctrines and philosophy of the Seventh-day Adventist Church (Deuteronomy 12:1–31; Isaiah 8:20).

6. Worship of our holy God is sacred and must exclude the secular, avoiding any association with common/profane styles, qualities, or performance techniques (Ezekiel 44:23).

7. Worship music should always be initiated with obedience, "in spirit and truth" (John 4:23, 24).

8. As communicators of God's Word, church musicians have a responsibility to maintain a growing relationship with Jesus Christ and should be held to the same standard of personal devotion to God as ministers and elders (1 John 2:3–6).

9. Worship should extol the attributes of God's character, the wonderful works that He has done in the past, and the victories of the future (Exodus 15:21; Isaiah 30:10).

10. Worship should include praise to God, self-sacrifice, confession, listening for God's voice, and a commitment to accept God's call (Psalm 66:4; Hebrews 10:19–22; Isaiah 6:5; Psalm 46:10; Joshua 24:15).[20]

While we hope that many benefit from the worship service, unfortunately, I've often seen the significance of the opening song service and worship overlooked. People are still rushing about doing their own thing because they reason, "Well, it's just song service, the church hasn't started yet!" But have we forgotten that song service is church—it is worship. This is preparing our hearts for what is to come. Let's not miss this special blessing!

Also, keep in mind that the true measure for success in a worship service is not if those in attendance had a powerful "feel good" experience, although the experience is important. But the true measure of success is if those in attendance were "convicted" by the Word of God and truth. If we are in the Living Word, if we are delighting in the Living Word, and if we are honoring the Living Word, we won't be dry. Our worship services will naturally overflow with life. They can do nothing else!

Worship lessons from Myanmar

A few years ago, while working in Myanmar with ASAP Ministries, I had the opportunity to visit one of the largest Buddhist pagodas in the region. Officially called Shwedagon Zedi Daw, but also known as the Great Dagon Pagoda, the golden mound-like structure dominates the Yangon skyline, measuring 326 feet tall.

However, upon entering the visiting center and paying our fee, we were greeted with a surprising sign. Under no conditions were shoes or socks to be worn as we walked the sacred worship place. Also, no miniskirts, shorts, spaghetti strap tops, or any other forms of nudity were allowed. I have to admit that I wasn't very excited about going barefoot, but I had no choice, so off my shoes came.

As we entered the large temple courtyard, everywhere, people were kneeling in worship. Some had tears coming down their cheeks, but no one was talking. There was a spirit of quiet, reverent awe. Many had their heads to the cold stone floor, while others kissed the floor several times before praying their silent prayers in front of the Buddha idols. My heart broke as I watched the idol worshipers who obviously have been deceived. But I also couldn't help thinking long and hard.

"How interesting," I remarked to my friend Julia, "that these heathen religions have such reverence and quiet awe as they approach their gods of stone, while we serve the living God of the universe, which we think we can approach any old way we want. It seems many of us have lost what it means to have true reverence and respect!"

As I look back on our experience at the Great Dagon Pagoda, my mind turns to Exodus 3:5. "Take your sandals off your feet, for the place where you stand is holy ground," God told Moses. I believe God is giving the same appeal for reverence today.

Unfortunately, in our desire to avoid the worldly worship practices, we often encourage another sin, and that is a spirit of cold, dry formalism that is uninviting and unattractive. I understand what this looks like, for I struggled as a youth attending church because of this dry formalism that I experienced.

"There are moral icebergs in our churches,"[21] Ellen White writes. "The cold formalism that is now prevailing among us must give place to the living energy of experimental godliness."[22] The good news is that, as we grow in our personal relationship with Jesus and as we prayerfully seek the Holy Spirit's leading, He will show us how to have a living, vibrant worship experience—both individually, and in the church. In fact, I've discovered that the more in tune my heart is with Jesus, the more alive I feel in my praise and worship on Sabbath.

The Bible tells us, "But the hour is coming, and now is, when the true worshipers will worship the Father in spirit and truth; for the Father is seeking such to worship Him" (John 4:23). What does it mean to worship in Spirit and in truth? I think Adam Clarke, in his Bible commentary, states it best: "A man worships God in spirit, when, under the influence of the Holy Ghost, he brings all his affections, appetites, and desires to the throne of God; and he worships him in truth, when every purpose and passion of his heart and when every act of religious worship, is guided and regulated by the Word of God."[23]

May Jesus help us learn what it means to keep holy things holy, honoring God in spirit and in truth, for His glory, and not our own (Psalm 115:1).

Daring to Live by Every Word—Going Deeper!
Keeping Holy Things Holy: 2 Chronicles 29:5

It's time to open our Bibles as we consider the following Going Deeper questions:

- Ephesians 5:26—How are we sanctified?
- Psalm 51:16, 17—What is an acceptable offering?

- Isaiah 58:13—How do we keep God's Sabbath holy?
- 2 Chronicles 29:5; Psalm 29:2—Is there rubbish in your heart that needs to be removed so you can worship God in the beauty of holiness?
- John 14:15–17—How can we love and worship God in our worship?
- Jeremiah 33:11; Psalm 135:3—What is a sacrifice of praise? How can we honor and praise God in our daily lives?
- 2 Timothy 3:16, 17; Isaiah 8:20—Should the truths of God's Word influence our daily music and listening choices, and if so, how?
- 1 Corinthians 10:23, 24; Romans 14:19—Do our music and worship choices draw others to a stronger faith, or are they a stumbling block?
- 2 Corinthians 7:10; Galatians 5:24—Do the music and worship styles we embrace lead us to a deeper recognition of the holiness of God, or do they lead us to wallow in our weaknesses and shortcomings?
- 1 John 1:5; 2 Corinthians 4:6–10—Do the music and worship styles we embrace exalt the sinfulness of our hearts, or do they point to victory in Jesus?
- Sing or reflect on the song, "Don't Forget the Sabbath," hymn no. 388.

I love the following thought from Inspiration: "The religion that comes from God is the only religion that can lead to God. In order to serve Him aright, we must be born of the divine Spirit. This will lead to watchfulness. It will purify the heart and renew the mind, and give us a new capacity for knowing and loving God. It will give us willing obedience to all His requirements. This is true worship."[24]

Time to dig deep into God's Word, get on our knees, and allow the Holy Spirit to take this message deeper into our hearts!

Chapter 20

Daring to Ask for Even More

Unleashing God's Power for Mission

> *"But you shall receive power when the Holy Spirit has come upon you."*
>
> —Acts 1:8

It all started back in 2011, when a couple in Eldoret, Kenya, eager for a deeper experience with God, embraced the new Revival and Reformation emphasis encouraged by the world church. Hungry for more of the Holy Spirit, this couple began gathering a small group of five people to pray for two to four hours every Monday. Not long after, when the 777 and 10 Days of Prayer[1] programs were introduced in the world church, the group enthusiastically adopted these initiatives.

In February 2014, after nearly three years of praying and studying the Bible together as a small group, the Kenyan couple were convicted that God wanted them to ask for even more, so they began placing an even greater emphasis on prayer. In order to make room for additional people to be involved, they organized a second prayer group in a larger Adventist-owned building. As a result, attendance at their weekly prayer meetings began to rise dramatically. First, there were fifty coming to pray, and then one hundred and fifty. By the 10 Days of Prayer in January of 2015, more than two hundred people were gathering together to pray.

Three months later, the world church launched the 100 Days of Prayer program.[2] Embracing this prayer initiative as well, the Eldoret prayer group grew to three hundred and then four hundred people. Soon friends from the community and members of other denominations were joining the prayer meetings. These visitors were so blessed that, when an all-night prayer session was announced, twelve pastors from other denominations were invited to attend.

By the time I met Philip and Chepchumba Rono, in San Antonio, Texas, at the General Conference Session in the summer of 2015, they were overflowing with excitement. "You will not believe what God is doing in our community in Eldoret, Kenya!" they told me enthusiastically.

Having been so blessed in the ongoing prayer meetings, many of the pastors from the other churches had asked to learn more about the Seventh-day Adventist Church and what Adventist believe. So the Rono's had organized a three-day seminar. At the end of the seminar, recognizing that God's Word truly is the foundation of all our doctrines and teachings, sixteen of the nearly fifty pastors in attendance had decided to be baptized as Seventh-day Adventists. Not long after, two of the churches where these ministers of the gospel had been pastoring also decided to become Seventh-day Adventist congregations. But this was only the beginning of blessings.

"We have a revival happening in Western Kenya!" Chepchumba told me excitedly. "God is working! And it is all because of prayer. We need to take prayer very, very seriously, especially as the church is calling for deeper revival and reformation. We have already witnessed so many miracles."

While we were in San Antonio, Mr. and Mrs. Rono shared with me that they were also setting up a "center of influence"—a wellness center with treatment rooms, a library, a chapel for daily prayers, and a restaurant in downtown Eldoret—as they were adopting another world church program, Mission to the Cities. The couple had already toured several wellness centers in the United States to get ideas and advice.[3]

It's been nearly five years now since I first met the Ronos, and the miracles continue. Their wellness center is making a big impact in their community, being recognized even by the county government, and now already nearly one hundred pastors of other faiths and denominations have made the decision to accept the biblical teachings of the Seventh-day Adventist Church and have been baptized. Family members as well as many in their different congregations have followed these pastors' example. Regularly there are new baptisms. In fact, there are so many stories and testimonies that there is not space to share them all here. Obviously, God is waking up His church!

But it's not just in Kenya that God is pouring out His Holy Spirit. In the jungles of the Philippines, there are whole groups of communist rebel leaders who are laying down their guns and asking for Bibles as they make the decision to be baptized. Those who once killed are now eagerly training to become soul winners, and God's Word is spreading. Already thousands have been baptized in more than a hundred villages, where just a couple years ago, there was no Adventist presence.[4]

In an unnamed country, hundreds of soldiers and generals of anti-government forces have been secretly listening to Adventist World Radio. Recognizing the hope that only Jesus can bring, many of these are also making decisions for God. One young man from another difficult territory, wanting to do something for Jesus, decided to experiment with cell-phone evangelism. He was hoping he could get maybe one hundred people to sign up for inspiring Bible messages. This man now has thousands receiving his daily messages of hope via their cell phones, and he has trained others to do the same.[5] As a result, nearly 80,000 people are being reached via cell-phone evangelism, just because of this man's desire to be used by God.

In Rwanda, not too long since the time of this writing, one of the largest evangelistic campaigns ever held by the Adventist Church brought in more than one hundred thousand baptisms. The event was nothing short of a complete miracle. "We have worked for years in Rwanda and have never seen anything like this," church leaders said in amazement. Of course, the leaders credit prayer and the willingness of new members to take part in Total Member Involvement for the record number of baptisms being seen. As people are coming to faith, they are bringing many with them.

As I write this chapter, in Papua New Guinea, more than fifty thousand people are currently participating in baptismal classes in preparation for a large upcoming evangelistic series. And thirteen prot-estant churches in this country recently became Adventist congrega-tions.

The stories go on and on, from the Middle East to Asia, to Europe, and even in the difficult countries of the world that we might consider closed and inaccessible, God's Word is spreading in remarkable ways. However, I believe what we are seeing is still only a drop in the bucket with what is to come.

Ellen White writes, "The Lord did not lock the reservoir of heaven after pouring His Spirit upon the early disciples. We, also, may receive of the fullness of His blessing. . . . If we do not have His power, it is because of our spiritual lethargy, our indifference, our indolence. Let us come out of this formality and deadness. There is a great work to be done for this time, and we do not half realize what the Lord is willing to do for his people."[6]

So how can we get on board with what God is longing to do?

Furthermore, how can we work and minister in places where the church seems cold, and in our own home territories, where the doors around us seem closed? Well, one thing is certain, we can't keep doing what we've been doing. Something needs to change!

I wonder how God might work if we looked at mission as a *divine* endeavor rather than a human endeavor? Instead of coming up with a plan, entering a target area, and then trying to execute that plan (as we usually do), what if our first and only real agenda was to go pray and then follow the Holy Spirit's leading from there?

As we consider this idea, let me share about a group of young people who decided to try just such an experiment.

Melting Iceland

In the summer of 2019, my friend Jonathan Walter, and other leaders from the GYC[7] Executive Committee, made a radical decision. They decided to take a group of young people to Iceland on a mission trip. But this was not going to be any ordinary mission trip for they had a different agenda—and what was their agenda? Their agenda was simple—prayer! They would go and pray—person-by-person, street-by-street, and town-by-town.

To give a little background, Iceland has a population of a little more than 330,000 people, but the majority of the population lives in one location, in the capital region of Reykjavík. However, Iceland is a very secular, humanistic culture with a very small Adventist presence. To some, going on a mission trip here might seem like a setup for failure. However, after much deliberation, the GYC team decided to move forward.[8]

Jonathan Walter recounts what happened in his own words:

After arriving in Iceland, we began each morning by spending hours in prayer as a group. Although most of us were complete strangers, from six different continents, this beautiful united prayer time bonded us together in unity. The Holy Spirit was there. It was powerful.

After this time in prayer, we headed to the streets with GLOW tracts in hand. Since we had mapped out the entire city of Reykjavík, as well as the surrounding territory, our hope was that no place would be left untouched. As we walked and prayed and began knocking on doors, we were shocked and amazed how receptive people were and how positively they responded to our asking if we could pray for them. It didn't matter that they were from one of the most liberal and post-Christian countries in the world. We saw God working time and time again, from conversations with a Freemason leader, to being able to give hope to hurting teens, to even visiting the home of the president of Iceland. Openly, people shared their needs, often with tears of gratitude in their eyes, and it quickly became evident that behind the mask of secular life, there was a great spiritual longing for something more.

Amazingly, without our offering, some people even asked for Bible studies and others expressed a desire to become connected to a group of believers. We've since heard that some have started attending the local church or now have enrolled their children in our Adventist school. In one city we prayed specifically for revival in the local churches. The next day church attendance in that city went up dramatically. We were amazed! If we as Christians only realized that the Holy Spirit can accomplish in a moment what we cannot do in a lifetime, wouldn't we be on our knees more?

As I look back on our trip, there are many testimonies that I could share. By the time our ten-day mission trip was over, 150,000 GLOW tracts had been distributed and our group of nearly fifty prayer warriors had reached over half the population of the country. With few exceptions, nearly every home, apartment, and person in Reykjavík and the surrounding cities were offered prayer personally, prayed over, or else received a GLOW tract. It was a miracle!

But the most amazing part of the experience was what happened in our own lives as a group. God gave our group revival and unity and love that reflect what we read about in the book of Acts. It was a price-less gift. In fact, the members of the Iceland Conference were inspired as well, so inspired that in their constituency meeting they voted that all three top executive officers of the conference would be in charge of prayer ministries for the church. Of course, only time and eternity will tell the results of our prayers, but for those of us who went on this trip, we have been forever changed.

What a beautiful testimony. As I reflect on Jonathan's experience in Iceland, I'm reminded of the following thought from Inspiration. "It is not the capabilities you now possess or ever will have that will give you success. It is that which the Lord can do for you. We need to have far less confidence in what man can do and far more confidence in what God can do for every believing soul. He longs to have you reach after Him by faith. He longs to have you expect great things from Him."[9]

Prayer is the main program!

We talk a lot, as a church, about our need for a deeper outpouring of the Holy Spirit. We preach about it from the pulpits, and we mention it again and again in prayer. But I'm afraid our talk of the Holy Spirit has also become merely another popular phrase. While the words roll easily off our lips, unfortunately, we still seem very content to live and work without the Holy Spirit's power.

To illustrate, not long ago, I was asked to lead a prayer meeting before a Sabbath morning service. As requested, the prayer meeting would occur in the main sanctuary and would last about thirty min-utes. However, as the time got closer, there began to be some differing opinions among the church programming committee about where this prayer meeting should take place. Should it stay in the main sanctuary, where everyone would see it happening as they came into the church and thus be encouraged to join, or should it occur in a side room where things would be a bit quieter and out of the way?

One man on the committee spoke up, voicing his strong opinion that it would be best not to have it in the main sanctuary, because, after all, there would be microphone sound checks going on, preservice music practice, and having the prayer meeting in the sanctuary might delay the start of Sabbath School. "The program cannot be held up just because of the prayer meeting," he said firmly.

As I walked away from the conversation, I was deeply disturbed. I couldn't get over the irony of it all. Here the church was asking me to lead a prayer meeting because they wanted more of the Holy Spirit, but they didn't want the prayer meeting to get in the way of *the program*.

When are we going to realize that our main program as a church is not *more programs*? Our greatest need is not more committees or better plans. (Not that committees or planning are always wrong.) But our biggest and most important program as a church should be to seek the Holy Spirit, and until we have the Holy Spirit, we will have no program—at least not as God intended.

As I reflect on our current state of affairs, I can't help but resonate with the following:

We do not live in a praying age. . . . I think it would be perfectly safe to say that the church of Christ was never in all its history so fully, so skillfully and so thoroughly and so perfectly organized as it is today. Our machinery is wonderful; it is just perfect, but, alas, it is machinery without power; and when things do not go right, instead of going to the real source of our failure, our neglect to depend on God and look to God for power, we look around to see if there is not some new organization we can get up, some new wheel that we can add to our machinery. We have altogether too many wheels already. What we need is not so much some new organization, some new wheel, but the "Spirit of the living creature in the wheels," we already possess. . . . Prayer has as much power today, when men and women are themselves on praying ground and meeting the conditions of prevailing prayer, as it ever had.[10]

As we consider our need for more of the Holy Spirit, let's turn back to the book of Acts.

Acts 1:4, 5, 8 tells us, "And being assembled together with them, [Jesus] commanded them not to depart from Jerusalem, but to wait for the Promise of the Father, 'which,' He said, 'you have heard from Me; for John truly baptized with water, but you shall be baptized with the Holy Spirit not many days from now.' . . . But you shall receive power when the Holy Spirit has come upon you; and you shall be witnesses to Me in Jerusalem, and in all Judea and Samaria, and to the end of the earth."

What a mission the disciples were given—to the ends of the earth. "I'm ready, let's go!" I can hear Peter saying. "Yes, me too!" John echoes. But this isn't about going, at least not yet. The agenda is about staying and waiting and *praying*.

But we humans aren't good at *staying*. We aren't good at waiting. Waiting drives us crazy! And we definitely aren't good at praying, at least not for very long. We are movers and doers and organizers. Yes, we have all those things down to a science. But God isn't looking for more organizers. He's looking for more *agonizers*!

Ellen White writes, "The greatest victories to the church of Christ or to the individual Christian are not those that are gained by talent or education, by wealth or the favor of men. They are those victories that are gained in the audience chamber with God, when earnest, *agonizing faith* lays hold upon the mighty arm of power."[11]

In another place, we read, "The descent of the Holy Spirit upon the church is looked forward to as in the future; but it is the privilege of the church to have it now. Seek for it, pray for it, believe for it. We must have it, and Heaven is waiting to bestow it."[12]

If heaven is waiting to bestow the Holy Spirit, why do we not have His full power? Could it be that we have yet to obey what He's already shown us?

Ten days of heart searching

As we reflect on our need for the Holy Spirit, it is significant that we understand the Holy Spirit is not just a mysterious power floating around that we need to somehow capture. No, the Holy Spirit is a Person—a Person who leads us, guides us, speaks to us, and ultimately draws us to Jesus and a deeper understanding of His Word (John 16:7–14; 14:26). "We cannot use the Holy Spirit. The Spirit is to use us," Ellen White writes.[13] With this in mind, instead of asking, "How can I have more of the Holy Spirit?" we should be daily asking, "How can the Holy Spirit have more of me?"[14]

Unfortunately, many look for sensational thrills, miracles, and fireworks, and if they find these, they assume the Holy Spirit is working, even if what is happening does not align with Scripture. But while miracles may occur, these cannot be the litmus test of the Holy Spirit's leading. A genuine work of the Holy Spirit will never contradict the Bible in any way. We are told, "The Spirit was not given—nor can it ever be bestowed—to supersede the Bible; for the Scriptures explicitly state that the word of God is the standard by which all teaching and experience must be tested."[15]

While no fireworks were taking place leading up to the actual Day of Pentecost, the Holy Spirit was already working powerfully. In fact, it was these ten days of deep heart searching and repentance that are most significant, for they prepared the disciples for the great visible outpouring that came on the actual Day of Pentecost.

Let's review what happened with the disciples during these ten days.

- They gathered together to wait for the promise.
- They humbled their hearts in true repentance.
- They confessed their unbelief.
- They recalled the words of Jesus regarding His sacrifice.
- They repeated to one another truths they remembered.
- They meditated upon Jesus' holy life.
- They determined to share Jesus with the world.
- They prayed with intense earnestness to lead sinners to Jesus.
- They put away differences and came close together in fellowship.
- They praised Jesus in song for sins forgiven.
- They contemplated with wonder the love of God.
- They took hold of the imparted gift.[16]

And what was the result? "The Spirit came upon the waiting, praying disciples with a fullness that reached every heart. . . . Lost in wonder, the apostles exclaimed, 'Herein is love.' They grasped the imparted gift.

And what followed? . . . Thousands were converted in a day."[17]

It's amazing to think that even greater days of Holy Spirit outpouring lie just ahead for us as a church. However, while people pray for the power of Pentecost to be repeated, the reality is that they aren't willing to surrender *to the degree* that the disciples surrendered during those ten days of preparation in the upper room. And yet they wonder why they have no power!

Unfortunately many think that their lack of spiritual power

> will be supplied by the latter rain. When the richest abundance of grace shall be bestowed, they intend to open their hearts to receive it. [But] they are making a terrible mistake. . . . [Even now] the heart must be emptied of every defilement and cleansed for the indwelling of the Spirit. It was by the confession and forsaking of sin, by earnest prayer and consecration of themselves to God, that the early disciples prepared for the outpouring of the Holy Spirit on the Day of Pentecost. *The same work, only in greater degree, must be done now.*[18]

The famous evangelist Dwight L. Moody once said, when reflecting on the church's great need, "God has got a good many children who have just barely got life, but not power for service. You might say safely, I think, without exaggeration, that nineteen out of every twenty of professed Christians are of no earthly account so far as building up Christ's kingdom; but on the contrary they are standing right in the way, and the reason is because they have just got life and have settled down, and have not sought for power."[19]

Although Dwight L. Moody was highly sought after as a speaker and evangelist and is known for reaching thousands for Jesus, he continually prayed daily for the Holy Spirit's filling. "Why do you keep praying to be full of the Holy Spirit when it's obvious you already have it?" a young student once asked him. "It's because I leak," Moody replied. "We are all leaky vessels and we have to stay under the fountain all the time in order to keep full."[20]

We have much to learn from Moody's example, for we are in a crisis right now in our world, in our homes, and in our church. We have no strength to stand in this crisis. Yet I take comfort that God will work if we step forward in faith and fervent prayer.

Ellen White writes,

It was because Elijah was a man of large faith that God could use him in this grave crisis in the history of Israel. As he prayed, his faith reached out and grasped the promises of Heaven, and he persevered in prayer until his petitions were answered. . . . And yet what he was enabled to do under God, all may do in their sphere of activity in God's service. . . . Faith such as this is needed in the world today— faith that will lay hold on the promises of God's word and refuse to let go until Heaven hears.[21]

What if we were willing to take the same steps as the disciples in that upper prayer room? What if instead of sandwiching a few minutes of prayer into our already packed schedules and programs, we just set aside the schedules and the programs and dedicated whole meetings, and whole days just to pray and to make things right with one another? Might what happened in the book of Acts happen again?

Inspiration tells us, "Just as long as the church is satisfied with small things, they are disqualified to receive the great things of God."[22] Let's not be satisfied with small things anymore. Let's dare to ask for even more!

Daring to Live by Every Word—Going Deeper!
Daring to Ask for Even More: Luke 11:13

As you reflect on the message of this chapter, remember our first work in preparing for the latter rain is getting our heart right with God and with one another, just like the disciples did in that upper room.

Ellen White writes,

When the Holy Spirit was poured out upon the early church, "the multitude of them that believed were of one heart and of one soul" (Acts 4:32). The Spirit of Christ made them one. This is the fruit of abiding in Christ. . . . Every individual is striving to become a center of influence, and until God works for his people, they will not see that subordination to God is the only safety for any soul. His transforming grace upon human hearts will lead to unity that has not yet been realized, for all who are assimilated to Christ will be in harmony with one another. The Holy Spirit will create unity.[23]

As you pray for a heart to receive the latter rain, I encourage you to sing the song, "Showers of Blessing," hymn no. 195. Then open your Bible and take some time to dig deeply in God's Word.

- Luke 11:13—How eager is Jesus to give us the Holy Spirit?
- Zechariah 10:1—What kind of rain should we be praying for?
- Galatians 5:22–26; Romans 8:14–17—What is evidence of the Holy Spirit in our life?
- Romans 5:5; Ephesians 2:18, 19—How are the Holy Spirit and God's love intertwined?
- Jude 18–21—Why do we need to be cleansed of all impurity if we want to be filled by the Holy Spirit?
- 1 Thessalonians 5:19–21—How can we quench the Holy Spirit?
- 1 Corinthians 12:13; Romans 6:3–7—What is the significance of baptism as it relates to receiving the Holy Spirit?
- Acts 1—What can we learn from the disciples' example?
- Acts 2, 3—What will be the result of our coming together in love and unity?
- Acts 4, 5—Will the Holy Spirit's work be accepted by everyone, or will there be persecution? If so, what might we expect in the coming days?

In taking this message deeper, I'd like to encourage you to watch a short YouTube video by David Wilkerson called "A Call to Anguish."[24] Also, I encourage you to take some time to prayerfully read chapter 4, titled "Pentecost," in Ellen White's book *The Acts of the Apostles*. This book can be accessed online if you don't have a physical copy.[25]

Time to dig deep into God's Word, get on our knees, and allow the Holy Spirit to take this message deeper into our hearts!

Chapter 21

Becoming a Living Sacrifice

Finding Hope in the Midst of Suffering

For I consider that the sufferings of this present time are not worthy to be compared with the glory which shall be revealed in us.
—Romans 8:18

One morning, a few months ago, I woke up to the soft beep of a text message that had come in on my phone. It was the kind of text message that no one wants to receive. As I rubbed my sleepy eyes trying to read the message, suddenly the words *terrible accident, broken neck,* and *died* leaped off my phone screen. I swallowed hard as tears came to my eyes! "Oh, no. Please, Jesus. No!" I cried.

My dear friend MaryAnn, along with her three daughters, had just a few hours earlier been in a horrific car accident. In the crash, Mary-Ann's oldest daughter, nine-year-old Sierra, had been killed. While her two younger daughters escaped with relatively minor injuries, Mary-Ann herself had suffered a C-6 cervical fracture and, as a result, was paralyzed from the neck down.

MaryAnn and her husband, T. J., are good friends of mine from my years living in Southern California. At the time we first met, T. J. had been a medical student at Loma Linda University School of Medicine, and MaryAnn had been a teacher in the local Adventist elementary school. They were fresh in love as young newlyweds and full of life, energy, faith, and hope for a bright future.

Now, almost thirteen years later, T. J. was working as a successful and respected ER physician, and MaryAnn was a busy stay-at-home mom, raising and homeschooling their four beautiful children while keeping up the gardens on their country farm. While life was not without its challenges, things were going very well for the Knutson family. That is, until suddenly, on July 28, 2019, their world was turned completely upside down, and life as they had known it was forever changed.

Can you imagine the intense pain of losing your firstborn child? Can you imagine being a devoted wife and mother, energetic hiker, gardener, cook, pianist, teacher, and so much more—and suddenly you can no longer even move a finger to wipe your own tears, let alone take care of your family? And what about being a working father who now suddenly finds himself without the helping hands of his wife and partner, with the constant needs of three energetic young children? What are you to do? How do you cope with such a tragedy?

Of course, we know that no tragedy ever catches God by surprise. No death, no heartache, no hurricane, no earthquake, no tornado or fire, no pain or paralysis or persecution escapes God's notice. In fact, God's Word reminds us, again and again, that while all things are not good, God is always good, and *all things will work together for good* to those who love Him and are called according to His purpose (Psalms 34:8; 100:5; Nahum 1:7; Romans 8:28). So this means even in our worst nightmares and most difficult trials, His faithfulness never changes (Lamentations 3:22, 23).

But knowing the truth spoken in God's Word and living the truth in the midst of life-shattering events are often very different experiences. And so my heart cried, *Would T. J. and MaryAnn sense God's nearness, even in the midst of their tragedy? Would they be able to hold on to Him in strong faith?* The words of comfort I tried to share sounded so empty, so shallow, and so trite. How could I do more?

A few weeks after the accident, I flew out to California for a few days to be with MaryAnn in the hospital, while T. J. traveled home (three hours north) along with his family to bury their daughter Sierra, who had been killed in the accident.

The intense pain I experienced with MaryAnn during that weekend is hard to describe. MaryAnn couldn't talk due to the tracheostomy tube that was still necessary for her breathing, and so our only communication was through her mouthed words. But the tears flowed freely. And yet through the tears, I was amazed as she continually expressed the belief that God works all things together for good. "God knows what He's doing," MaryAnn confided as I wiped tears from her eyes. "If our pain can be used to point someone's eyes toward Jesus, then all our suffering will be worth it."

The final evening before I left California to fly home, several of us were talking around MaryAnn's hospital bed about what had happened. At this moment, MaryAnn earnestly mouthed the following words to those of us surrounding her: "When you tell people our story, be sure to tell them that God is good! And He's been so good to me," she mouthed clearly. "Tell them that He's been merciful and faithful to our family in so many ways, each step of our painful journey. Also, plead with them to put away anything that comes between them and God because we don't have much time. He's coming soon to take us home, and we need to be ready to meet Him."

As MaryAnn mouthed the words of faith and trust, tears came to my eyes, and all I could do was look heavenward in awe. You see, when I bought my airline tickets to go spend time with MaryAnn, it was my heart prayer that I could somehow strengthen her and her husband's faith during their great trial, but the reality of our time together was that their faith strengthened mine.

Yes, we all cried together—buckets of tears! The pain was and is very deep and very real, and the difficult journey that lies ahead is scary for everyone to embrace. Yet through it all, T. J. and MaryAnn's trust and faith in God's goodness continues unwaveringly.

Romans 8:18 tells us, "For I consider that the sufferings of this present time are not worthy to be compared with the glory which shall be revealed in us." Could it be that MaryAnn and T. J. already catch a glimpse of a coming glory that many of us cannot yet see?

Coping with the unexplained

So what do we do when life doesn't make sense? How do we find hope when there seems no purpose or explanation behind our suffering? I believe there's only one answer. We must root our hope in Jesus, surrendering our lives into His hands as living sacrifices, trusting that someday, the unexplained will be explained, and the brokenness will be made beautiful.

Ellen White writes, "All that has perplexed us in the providences of God will in the world to come be made plain. The things hard to be understood will then find explanation. The mysteries of grace will unfold before us. Where our finite minds discovered only confusion and broken promises, we shall see the most perfect and beautiful harmony. We shall know that infinite love ordered the experiences that seemed most trying. As we realize the tender care of Him who makes all things work together for our good, we shall rejoice with joy unspeakable and full of glory."[1]

As we talk about suffering, I'm reminded of the story of Job, who, instead of cursing God or renouncing his faith during his most difficult hour, cried out, "Though He slay me, yet will I trust Him" (Job 13:15). Job knew that God loved him, and although all his circumstances made it seem otherwise, he refused to let go of that trust.

Inspiration tells us, "Above the distractions of the earth [God] sits enthroned; all things are open to His divine survey; and from His great and calm eternity He orders that which His providence sees best."[2]

I've heard it said that we should praise the Lord for whatever it is that pushes us into the arms of our Savior. Unfortunately, in the midst of trials and suffering, instead of running to Jesus, we often run away, questioning His goodness and doubting His love, and asking "why" He's even allowing the trials in the first place. But the Bible tells us, "Beloved, do not think it strange concerning the fiery trial which is to try you, as though some strange thing happened to you" (1 Peter 4:12). In other words, we shouldn't be surprised when trials come. We shouldn't be shocked when pain and suffering wound our soul. They are part of the results of living in a broken, sinful world. They are also the refiner's fire that God uses to purge away the dross of earthliness from our hearts so that we can reflect Jesus and be prepared to meet Him when He comes.

I still remember one of the first significant trials that God used in my own journey. It happened more than twenty years ago. One of my best friends had just been diagnosed with colon cancer, and the doctor's prognosis for her survival was not very hopeful. At the time, I was in the middle of my sophomore year in college and was living in my friend's home. She and her husband were like a second family to me and had been mentoring me and helping me grow in my walk with God. And that's when the dreadful cancer diagnosis came. Suddenly, I felt like the bottom had fallen out from my world. "God, how can You let this happen?" I wailed. "What are You doing?"

I cried as I'd never cried before, trying to cope with the crisis and, at the same time, be supportive of my friend Karen and her husband. However, the biggest crisis was not that Karen had cancer, but that my trust in God was weak.

One morning, while driving to the hospital to see Karen, I'd been having a serious weeping session and was feeling quite abandoned by God, when suddenly, the story flashed across my mind of Shadrach, Meschach, and Abednego and how they refused to bow down and worship the golden image. As a result, King Nebuchadnezzar had given them a simple ultimatum. Either you bow down, or you go into the furnace. There was no negotiation. The Bible tells us their bold response: "Our God whom we serve is able to deliver us from the burning fiery furnace, and He will deliver us from your hand, O king. *But if not*, let it be known to you, O king, that we do not serve your gods, nor will we worship the gold image which you have set up" (Daniel 3:17, 18; emphasis added).

As I thought about the story that morning, I heard God's still small voice speaking to my heart. "Melody, I see your pain. I haven't forsaken you. I care about Karen, and I'm able to spare her life. However, even if I don't work a miracle, will you still trust Me?"

Fresh tears poured down my face as I cried out to God that morning, "Please, Lord, don't take her life! Please, Lord!" There was silence, then the Holy Spirit spoke again, "But will you still trust Me, *even if . . .* ?" Oh, how I wept. Finally, with a shaking voice, I surrendered, "I will trust You, Lord! I know You are able to deliver and to heal Karen, *but even if You don't*, I will still trust You, and I will still praise You!"[3]

That day was a significant turning point in my young, growing faith.

However, God has continued to ask me this same difficult, faith-testing question again and again through the years, "Melody, will you trust Me, even if . . . even if I don't answer your prayers in the way that you desire, even if your plans don't work out as you hope, even if your loved ones die, even if your heart is broken?"[4]

Just recently, when my mother was diagnosed with stage 4 lung cancer, I felt the piercing question once again, and I cried fresh tears as I told the Lord, "Yes, I will trust You and praise You, even if . . . "

I once read that a bar of steel is worth five dollars, but when beat into horseshoes, it is worth ten dollars. "If made into needles, it is worth three hundred and fifty dollars; if into penknife blades, it is worth thirty-two thousand dollars; if into springs for watches it is worth two hundred and fifty thousand dollars. What a drilling the poor bar must undergo to be worth this! But the more it is manipulated, the more it is hammered and passed through the fire, and beaten and pounded and polished, the greater the value."[5]

Perhaps this is why James tells us, "My brethren, count it all joy when you fall into various trials, knowing that the testing of your faith produces patience. But let patience have its perfect work, that you may be perfect and complete, lacking nothing" (James 1:2–4).

Let me share a couple more stories that have helped me in how I approach suffering.

Praising God in the midst of pain

Happily married, and with an energetic two-year-old toddler underfoot, my friend Janet was living her dream. She and her husband Mike, who was a pastor, were just beginning their life together in ministry. Then one day, tragedy struck when Janet found Mike submerged at the bottom of their apartment swimming pool. For no explainable reason, he had passed out while swimming and drowned. Unable to resuscitate him, Janet watched in shock as the paramedics carried Mike's cold body away.

Suddenly Janet was a widow, and a single mom, with no means of support for her and her young son. What was she to do? To make matters worse, just months before, in an effort to cut expenses, she and Mike had decided to cancel Mike's life insurance policy. Oh, how she regretted that decision now.

Crying out in desperation to the Lord, Janet felt God telling her to praise Him—not praise Him that her husband died, but praise Him that He, God, was still in control, and He could provide even through this great loss. And so even through her heartache and tears of pain, she began to praise God. As she did, God slowly began to provide.

As it turned out, her parents had just built a new home with an extra room. It didn't really make sense for them to include the extra room in their building plans, as their children were all grown and gone. But they did it anyway. Just a few months later, they knew why, as they were able to offer Janet and her son a place to live.

When people heard about Janet's loss, they began sending funds to help her pay her bills. Slowly and gradually, she began to rebuild her shattered life as she clung to her Savior.

Almost a year after Mike's death, Janet was going through her financial records one day and decided to add up all the donations that had come in from generous friends and donors during her time of hardship. She was shocked to discover that all the donations she had received added up to the exact penny of the amount her husband's life insurance had been worth. As she had been worshiping and praising God, even in her pain, God had faithfully provided for her every need.

Today Janet Page and her new husband, Jerry (of over thirty-five years now), travel the world working for the General Conference of Seventh-day Adventists,[6] sharing their testimony of God's faithfulness, and seeking to inspire others to have a deeper, closer walk with God. Thousands have been blessed through their encouragement.

Sometimes when I'm tempted to complain about my struggles or problems, Janet will remind me, "We need to stop telling God how big our problems are and start telling our problems how big our God is! Nothing is too hard for Him!"

Maybe you are overwhelmed by the struggles in your life; maybe you face mountains on every side. Maybe God appears silent, or you don't understand why He's not answering your prayers. As Janet would encourage, don't just keep praying through, but keep *praising through.* When we have problems or trials, our natural default is to think, *I have to find someone who I can talk to about this problem. I need to find books about this or Google my problem and see what the experts say.* But rather than turning to human solutions, we should be going to God with open hands saying,

"I praise You, I trust You, I worship You, even if I don't understand what You're doing in my life, and I give my body as a living sacrifice."

I'm reminded of an illustration Ellen White once gave about a plow and an altar. "There is a picture representing a bullock standing between a plow and an altar, and with the picture is the inscription, 'Ready for either.' Thus we should be ready to tread the weary furrow or to bleed on the altar of sacrifice. This singleness of purpose, this devotion to duty, is to be expressed in the life of every child of God. This was the position our Saviour occupied while upon the earth; it is the position that every follower of His will occupy."[7]

Remember, a living sacrifice always has the freedom to crawl off the altar. As a living sacrifice, we have the freedom to walk away. But it takes a truly committed Christian to stay on the altar, even when the heat of pain and suffering increase.

Richard Wurmbrand, founder of Voice of the Martyrs, who I shared about in earlier chapters, was a genuine testimony of what it means to be a living sacrifice. He was ready for the plow (to serve the church of Romania in the midst of great Communist oppression) or to go to the altar (to die or spend his years in prison). As a result of His stand for Jesus during this difficult time, he was called to do the latter—to spend fourteen years in a Communist prison. Torture was routine, and things got so bad at one point that he nearly died. Yet, despite his years of hardship and suffering, his faith remained strong, and he had no bitterness over what he endured.

In fact, not long after his release, his friends gathered around Richard, asking him what it was like in prison. "Oh, they gave us instruments," he said, smiling.

"Instruments?" his friends asked incredulously.

"Yes, instruments with which we sang praises to our God. The instruments were our chains."

The Communist leaders had done everything they could to break Richard's spirit, and yet all they could do was make Richard praise God more.

In *The Desire of Ages*, we read,

God never leads His children otherwise than they would choose to be led if they could see the end from the beginning, and discern the glory of the purpose which they are fulfilling as co-workers with Him. Not Enoch, who was translated to heaven, not Elijah, who ascended in a chariot of fire, was greater or more honored than John the Baptist, who perished alone in the dungeon. "Unto you it is given in the behalf of Christ, not only to believe on Him, but also to suffer for His sake." Philippians 1:29. And of all the gifts that Heaven can bestow upon men, fellowship with Christ in His sufferings is the most weighty trust and the highest honor.[8]

Are we willing to accept this weighty trust and high honor? Are we willing to praise and worship God, even in our suffering, even when life doesn't make sense?

Suffering is not easy, but when we place our hope in the Lord, He will take our pain and use it to make beautiful instruments of praise for His glory. Then just like Job, we can say, "But He knows the way that I take; when He has tested me, I shall come forth as gold" (Job 23:10).

Daring to Live by Every Word—Going Deeper!
Finding Hope in Suffering: Romans 8:18

Dane Griffin, while facing a battle with cancer that would eventually take his life, wrote the following:

I realize now that faith is not about the outcome: Faith is about growing from trial to trial ("from faith to faith," Romans 1:17), in order to be ready for the outcome that God permits. Faith is not an insurance policy against unwanted troubles. Faith is a road map that will lead us unfailingly to God's perfect destination for us. . . . Where will my journey take me? That's up to God. I just want His faith that overcomes the world, His faith that develops me to meet each new trial, His faith that prepares me for the only guarantee faith offers. "For by grace you have been saved through faith" (Ephesians 2:8).[9]

I don't know what trial or test of faith you might be going through, but know that Jesus is near. He will not forsake you in the refiner's fire.

Ellen White writes, "The fact that we are called upon to endure trial shows that the Lord Jesus sees in us something precious which He desires to develop. If He saw in us nothing whereby He might glorify His name, He would not spend time in refining us. He does not cast worthless stones into His furnace. It is valuable ore that He refines."[10]

Consider the following Bible passages, as you reflect on what it means to trust God in the midst of suffering:

- Romans 8:14–39—What does God promise through our trials and pain?
- 2 Corinthians 4:7–10—What does God wish to reveal in our characters?
- Isaiah 61:3—How can we love and worship God in times of suffering?
- Matthew 15:25—When it didn't look as though Jesus was going to answer the Canaanite woman's prayer, what was her response?
- Malachi 3:2, 3—Why does God use fire (suffering) to purify us?
- Hebrews 11—What courage can we gain from the heroes of faith?
- Genesis 50:20—How can what the enemy has intended for evil in your life be turned to good?
- Psalm 56:8—Are any of our tears lost or overlooked by God?
- Revelation 21:4; Jeremiah 31:13—What is God going to do with all our sorrows?
- Sing or reflect on the song, "Be Still, My Soul," hymn no. 461.

Keep pressing close to Jesus. The Lord is on your side, and thorny ways will lead to a joyful end! As Inspiration reminds us, "How many there are who would never have known Jesus had not sorrow led them to seek comfort in Him!"[11]

Time to dig deep into God's Word, get on our knees, and allow the Holy Spirit to take this message deeper into our hearts!

Chapter 22

It's OK to Die!

The Best Is Yet to Come

> *"For whoever desires to save his life will lose it, but whoever loses his life for My sake and the gospel's will save it."*
> —Mark 8:35

When I hear the testimonies of those who have stood firm for their faith over the centuries, even in the face of death, my pulse quickens, and my heart burns with a strengthened resolve. "If God brings me to such a test, I want to have faith like that!" I tell myself. "I want to be able to lay *everything* on the altar for Jesus, even if it means my life."

As we know, all of the disciples of Jesus, except for John, died as martyrs for the sake of the gospel. Clear to the end, their faith remained strong. As a result, their testimony is still shaking our world today. Of course, the apostle John, while he did not die as a martyr, lived a martyr's life as his final years were spent in exile. However, it was his testimony and personal discipleship that encouraged a young man named Polycarp to be faithful unto death.

Polycarp, a Christian from his youth, served as a bishop in Smyrna, Turkey, about one hundred years after the time of Christ. It was not until his elderly years, in A.D. 155, that he was arrested for refusing to burn incense to the Roman emperor. Knowing he would most likely die, he requested permission to pray for one hour before they took him away. The soldiers honored his request and stood by watching. When that hour was up, he was hauled to prison.

A few days later, on the Sabbath, as the authorities prepared to tie Polycarp to the stake, he was given one last opportunity to recant his faith. Courageously he spoke to all those looking on. "Eighty-six years, I have served the Lord, and He never once wronged me. How then shall I blaspheme my King, who has saved me?"

Then turning his eyes toward heaven, Polycarp prayed, "I bless thee, because thou hast deemed me worthy of this day and hour, to take my part in the number of the martyrs, in the cup of thy Christ, for resurrection to eternal life."[1]

The flame was lit, but it encircled Polycarp and did not touch him. In consternation, one standing nearby pierced him through with a sword. As a result, the blood that gushed forth extinguished the fire. The soldiers had to light the fire again before it did its work. However, there is no record of Polycarp ever faltering or crying out in pain. Later, many of the soldiers who had witnessed his last hour of prayer repented of their crime and gave their lives to Jesus. Polycarp's courageous witness has gone on to strengthen countless others in the centuries since.

There are many stories of courageous martyrs like that of Polycarp, but one of my favorite testimonies is of two young women named Perpetua and Felicitas.

Perpetua, whose painting is pictured in the book *The Triumph of God's Love*,[2] was born into nobility in the second century A.D., but somehow came to accept Jesus as her Lord and Savior. This brought great consternation to her family. She was twenty-two years of age and nursing an infant son at the time of her arrest, and her family pleaded that she renounce her faith, for the sake of her child. But she stood steadfast, refusing to deny her Lord. As a result, she was sentenced to be thrown to the wild beasts in a Roman coliseum.

Her companion Felicitas was a slave girl and was eight months pregnant when she was imprisoned along with Perpetua. Since it was illegal to execute a pregnant woman, it seemed that Felicitas would avoid being executed with Perpetua and the other Christians condemned to die. But instead of being relieved, Felicitas was deeply grieved that her pregnancy might prevent her from joining her companions in martyrdom. So three days before the scheduled execution Felicitas and her companions prayed earnestly, asking God to give her an early labor so she could face the wild beasts with her fellow Christians. Felicitas went into labor immediately.

As she cried out in labor pains, the prison guards yelled at her, "If you think you are hurting now, what will you do when we throw you to the wild beasts because you refuse to sacrifice to Cesar?" Felicitas bravely responded, "Now it is I that suffer what I suffer. But then there will be Another by my side who will suffer for me because I shall suffer for Him." She gave birth to a baby girl whom her sister took to raise.

Perpetua and Felicitas bravely approached their execution day not long after, calling it the day of their victory. Knowing God was with them, Perpetua was singing a song as they entered the arena where the wild beasts waited.

The two women, along with several others, received the mauling from the wild beasts in prayer and silence, without any outcry and were scarcely aware of what was happening. In fact, Perpetua felt no pain and did not believe that she was even touched until someone pointed out her bleeding wounds.

While Perpetua and Felicitas perished that day, along with others, their legacy lives on to give us courage and to remind us that it's okay to die. This world is not our home. We have a better home above.

The Bible tells us, "He who loves father or mother more than Me is not worthy of Me. And he who loves son or daughter more than Me is not worthy of Me. And he who does not take his cross and follow after Me is not worthy of Me" (Matthew 10:37, 38).

Are we willing to obey God's Word and take up our cross, even if it eventually means being a martyr for Jesus? This may seem like a hard call, but we must remember that persecution, suffering, and even death have always been the lot of Christians ever since the early church was formed. Stephen was the first martyr (Acts 7:59), and countless millions have followed in his footsteps.

I'm reminded of one Waldensian pastor who was captured along with his family in the mountains of Italy during the time of great persecution to the Waldenses. While binding his hands, his captors taunted him, "Unless you renounce your faith in Christ, we are going to torture you and your family to death."

The pastor bravely replied, "I love my Lord. Ten thousand deaths of such kind would be too few to die on behalf of the One who gave His all for me."[3]

As I type these testimonies, tears come to my eyes. It was sacrifices such as these and that of countless forgotten others,[4] that paved the way for God's church to continue growing despite all obstacles and despite much persecution and oppression.

> History bears record to the fortitude and heroism of these men [and women]. Like the apostles, many of them fell at their post. . . . The workmen were slain, but the work advanced. The Waldenses, John Wycliffe, Huss and Jerome, Martin Luther and Zwingli, Cranmer, Latimer, and Knox, the Huguenots, John and Charles Wesley, and a host of others brought to the foundation material that will endure throughout eternity. And in later years those who have so nobly endeavored to promote the circulation of God's word, and those who by their service in heathen lands have prepared the way for the proclamation of the last great message—these also have helped to rear the structure [of God's church].[5]

James and Mary Calvert, natives of Yorkshire England, in 1830, sailed as missionaries to work among the cannibals of Fiji. When they arrived on the island, they were questioned, "Aren't you afraid to be here? This is cannibal territory." James replied, unflinchingly, "We died before we came here."[6]

It's easy to be fearful about the future. None of us like the thought of suffering or pain. But the Bible tells us, "For God has not given us a spirit of fear, but of power and of love and of a sound mind" (2 Timothy 1:7). He also hasn't given us strength today for tomorrow's trials. However, we can be confident that when He asks us to walk through the fire, He will walk with us, just as He has countless others who have walked this path before. "As your days, so shall your strength be" (Deuteronomy 33:25), He reminds us.

To the church in Smyrna, Jesus sent the message, "Do not fear any of those things which you are about to suffer. Indeed, the devil is about to throw some of you into prison, that you may be tested, and you will have tribulation ten days. Be faithful until death, and I will give you the crown of life" (Revelation 2:10).

In the Bible, Paul reminded the early Christians, "All that will live godly in Christ Jesus shall suffer persecution" (2 Timothy 3:12). Responding to this passage, Ellen White writes:

Why is it, then, that persecution seems in a great degree to slumber? The only reason is that the church has conformed to the world's standard and therefore awakens no opposition. The religion which is current in our day is not of the pure and holy character that marked the Christian faith in the days of Christ and His apostles. It is only because of the spirit of compromise with sin, because the great truths of the word of God are so indifferently regarded, because there is so little vital godliness in the church, that Christianity is apparently so popular with the world. Let there be a revival of the faith and power of the early church, and the spirit of persecution will be revived, and the fires of persecution will be rekindled.[7]

Are we willing to embrace a primitive godliness that will rekindle the fires of persecution? Remember, death is not to be feared. It's OK to die. In fact, we must die, die to self, die to the world, and die to all that separates us from God, if we want to truly live. "For whoever desires to save his life will lose it, but whoever loses his life for My sake and the gospel's will save it" (Mark 8:35).

As one brave Christian said before his own death, "When Christ calls a man, He bids him come and die."[8] But death doesn't start on the way to the martyr's grave. Death starts today!

Final words

As we bring this book to a close, I think it's very fitting that I share a few of the final words Ellen White wrote to the church before her death. This is a message filled with hope and encouragement. It's a message for you and me! Take to heart the following:

Dear Friend,

The Lord has given me a message for you, and not for you only, but also for other faithful souls who are troubled by doubts and fears regarding their acceptance by the Lord Jesus Christ. His word to you is, "Fear not: for I have redeemed thee, I have called thee by thy name; thou art Mine." You desire to please the Lord, and you can do this by believing His promises. He is waiting to take you into a harbor of gracious experience, and He bids you, "Be still, and know that I am God." You have had a time of unrest; but Jesus says to you, "Come unto Me, . . . and I will give you rest." The joy of Christ in the soul is worth everything. "Then are they glad," because they are privileged to rest in the arms of everlasting love.

Put away your distrust of our heavenly Father. Instead of talking of your doubts, break away from them in the strength of Jesus, and let light shine into your soul by letting your voice express confidence and trust in God. . . .

It is your privilege to trust in the love of Jesus for salvation, in the fullest, surest, noblest manner; to say, He loves me, He receives me; I will trust Him, for He gave His life for me. Nothing so dispels doubt as coming in contact with the character of Christ. He declares, "Him that cometh to Me I will in no wise cast out;" that is, there is no possibility of My casting him out, for I have pledged My word to receive him. Take Christ at His word, and let your lips declare that you have gained the victory.

Is Jesus true? Does He mean what He says? Answer decidedly, Yes, every word. Then if you have settled this, by faith claim every promise that He has made, and receive the blessing; for this acceptance by faith gives life to the soul. You may believe that Jesus is true to you, even though you feel yourself to be the weakest and most unworthy of His children. And as you believe, all your dark, brooding doubts are thrown back upon the arch deceiver who originated them. You can be a great blessing if you will take God at His word. By living faith you are to trust Him, even though the impulse is strong within you to speak words of distrust.

Peace comes with dependence on divine power. As fast as the soul resolves to act in accordance with the light given, the Holy Spirit gives more light and strength. The grace of the Spirit is supplied to cooperate with the soul's resolve, but it is not a substitute for the individual exercise of faith. Success in the Christian life depends upon the appropriation of the light that God has given. It is not an abundance of light and evidence that makes the soul free in Christ; it is the rising of the powers and the will and the energies of the soul to cry out sincerely, "Lord, I believe; help Thou mine unbelief."

I rejoice in the bright prospects of the future, and so may you. Be cheerful, and praise the Lord for His loving-kindness. That which you cannot understand, commit to Him. He loves you and pities your every weakness. He "hath blessed us with all spiritual blessings in heavenly places in Christ." It would not satisfy the heart of the Infinite One to give those who love His Son a lesser blessing than He gives His Son.

Satan seeks to draw our minds away from the mighty Helper, to lead us to ponder over our degeneration of soul. But though Jesus sees the guilt of the past, He speaks pardon; and we should not dishonor Him by doubting His love. The feeling of guiltiness must be laid at the foot of the cross, or it will poison the springs of life. . . .

. . . God rejoices to bestow grace upon all who hunger and thirst for it, not because we are worthy, but because we are unworthy. Our need is the qualification, which gives us the assurance that we shall receive the gift.

It should not be difficult to remember that the Lord desires you to lay your troubles and perplexities at His feet, and leave them there. Go to Him, saying: "Lord, my burdens are too heavy for me to carry. Wilt Thou bear them for me?" And He will answer: "I will take them. 'With everlasting kindness will I have mercy on thee.' I will take your sins, and will give you peace. Banish no longer your self-respect; for I have bought you with the price of My own blood. You are Mine. Your weakened will I will strengthen. Your remorse for sin I will remove."

"I, even I, am He," the Lord declares, "that blotteth out thy transgressions for Mine own sake, and will not remember thy sins. . . . Look unto Me, and be ye saved, all the ends of the earth: for I am God, and there is none else." Respond to the calls of God's mercy, and say: "I will trust in the Lord and be comforted. I will praise the Lord; for His anger is turned away. I will rejoice in God, who gives the victory."[9]

And so ends Ellen White's final words to our church. Isn't that message beautiful?

Perhaps you are thinking, *I want to follow Jesus all the way, but I keep falling. I'm such a sinner, I fear I will never make it.* Have courage, dear friend. Don't trust self. Trust Jesus!

In *Acts of the Apostles*, we are reminded, "None of the apostles and prophets ever claimed to be without sin. Men who have lived the nearest to God, men who would sacrifice life itself rather than knowingly commit a wrong act, men whom God has honored with divine light and power, have confessed the sinfulness of their nature. They have put no confidence in the flesh, have claimed no righteousness of their own, but have trusted wholly in the righteousness of Christ."[10]

The work that God has begun in us He will be faithful to complete (Philippians 1:6). In Jesus' final prayer before going to His crucifixion, He reminded God, "Of those whom You gave Me I have lost none" (John 18:9). That's right, *none*!

If we are trusting in the blood of Jesus, we can have full assurance that when He comes back in the clouds of glory for His redeemed, He will be coming for you and me (1 John 1:9; Isaiah 25:9; Revelation 3:5).

It's time to take up our cross joyfully! Soon God's voice is going to ring from heaven,

"He who is unjust, let him be unjust still; he who is filthy, let him be filthy still; he who is righteous, let him be righteous still; he who is holy, let him be holy still.

"And behold, I am coming quickly, and My reward is with Me, to give to every one according to his work. I am the Alpha and the Omega, the Beginning and the End, the First and the Last."

Blessed are those who do His commandments, that they may have the right to the tree of life, and may enter through the gates into the city (Revelation 22:11–14).

This world is not our home. This life is not the end of our story. The best is truly yet to come![11] The best is Jesus—and He's coming for you and for me!

And it will be said in that day:
"Behold, this is our God;
We have waited for Him, and He will save us.

This is the LORD;
We have waited for Him;
We will be glad and rejoice in His salvation" (Isaiah 25:9).

Daring to Live by Every Word—Going Deeper!
The Best Is Yet to Come: Mark 8:35

As we close this book, asking ourselves, how can we love and worship God even while dying, I want us to picture the new chapter that is to come very soon in God's heavenly book. I want us to imagine the joys and glories of going home and of meeting Jesus face to face! As you read the following, sing the song or find the music for "When We All Get to Heaven," hymn no. 633.

In this final reflection consider the following questions and passages about heaven!

- What is the first thing you want to do when you get to heaven?
- Have you ever taken time to dream about heaven or what your home will be like there? If not, take some time to do that with a friend or loved one.
- What are you looking forward to most?
- What do you want to do that you could not do here on earth?
- What type of questions do you have for Jesus?
- Which Bible hero are you most looking forward to meeting?
- Who are you praying will be in heaven with you?
- Isaiah 65:17–25—What do we learn about heaven from this passage?
- Revelation 21:1–7—What will it be like when all things are made new?
- 1 Corinthians 2:9—Can we comprehend our coming reward?

A fear of making the future inheritance seem too material has led many to spiritualize away the very truths which lead us to look upon it as our home. Christ assured His disciples that He went to prepare mansions for them in the Father's house. Those who accept the teachings of God's word will not be wholly ignorant concerning the heavenly abode. . . . Human language is inadequate to describe the reward of the righteous. It will be known only to those who behold it. No finite mind can comprehend the glory of the Paradise of God. . . .

There are homes for the pilgrims of earth. There are robes for the righteous, with crowns of glory and palms of victory. . . .

We are homeward bound [friends]. He who loved us so much as to die for us hath builded for us a city. The New Jerusalem is our place of rest. There will be no sadness in the City of God. No wail of sorrow, no dirge of crushed hopes and buried affections, will evermore be heard. Soon the garments of heaviness will be changed for the wedding garment. Soon we shall witness the coronation of our King. Those whose lives have been hidden with Christ, those who on this earth have fought the good fight of faith, will shine forth with the Redeemer's glory in the kingdom of God. . . .[12]

"[There] on those peaceful plains, beside those living streams, God's people, so long pilgrims and wanderers, shall find a home."[13] It's time to prepare to meet our Savior. It's time to get ready to go home!

Chapter 23

Closing Thoughts

As I make the final edits on this manuscript, I have to share something personal. Writing this book has not been an easy journey. In fact, I'm not sure if I've ever attempted to do something that was more physically, mentally, spiritually, and emotionally exhausting. The enemy knows how to attack, and attack he has, over and over. The Bible tells us, "Be sober, be vigilant; because your adversary the devil walks about like a roaring lion, seeking whom he may devour" (1 Peter 5:8).

Time and time again, as I was writing the various chapters throughout this book, I would unexpectedly find myself struggling with the very issues I was addressing.

For example, when I was writing on the topic of forgiveness, suddenly, an incident that happened years ago came to my mind, and bitterness overwhelmed me as I remembered how I had been wronged. I thought I had forgiven, I thought the past was behind me, but God showed me that I hadn't fully let it go. So I had to put my writing aside and spend significant time on my knees, pleading that God would change my own heart and give me a spirit of forgiveness and mercy. He did!

When I was writing about grace and love in the family, I found myself challenged to put that very grace and love into practice. It was painful and difficult. And truth be told, I wanted to avoid certain issues and just go on. But God put His finger on specific attitudes I had and

240

said, "No Melody, you need a change of heart. What you are writing about needs to be applied to this difficult situation in your life right now." Oh, how I did not want to obey. But once again, God changed my heart.

There were a few weeks while writing this book when I really began murmuring and complaining about some specific things that were happening in my life. Being grateful and praising God was the last thing on my mind. But God began to remind me that as I'm encouraging others to praise Him, I need that same spirit myself. So one day I spent a couple hours on my knees, crying as I claimed God's promises, asking that He would restore my spirit of thankfulness and give me a heart of genuine gratitude. Not only did He do that, but after I had finished praying, I opened a gift bag from my neighbor Jody to discover a beautiful painted heart with the word "GRATITUDE" engraved across it! Jody had no idea what I was going through, but I was moved to tears that God would answer my prayer in such a personal and visible way.

Again, while I was writing about the battle we have in appetite, suddenly I found myself splurging on things I didn't need to be eating. "What am I doing?" I asked myself. Then it hit me! Right then, I was working on the chapter "Entertainment Center Versus Holy Temple," and Satan was attacking me because he knows how powerful our health message is. He knows that if he can lead me to indulgence, I will not be so in tune with the Holy Spirit's voice, nor will I be able to share with the same enthusiasm and passion. And so God once again opened my eyes to my fleshly weaknesses and my great spiritual need.

On and on the attacks came—from painful disappointments, to family health challenges, and to many other difficult circumstances that have been outside my control. So many times, I felt discouraged and was tempted to give up this whole *Daring to Live by Every Word* project, especially as I was painfully reminded of the many shortcomings in my own life. But through it all, God has held me, and day-by-day He has continued to sustain me. When I was dry and void of inspiration, He filled my cup. When I was tired and weary and felt as though I couldn't keep my eyes open, He sent me promises of strength (Psalm 77:4).[1] He is so good. And the fact that this book is finally completed is a testament to His amazing and sustaining grace. This book is His miracle, and He must get all the glory (Psalm 115:1).

In fact, right now, why don't we pause and sing, "To God be the glory, great things He hath done!"[2]

While I continue to fall short in many ways, I praise the Lord that I have a perfect Advocate in heaven who is fighting on my behalf. He's fighting on your behalf too. Although I know the spiritual battles will become even more intense in the days ahead, we can take courage that our final victory is promised. So let us keep moving forward, knowing that this is a lifelong journey of faith.

Ellen White writes:

Sanctification is not the work of a moment, an hour, a day, but of a lifetime. It is not gained by a happy flight of feeling, but is the result of constantly dying to sin, and constantly living for Christ. Wrongs cannot be righted nor reformations wrought in the character by feeble, intermittent efforts. It is only by long, persevering effort, sore discipline, and stern conflict, that we shall overcome. We know not one day how strong will be our conflict the next. So long as Satan reigns, we shall have self to subdue, besetting sins to overcome; so long as life shall last, there will be no stopping place, no point which we can reach and say, I have fully attained. Sanctification is the result of lifelong obedience.[3]

And I might add, sanctification is the result of lifelong trust in Jesus, who alone can make our obedience acceptable to God. So let's keep walking! Let's keep trusting in Jesus' righteousness! He will see us safely through to the completion of our journey.

"For by grace you have been saved through faith, and that not of yourselves; it is the gift of God, not of works, lest anyone should boast. For we are His workmanship, created in Christ Jesus for good works, which God prepared beforehand that we should walk in them" (Ephesians 2:8–10).*

---

* If you'd like more inspiration and testimonies of God's faithfulness, you can follow Melody's adventures on Instagram @melodiousecho. You can also find her on Facebook under the name "Melodious Echo Mason."

Recommended Books and Resources

Books and Resources by Adventist Authors

Many books have shaped my life over the years, but these are a few that I've been blessed by in more recent times. I pray you are blessed as well as you read them!

- *Adventism's Greatest Need: The Outpouring of the Holy Spirit*, by Ron E. M. Clouzet
- *Almost Home: A Call to Reformation and Revival*, by Ted N. C. Wilson
- *As Light Lingers: Basking in the Word of God*, by Nina Atcheson
- *At Jesus Feet*, by Doug Batchelor
- *The Big Four: Secrets to a Thriving Church Family*, by S. Joseph Kidder
- *Boot Camp for the Last Days: Living for Jesus in the Judgment Hour of Earth's History*, by Randy Maxwell
- *The Called . . . the Chosen: God Has Always Had a People*, by Ken McFarland
- *Commentary on the Book of Daniel: Practical Living in the Judgment Hour*, by Norman McNulty
- *The Dangers of Contemplative Prayer*, by Howard Peth
- *Delighting in the Almighty: A Practical Guide to Primitive Godliness*, by Michael Dant
- *Discipleship Handbook: A Resource for Seventh-day Adventist Church Members*, by Jim Howard
- *Exalting His Word*, by Shelley Quinn
- *Getting to Know the Holy Spirit*, by Ron E. M. Clouzet
- *Heart Lift: Experiencing God's Freedom*, by Jill Morikone
- *Home at Last*, by Walton J. Brown
- *How to Interpret Scripture*, by Frank M. Hasel and Michael G. Hasel
- *If My People Pray*, by Randy Maxwell
- *The Law of Life: Heal From Disease, Depression, and Damaged Relationships*, by Mark Sandoval
- *Lessons on Faith*, by Alonzo T. Jones and E. J. Waggoner

243

- *Living for God: Reclaiming the Joy of Christian Virtue*, by Frank M. Hasel
- *A Living Sacrifice: Unsung Heroes of Adventist Missions*, by D. J. B. Trim
- *Longing for God: A Prayer and Bible Journal*, by Frank M. Hasel
- *One Miracle After Another: The Pavel Goia Story*, by Greg Budd
- *Optimize Your Brain* (DVD series), by Neil Nedley
- *Pray Big: God Can Do So Much More*, by Cindy Mercer
- *A Prophet for This Generation*, by Joakin Hjortland
- *Radical Evidence*, by Derek Morris
- *Revival for Mission*, by Mark Finley
- *Revive us Again*, by Mark Finley
- *Steps to Personal Revival*, by Helmut Haubeil
- *Story Catcher: Powerful Stories That Will Impact Your Spiritual Journey*, by Richard Duerksen
- *Surrender: The Secret to Perfect Peace and Happiness*, by Gregory L. Jackson
- *A Thoughtful Hour: Tracing the Final Footsteps of Jesus*, by Jerry D. Thomas
- *A Thousand Shall Fall*, by Susi Hasel Mundy

Books by Ellen White

There are too many to list, but if you aren't in the habit of reading from Ellen White, I highly encourage you to give her books a try. Ellen White's writings are pure gold. Below I list a few of my favorite titles.

- *The Acts of the Apostles*
- *The Adventist Home*
- *Christian Service*
- *Christ's Object Lessons*
- *The Desire of Ages*
- *Faith and Works*
- *The Great Controversy*
- *Help in Daily Living*
- *Last Day Events*
- *Living the Life of Enoch*

- *The Ministry of Healing*
- *Patriarchs and Prophets*
- *Prophets and Kings*
- *Steps to Christ*
- *Testimonies for the Church, vols. 1–9*
- *Thoughts From the Mount of Blessing*

Excellent Resources by Other Authors

While I do not endorse all the works, beliefs, or ideas of these named authors, these particular titles have been extremely beneficial in helping me go deeper in my walk with God, and I highly recommend them! However, as you read, keep in mind 1 Thessalonians 5:21, which says, "Test all things, hold fast what is good."

- *Absolute Surrender*, by Andrew Murray
- *Beholding and Becoming: The Art of Everyday Worship*, by Ruth Chou Simons
- *Brokenness, Surrender, Holiness: A Revive Our Hearts Trilogy*, by Nancy Leigh DeMoss
- *Calm, Cool, and Connected: 5 Digital Habits for a More Balanced Life*, by Arlene Pellicane
- *Crazy Love: Overwhelmed by a Relentless God*, by Francis Chan
- *Continuous Revival: The Secret of Victorious Living*, by Norman Grubb
- *The Daniel Fast for Spiritual Breakthrough*, by Elmer L. Towns
- *Discipline: The Glad Surrender*, by Elizabeth Elliot
- *The Effects of Praise*, by Andrew Wommack
- *Evidence Not Seen: A Woman's Miraculous Faith in the Jungles of World War II*, by Darlene Deibler Rose
- *Free to Live: The Utter Relief of Holiness*, by John Eldredge
- *Give Me Jesus: Bible Journal*, by Gretchen Saffles
- *The Good Portion*, by Heidi Baird
- *The Gospel's Power and Message*, by Paul Washer
- *The Heavenly Man: The Remarkable True Story of Chinese Christian Brother Yun*, by Paul Hattaway
- *Humility*, by Andrew Murray

- *In His Image: 10 Ways God Calls Us to Reflect His Character,* by Jen Wilkin
- *The Insanity of Obedience: Walking With Jesus in Tough Places,* by Nik Ripken
- *Kept for the Master's Use,* by Frances Ridley Havergal
- *Lies Men Believe: And the Truth That Sets them Free,* by Robert Wolgemuth
- *Lies Women Believe: And the Truth that Sets them Free,* by Nancy De-Moss Wolgemuth
- *Moments With the Savior,* by Ken Gire
- *Not a Fan: Becoming a Completely Committed Follower of Jesus,* by Kyle Idleman
- *Passion and Purity,* by Elisabeth Elliot
- *The Practice of Godliness,* by Jerry Bridges
- *Praying Hyde: The Life of John Praying Hyde,* by Captain E. G. Carre
- *The Pursuit of Holiness,* by Jerry Bridges
- *Radical: Taking Back Your Faith From the American Dream,* by David Platt
- *Rees Howells, Intercessor: The Story of a Life Lived for God,* by Norman Grubb
- *Rescue the Captors: The True Story of a Kidnapped Jungle Pilot,* by Russel Stendal
- *Respectable Sins: Confronting the Sins We Tolerate,* by Jerry Bridges
- *Streams in the Desert: 365 Devotional Readings,* by L. B. Cowman
- *Suffering Is Never for Nothing,* by Elisabeth Elliot
- *The Set-Apart Woman: God's Invitation to Sacred Living,* by Leslie Ludy
- *The Scars That Have Shaped Me: How God Meets Us in Suffering,* by Vaneetha Rendall Risner
- *They Found the Secret: 20 Transformed Lives That Reveal a Touch of Eternity,* by V. Raymond Edman
- *Tramp for the Lord,* by Corrie Ten Boom
- *12 Ways Your Phone Is Changing You,* by Tony Reinke
- *Virtuous Minds: Intellectual Character Development,* by Philip E. Dow
- *When God Writes Your Life Story: Experience the Ultimate Adventure,* by Eric and Leslie Ludy
- *Why Revival Tarries,* by Leonard Ravenhill
- *Women of the Word: How to Study the Bible With Both Our Hearts and Our Minds* by Jen Wilkin
- *Worldliness: Resisting the Seduction of a Fallen World,* by C. J. Mahaney

The Humility "Heart Challenge"

Humble yourselves in the sight of the Lord, and He will lift you up.
—James 4:10

T he following may be hard to digest all in one reading. I encourage you to take your time (maybe even a few days or more) as you pray and reflect on the truths of God's Word in the following comparisons. And don't despair as you realize all the ways you fall short. We all fall short, so we are in this together. But the good news is that God promises that He can change our hearts (1 John 1:9, 10; Ezekiel 36:26).

We are told, "There is nothing that Satan fears so much as that the people of God shall clear the way by removing every hindrance, so that the Lord can pour out His Spirit upon a languishing church. . . . The latter rain will come, and the blessing of God will fill every soul that is purified from every defilement. It is our work today to yield our souls to Christ, that we may be fitted for the time of refreshing from the presence of the Lord—fitted for the baptism of the Holy Spirit."[1]

The Bible tells us to search our hearts (Psalm 139:23, 24). But we search our hearts not so we can dwell on our weaknesses, but so we can recognize our great need and flee to Jesus. With this in mind, let's go. Here is the no-sugar-added, straight-to-the-point contrast between pride and humility.

The Beauty of Humility

- Proud, self-filled people see all the good they do and feel worthy of salvation.
- **Humble, selfless people know that only through Christ's righteousness can they gain salvation.**

"Not by works of righteousness which we have done, but according to His mercy, He saved us, through the washing of regeneration and renewing of the Holy Spirit" (Titus 3:5).

- Proud, self-filled people feel confident and proud of how much they know.
- **Humble, selfless people feel humbled by how much they have yet to learn.**

"Then King David went in and sat before the LORD; and he said: 'Who am I, O Lord GOD? And what is my house, that You have brought me this far?' " (2 Samuel 7:18).

- Proud, self-filled people thank God that they aren't like the world around them.
- **Humble, selfless people realize that "pride" itself is as deadly as the sins of the world.**

"Everyone proud in heart is an abomination to the LORD; though they join forces, none will go unpunished" (Proverbs 16:5).

- Proud, self-filled people carry grudges because they have difficulty saying, "I was wrong. Will you forgive me?"
- **Humble, selfless people are quick to say, "I'm sorry; let's work this out."**

"Therefore if you bring your gift to the altar, and there remember that your brother has something against you, leave your gift there before the altar, and go your way. First be reconciled to your brother, and then come and offer your gift" (Matthew 5:23, 24).

- Proud, self-filled people tend to focus on the failures and weaknesses of others and are unmoved by others' brokenness.
- **Humble, selfless people feel their own weaknesses and great spiritual need deeply and are sensitive to those who are broken.**

"This is a faithful saying and worthy of all acceptance, that Christ Jesus came into the world to save sinners, of whom I am chief" (1 Timothy 1:15).

- Proud, self-filled people have to prove they are right and save face even when they are wrong.
- **Humble, selfless people are willing to yield the "right to be right" in situations even when they are right, as they are more worried about being righteous before God than being right before men.**

"For it is better, if it is the will of God, to suffer for doing good than for doing evil" (1 Peter 3:17).

- Proud, self-filled people are selfishly protective of personal space, time, and their reputation.
- **Humble, selfless people have a generous giving spirit and are willing to be inconvenienced, allowing God to protect their space, time, and reputation.**

"Give, and it will be given to you: good measure, pressed down, shaken together, and running over will be put into your bosom. For with the same measure that you use, it will be measured back to you" (Luke 6:38).

- Proud, self-filled people are too busy to notice or reach out to the "small people" in their lives, those who can't benefit them in some way.
- **Humble, selfless people are always seeking to serve and minister to even the "least of these" as unto Jesus.**

"And the King will answer and say to them, 'Assuredly, I say to you, inasmuch as you did it to one of the least of these My brethren, you did it to Me' " (Matthew 25:40).

- Proud, self-filled people desire to be recognized and applauded, and they covet promotions, trophies, and awards.
- **Humble, selfless people desire to be faithful so that God's glory may be seen, and they shy away from recognition or applause.**

"Not unto us, O LORD, not unto us, but to Your name give glory, because of Your mercy, because of Your truth" (Psalm 115:1).

- Proud, self-filled people are quick to flaunt their titles and great achievements and feel entitled to special treatment.
- **Humble, selfless people don't need to speak of their titles or achievements, and they are content to go unnoticed as long as God gets the glory.**

"Most men will proclaim each his own goodness, but who can find a faithful man?" (Proverbs 20:6).

- Proud, self-filled people use their life and any influence they've received as a stage to showcase themselves.
- **Humble, selfless people use the stage and influence God has given to seek to exalt Christ and make sure only He is seen.**

"He must increase, but I must decrease" (John 3:30).

- Proud, self-filled people have difficulty serving and submitting to others, especially those in positions of authority or leadership.
- **Humble, selfless people, such as Jesus, serve all in humility, without regard to status or position. They lift up those who can do them no benefit, as well as respectfully seeking to hold up those who have authority above them.**

"And whoever desires to be first among you, let him be your slave—just as the Son of Man did not come to be served, but to serve, and to give His life a ransom for many" (Matthew 20:27, 28).

- Proud, self-filled people are always thinking about the good things they do for God, and how the church or ministry couldn't do without them.
- **Humble, selfless people realize that without God, they can do nothing of value for His kingdom. They feel humbled just to be used at all.**

"For it is God who works in you both to will and to do for His good pleasure" (Philippians 2:13).

- Proud, self-filled people are often cold, distant, rigid, unforgiving, and unapproachable. When misunderstandings occur, they wait for others to make the first move.
- **Humble, selfless people are warm, loving, welcoming in their manners, forgiving, and easy to be entreated. They are quick to make amends.**

"Let all bitterness, wrath, anger, clamor, and evil speaking be put away from you, with all malice. And be kind to one another, tenderhearted, forgiving one another, even as God in Christ forgave you" (Ephesians 4:31, 32).

- Proud, self-filled people are often defensive when criticized, and don't want others to know when they have made a mistake or done wrong.
- **Humble, selfless people receive criticism with a humble, open heart and seek to grow by it. They are not overly concerned when others see their failures.**

"For whom the LORD loves He corrects, just as a father the son in whom he delights" (Proverbs 3:12).

- Proud, self-filled people tend to walk alone and have difficulty sharing their spiritual struggles and needs with others.
- **Humble, selfless people are willing to be open, vulnerable, and real before others. They aren't concerned about appearing weak but want to be genuine so that God's strength can be glorified even in their times of weakness.**

"And He said to me, 'My grace is sufficient for you, for My strength is made perfect in weakness.' Therefore most gladly I will rather boast in my infirmities, that the power of Christ may rest upon me" (2 Corinthians 12:9).

- Proud, self-filled people, when confessing sins to God, tend to confess in vague generalities. "Dear God, please forgive me for all my sins."
- **Humble, selfless people, when confessing sins to God, always confess specific sins. "Dear God, please forgive me for _____."**

"Confess your trespasses to one another, and pray for one another, that you may be healed. The effective, fervent prayer of a righteous man avails much" (James 5:16).

- Proud, self-filled people are concerned with being respectable and not a spectacle, and thus they often live a self-righteous façade.
- **Humble, selfless people are more concerned with being right with God, and they shun all forms of hypocrisy or double living.**

"For the LORD *does not see as man sees; for man looks at the outward appearance, but the* LORD *looks at the heart"* (1 Samuel 16:7).

- Proud, self-filled people compare themselves to others and feel deserving of honor and salvation.
- **Humble, selfless people recognize their true sinful condition and praise God that He sent His Son so that, though undeserving, they could receive salvation and honor.**

"But God demonstrates His own love toward us, in that while we were still sinners, Christ died for us" (Romans 5:8).

- Proud, self-filled people think they are pretty much OK, but they are blind to their true heart condition.
- **Humble, selfless people have a continual attitude of "God be merciful to me a sinner!"**

"And the tax collector, standing afar off, would not so much as raise his eyes to heaven, but beat his breast, saying, 'God, be merciful to me a sinner!' " (Luke 18:13).

- Proud, self-filled people don't think they need revival, but they think everyone else does. (In fact, right about now, they are making a mental list of all those who need to read this list.)
- **Humble, selfless people will be the first to acknowledge that they need daily spiritual revival! They are constantly sensing their need for a fresh outpouring of the Holy Spirit in their hearts and lives.**

"Will You not revive us again, that Your people may rejoice in You?" Psalm 85:6.

"Be merciful unto me, O Lord: for I cry unto thee daily" (Psalm 86:3, KJV).[2]*

---

* The "Beauty of Humility—Full Version" can be downloaded as a free handout from: www.revivalandreformation.org. (This pride versus humility comparison was originally written by Nancy DeMoss Wolgemuth and has been adapted with permission. Original copyright held by *Revive Our Hearts* © 2016, www.ReviveOurHearts.com)

What You Are in Christ!

Take time to look up each Bible verse referenced.

You are known!	Jeremiah 1:5
You are loved!	Jeremiah 31:3
You are chosen!	Ephesians 1:4
You are God's child!	1 John 3:1
You are the apple of God's eye!	Zechariah 2:8
You have been bought with a price!	1 Corinthians 6:20
You have been saved by grace!	Ephesians 2:8, 9
You have been redeemed!	Psalm 71:23
You are free from condemnation and sin!	Romans 8:1, 2
You are forgiven!	Ephesians 1:7
You are healed!	1 Peter 2:24
You are washed clean!	Isaiah 1:18
You are free from your past!	Galatians 5:1
You are rejoiced over!	Zephaniah 3:17
You are a masterpiece!	Ephesians 2:10
You are fearfully and wonderfully made!	Psalm 139:14
You are a crown of glory in God's hand!	Isaiah 62:3
You are adopted into God's family!	Romans 8:15
You have direct access to God through the Spirit!	Ephesians 2:18
You are a habitation of God through the Spirit!	Ephesians 2:22
You are a new creature in Christ!	2 Corinthians 5:17
You are made righteous in Christ!	2 Corinthians 5:21
You are complete in Christ!	Colossians 2:10

You are sanctified!	1 Corinthians 6:11
You are chosen and set apart!	1 Peter 2:9
You are a friend of Christ!	John 15:15
You are an ambassador of Christ!	2 Corinthians 5:20
You are a colaborer with Christ!	1 Corinthians 3:9
You are a coheir with Christ!	Romans 8:17
You can do all things through Christ!	Philippians 4:13
You are a minister of reconciliation!	2 Corinthians 5:17–20
You are a branch of the True Vine!	John 15:1, 5
You are enabled to bear fruit!	John 15:16
You have a secure future!	Jeremiah 29:11
You have grace and mercy in time of need!	Hebrews 4:16
You have been given all that you need!	Philippians 4:19
You are a citizen of heaven!	Philippians 3:20

"God so loved the world, that He gave His only-begotten Son." He gave Him not only to live among men, to bear their sins, and die their sacrifice. He gave Him to the fallen race. Christ was to identify Himself with the interests and needs of humanity. He who was one with God has linked Himself with the children of men by ties that are never to be broken. Jesus is "not ashamed to call them brethren" (Hebrews 2:11); He is our Sacrifice, our Advocate, our Brother, bearing our human form before the Father's throne, and through eternal ages one with the race He has redeemed—the Son of man. And all this that man might be uplifted from the ruin and degradation of sin that he might reflect the love of God and share the joy of holiness. . . .

Such love is without a parallel. Children of the heavenly King! Precious promise! Theme for the most profound meditation! The matchless love of God for a world that did not love Him![1]

Appendix 3

The Sentinel at the Door

The year was 1899, and Ellen White was in attendance at a camp meeting in Newcastle, Australia. The meetings were so blessed by the spirit of God that she later wrote how she'd never attended a meeting where it was so evident that the heavenly host was walking among them. God's Spirit was indeed poured out in many ways, and the interest of the meetings even extended to other towns and cities, as those of other faiths joined the congregation.

However, during this very special camp meeting, Ellen White spoke and shared a dream that God had recently given her. She relayed the dream as follows:

In my dream a sentinel stood at the door of an important building, and asked every one who came for entrance, "Have ye received the Holy Ghost?" A measuring-line was in his hand, and only very, very few were admitted into the building. "Your size as a human being is nothing," he said. "But if you have reached the full stature of a man in Christ Jesus, according to the knowledge you have had, you will receive an appointment to sit with Christ at the marriage supper of the Lamb; and through the eternal ages, you will never cease to learn of the blessings granted in the banquet prepared for you.

"You may be tall and well-proportioned in self, but you cannot enter here. None can enter who are grown-up children, carrying with them the disposition, the habits, and the characteristics, which pertain to children. If you have nurtured suspicions, criticism, temper, self-dignity, you cannot be admitted; for you would spoil the feast. *All who go in through this door have on the wedding garment, woven in the loom of heaven.* Those who educate themselves to pick flaws in the characters of others, reveal a deformity that makes families unhappy, that turns souls from the truth to choose fables. Your leaven of distrust, your want of confidence, your power of accusing, closes against you the door of admittance. Within this door nothing can enter that could possibly mar the happiness of the dwellers by marring their perfect trust in one another. You cannot join the happy family in the heavenly courts; for I have wiped all tears from their eyes. You can never see the King in His beauty if you are not yourself a representative of His character.

"When you give up your own will, your own wisdom, and learn of Christ, you will find admittance into the kingdom of God. He requires entire, unreserved surrender. Give up your life for Him to order, mold, and fashion. Take upon your neck His yoke. Submit to be led and taught by Him. Learn that unless you become as a little child, you can never enter the kingdom of heaven.

"Abiding in Christ is choosing only the disposition of Christ, so that His interests are identified with yours. Abide in Him, to be and to do only what He wills. These are the conditions of discipleship, and unless they are complied with, you can never find rest. Rest is in Christ; it cannot be as something apart from Him.

"The moment His yoke is adjusted to your neck, that moment it is found easy; then the heaviest spiritual labor can be performed, the heaviest burdens borne, because the Lord gives the strength and the power, and He gives gladness in doing the work. Mark the points: 'Learn of me; for I am meek and lowly in heart' (Matthew 11:29). Who is it that speaks thus?—The Majesty of heaven, the King of glory. He desires that your conception of spiritual things shall be purified from the dross of selfishness, the defilement of a crooked, coarse, unsympathetic nature. You must have an inward, higher experience. You must obtain a growth in grace by abiding in Christ. When you are converted, you will not be a hindrance, but will strengthen your brethren."

As these words were spoken [in my dream], I saw that some turned sadly away and mingled with the scoffers. Others, with tears, all broken in heart, made confession to those whom they had bruised and wounded. They did not think of maintaining their own dignity, but asked at every step, "What must I do to be saved?" (Acts 16:30). The answer was, "Repent, and be converted, that your sins may go beforehand to judgment, and be blotted out." Words were spoken which rebuked spiritual pride. This God will not tolerate. It is inconsistent with His Word and with our profession of faith. Seek the Lord, all ye who are ministers of His. Seek Him while He may be found, call upon Him while He is near. "Let the wicked forsake his way, and the unrighteous man his thoughts: and let him return unto the Lord, and he will have mercy upon him; and to our God, for he will abundantly pardon" (Isaiah 55:7).[1]

The dream Ellen White shares is sobering because it reminds us that God is calling us to a revival of primitive godliness such as has not been seen or experienced for centuries. This revival is coming! Will we be a part of it? Will we keep our wedding garments on?

We are told, "Before the final visitation of God's judgments upon the earth there will be among the people of the Lord such a revival of primitive godliness as has not been witnessed since apostolic times. The Spirit and power of God will be poured out upon His children. At that time many will separate themselves from those churches in which the love of this world has supplanted love for God and His word."[2]

As you consider God's call to a revival of primitive godliness, pray about the following heart-to-heart questions that Pastor Mark Finley put together to help keep our lives in check. These "self-examination" questions are designed to make sure the call to revival and reformation is ongoing and personal in our daily life.

1. Am I daily growing in grace?

2. Are there plague spots in my character that I see popping up over and over?

3. Am I still struggling with the same things today as I was years ago? If so, where is the victory and power that God tells us is available?

4. Does my heart beat with joy? Do I feel closer to God today than ten years ago?

5. Am I so exhausted and busy in life (or ministry) that I am really too tired to pray meaningful prayers?

6. Am I still thrilled each time I pick up God's Word? Does it bring me to closer intimacy with God? Is it the joy and rejoicing of my heart, or am I just checking off a "to-do" item on the agenda for my day?

7. Am I constantly finding and sharing (if in ministry) fresh material, or do I keep sharing the same materials? Does the discipline of Bible study leave me as though I just learned something new and I can't wait to share it?

You can find many more heart questions like these at www.revivaland reformation.org. Just search for "Questions of the Heart: Making God's Word Personal." Second Corinthians 13:5 tells us, "Examine yourselves as to whether you are in the faith. Test yourselves."

As you've prayerfully considered the questions, let me leave you with some more hope and courage as we turn our eyes to Jesus. Inspiration tells us, "Christ has pledged Himself to be our substitute and surety, and He neglects no one. There is an inexhaustible fund of perfect obedience accruing from His obedience. In heaven His merits, His self-denial and self-sacrifice, are treasured as incense to be offered up with the prayers of His people. As the sinner's sincere, humble prayers ascend to the throne of God, Christ mingles with them the merits of His own life of perfect obedience. Our prayers are made fragrant by this incense. Christ has pledged Himself to intercede in our behalf, and the Father always hears His Son."[3]

Aren't you thankful there's an inexhaustible fund of perfect obedience just waiting to cover your lack? Cling to Jesus—one day at a time, He will lead you safely home!

Appendix 4

"That We May Be One"

Compiled by Jerry and Janet Page

Think of the person you like the least, and ask yourself, "Why did Jesus come to this world?" The reality is that He came to save them, as well as you and me. Let's not forget Jesus' prayer for us "that they all may be one, as You, Father, are in Me, and I in You; that they also may be one in Us, that the world may believe that You sent Me" (John 17:21).

When we look at the Scriptures, we see two primary reasons Jesus came to earth. The first was to reconcile us to the Father by His perfect life and death so that we could spend eternity in heaven (Romans 3; 2 Corinthians 5:7–21). The second was to reconcile us to each other in perfect agape love relationships. And this is what shows that we have been restored to the image of God (John 17:21–23; Ephesians 2:13–18). When we are one in Christ, the world can believe in Him!

Ellen White writes, "It is not the opposition of the world that most endangers the church of Christ. It is the evil cherished in the hearts of believers . . . on the other hand, the strongest witness that God has sent His Son into the world is the existence of harmony and union among men of varied dispositions who form His church."[1]

7 Principles for Building Better Relationships

1. Intercede in prayer for people instead of trying to change them or trying to do the Holy Spirit's work yourself (claim promises such as 1 John 5:16; Isaiah 42:7, 16; Acts 26:18; Isaiah 65:1; Jeremiah 24:7; Jeremiah 3:22; Ezekiel 37:2, 3).
   - Keep in mind that as we spend time with the Lord, He may show us we are part of the problem or set a mirror before us so we can see our need for change (Galatians 6:1–3; Luke 6:37, 38, 41, 42).
   - Live the fruit of the Spirit more and "preach" at others less.
   - Take action only if the Holy Spirit leads.
2. Respect diversity of temperaments and God's created differences in people.
   - The Lord has created and gifted us differently, so the Body of Christ will have all its complementary parts (Ephesians 4:1–32).
   - Sacredly regard the feelings and respect the rights of those with whom God has placed us in a relationship.
3. Assume the best about others' motives and actions.
   - Listen more, seeking first to understand clearly and then to be understood. Don't take things secondhand from secondary sources.
   - "Christlike love places the most favorable construction on the motives and acts of others. It does not needlessly expose their faults; it does not listen eagerly to unfavorable reports, but seeks rather to bring to mind the good qualities of others."[2]
4. Follow Christ's specific instructions and do not talk to others about problems!
   - Never talk to those who are not part of the situation or solution process. Only say those things which can help build others up according to their needs. Even if something is "true," don't talk to others if it can't help or resolve the problem (Ephesians 4:29–32).
   - Follow the "gospel order" in all situations (Matthew 18:15–17). When a brother in Christ sins against you, go to the person "alone" first. If needed, take one or two others as witnesses. Lastly, if needed, take it to the church for discipline.
   - Seek reconciliation before you worship (Matthew 5:23, 24).
5. Yield your "rights" and "expectations" to God.
   - Jesus did not go around defending His rights or getting angry when His expectations weren't met. Many of our relationship problems

are caused by our concern for our "rights." The Bible tells us, "Great peace have they which love thy law and nothing shall offend them" (Psalm 119:165, KJV; Luke 6:27–36).

- There is a time for "tough love," but be sure it's the Lord's will, not self-centeredness, that is leading.

6. Praise God for the source of your irritations.

- Make a list of the good things about the other person and praise God for those things.
- Pray for the "problem person" to be blessed (Matthew 5:43, 44).
- Praise drives evil angels away. By beholding, we become changed— so dwell on the good (Philippians 4:4–9).

"When things go crossways at your homes, strike up a song about the matchless charms of the Son of God, and I tell you, when you touch this strain, Satan will leave you."[3]

7. Five minutes can solve most difficulties if self and pride are laid aside! "By pride comes nothing but strife, but with the well-advised is wisdom" (Proverbs 13:10).[4]

I saw that the remnant were not prepared for what is coming upon the earth. Stupidity, like lethargy, seemed to hang upon the minds of most of those who profess to believe that we are having the last message. My accompanying angel cried out with awful solemnity, "Get ready! get ready! get ready! for the fierce anger of the Lord is soon to come. His wrath is to be poured out, unmixed with mercy, and ye are not ready. Rend the heart, and not the garment. A great work must be done for the remnant. Many of them are dwelling upon little trials. Said the angel, "Legions of evil angels are around you, and are trying to press in their awful darkness, that ye may be ensnared and taken. Ye suffer your minds to be diverted too readily from the work of preparation and the all-important truths for these last days. And ye dwell upon little trials and go into minute particulars of little difficulties to explain them to the satisfaction of this one or that." Conversation has been protracted for hours between the parties concerned, and not only has their time been wasted, but the servants of God are held to listen to them, when the hearts of both parties are unsubdued by grace. If pride and selfishness were laid aside, five minutes would remove most difficulties. Angels have been grieved and God displeased by the hours which have been spent in justifying self. I saw that God will not bow down and listen to long justifications, and He does not want His servants to do so, and thus precious time be wasted that should be spent in showing transgressors the error of their ways and pulling souls out of the fire.[5]*

* This handout has been condensed. To download the full version along with additional quotes, please visit: www.revivalandreformation.org and search for "Experiencing God Through Prayer and Praise" by Jerry and Janet Page.

Biblical Tips for Managing Your Resources

- Live simply and within your means, and instead of spending all your money each month, learn to save (1 Timothy 6:6–8; Proverbs 21:20).
- Do not covet the possessions of others (Ephesians 5:5).
- Follow this advice: "Use it up, wear it out, make it do, or do without."
- When considering making a purchase, ask yourself, "Do I really need this?" Learn to discern between your needs and your wants (1 Timothy 6:8–10; Hebrews 13:5).
- Examine your home for evidence of hoarding (Luke 12:18).
- Actively de-accumulate by going through your closets, drawers, storage spaces, garage, basement, and so on (Matthew 6:19, 20).
- Give away anything that owns you. Give to others in greater need (Matthew 19:21; James 4:17).
- Do not fall for commercial advertising—shop wisely based on good counsel (Proverbs 11:14).
- Avoid fads; stick with classics that are always in style (Colossians 2:8; Romans 12:1, 2).
- Analyze the cost of seemingly small expenditures, such as eating out, buying name-brand clothing, et cetera. These purchases can add up to substantial sums of money (Proverbs 27:23, 24).
- Avoid impulse buying. In making major purchases, be sure to shop around, compare prices, gain knowledge, and get at least three prices or bids before making your final decision (Proverbs 24:4, 5).

- Try to avoid spending money before you have it, living on credit cards, or carrying a balance over each month. Only use credit cards when you already have money in the bank to pay it back (Proverbs 22:7).
- Be willing to pray before making special purchases. Give God the opportunity to lead you or provide for you in an unexpected but more affordable way (1 Peter 5:7).
- Be willing to purchase or use pre-owned items. Often you can save substantial money by getting what someone else previously paid full price for (Job 27:16; Proverbs 13:22).

For a practical and inspiring six-part online series by Alistair Huong called "Beyond the Tithe: Practical Lessons on Personal Finance," visit Audioverse.org. If you aren't familiar with Audioverse, it's time you get acquainted. There are hundreds of wonderful inspirational sermons and messages freely available here online. I highly recommend this website!

These tips, with slight modifications, have been taken from the booklet *The 7 Week Spiritual Journey to a More Generous Life*, page 30. This booklet comes from the Stewardship Ministries Department of the General Conference.

Practical Tips for Growing a Healthy Body

Applying wellness principles to your daily life! *
By Zeno Charles-Marcel, MD

Learning to live healthfully is not rocket science! It's rather simple! The following are some practical pointers in learning to be well physically. Incorporating these core choices into your daily life will help your heart, brain, and metabolism, improve your physique, and can increase the likelihood that you will live a long, healthy life. Yet, there is more to life than just good physical health. Our thinking, feelings, moods, relationships, and spiritual connectedness are equally important. Consider this fact: depression is the leading cause of ill health and disability worldwide. Also, doing everything right does not completely remove the possibility of physical illness or mental stress. Total restoration comes when Christ returns, and we are changed forever. Until then, remember, we don't promote being healthy in body and mind in order for us to be saved. We live a health-promoting life because we are saved!

Here is a simple, straightforward way to change your health status based on a few fundamental principles:

---

* **Doctor's Disclaimer Statement:** Please note that the information given here is provided for informational and educational purposes only and is not intended to diagnose or treat any disease or substitute for the attention of a competent physician or appropriate health professional.

- Correct CHOICE is key, appropriate ACTION is essential!
- Just as thoughts influence actions, actions influence thought.
- Any step in the right direction is better than no step at all.
- Repetition produces habits; habits produce a lifestyle.

Here are the Core Issues that I will address:

1. Be physically ACTIVE.

2. Eat REAL food, not too much, and on a regular schedule.

3. Get adequate, regular, rest and nighttime SLEEP.

4. PREVENT, MANAGE or REVERSE chronic diseases and risk factors.

5. PREVENT and TREAT addictions.

1. Be ACTIVE

Sitting or lying down for long periods increases your health risks: heart disease, diabetes, and some cancers, and is also bad for your mental health. Exercise is probably the most important single thing you can do to affect your longevity and quality of life.

Any type of exercise is better than none; however, aerobic exercise (swimming, walking, jogging, running, biking, etc.) increases the brain's gray matter. Mixed resistance and aerobic exercise, however, appears to be the best overall health regimen. This can be achieved through Intermittent Training (where you walk/run/walk/run, etc.).

- Get a minimum of thirty to forty-five minutes of exercise in the fresh air daily!
- Take a ten-minute stroll after each meal.
- Adopt a seven-minute morning exercise routine.
- Use the stairs instead of the elevator whenever possible.
- Walk whenever you're on an escalator.
- Exit the bus or taxi before your destination and walk a little when appropriate.
- Park away from where you're going and walk the rest of the way when appropriate.
- Organize walking meetings and walk to a colleague's desk rather than texting or emailing them.
- Use a standing desk if possible or stand and walk around for three to

five minutes every hour or so if you have a sitting job. (Put a reminder on your phone; it helps.)

- Make daily sun-exposure part of your routine. Fifteen to thirty minutes is usually sufficient for fair-skinned individuals in tropical climates to make enough vitamin D.

2. Eat REAL Food

Real food is food grown without much or any processing. Well-balanced, whole-food, plant-based diets have been shown to confer multiple health benefits. Our diet should include vegetables and fruits of all colors, nuts, seeds, and whole grains, and healthy fats should come from avocados and olives. This is helpful for our intestinal bacteria as well! Drinking pure water (unsweetened, not artificially adulterated) hydrates your body and may help with weight management when taken before meals.

- Eat to live; don't live to eat! Develop a healthy relationship with food. Pray for the Spirit and let Him bear fruit, then practice self-control.
- Eat as close to the natural food source as possible (e.g., eat the potato instead of the potato chip).
- Eat the rainbow: A wide variety of colorful fruits and vegetables should be part of your diet every day!
- Eat organic when possible and feasible; avoid pesticides and herbicides; exercise caution with genetically modified foods.
- Follow the old slogan: Eat like a king for breakfast, like a prince for lunch, and like a pauper for supper!
- Eat to 80 percent satiety and only at mealtimes, not in between!
- Don't eat close to bedtime, and consider taking a "Daniel's Fast" occasionally to give your body a rest. Intermittent fasting and short, water-only, supervised fasts have associated health benefits.
- Avoid drinking carbonated beverages and other sugary, high-fructose or artificially sweetened drinks.
- Try fruit-infused water for cool, healthy refreshment.

3. SLEEP Well, Rest Well!

Sleep is an underappreciated and underestimated health factor. Adequate, restful sleep restores strength, curbs inflammation, improves memory and sharpens attention, reduces stress, and provides a better quality of life with the bonus of helping you maintain a healthy weight. Lack of adequate rest affects the mind in a similar way as if you have been drinking alcohol.

- Avoid caffeine, alcohol, nicotine, and other chemicals that interfere with sleep.
- Lighten-up on evening meals (try to eat all meals before 6:00 p.m.).
- End strenuous exercising at least three hours before bedtime.
- Go to bed five or ten minutes earlier for a week or two and gradually increase the time until you reach the seven- to eight-hour optimal sleep time.
- Set a "go-to-bed" alarm rather than a "wake-up" alarm.
- Follow the old adage: Early to bed, early to rise makes you healthy, wealthy, and wise!
- Keep your internal clock set with a consistent sleep schedule once your routine is established.
- Listen to soothing music if that helps you to relax and fall asleep.
- Avoid looking at your phone or computer screen before bedtime. Instead, read a book, talk with family, take a short, calm, fresh air stroll, or enjoy a warm bath.
- Darken your bedroom for better sleep but let in the light first thing in the morning and schedule a sun break during the day.

Note: Many sleep problems are easily treated, but some could signify the presence of a sleep disorder such as apnea, restless legs syndrome, narcolepsy, or another clinical sleep problem. If your sleep difficulties don't improve with the above, please consult your physician or a sleep specialist.

4. Prevent, Manage, and Reverse Disease When Possible

Many of the so-called noncommunicable diseases (NCDs), such as type 2 diabetes, hypertension, and coronary artery disease, are associated with systemic inflammation. Poor oral hygiene is an often overlooked and underappreciated contributor to systemic inflammation. NCDs are often preventable and even reversible to a large extent, especially when detected early on in the predisease state. In these cases, often, intensive lifestyle intervention is needed, and that is most appropriately dealt with under the care of a trained professional or team at a lifestyle center. However, by following the above recommendations as part of a healthy lifestyle, most of these conditions can be prevented.

Don't forget to keep up with age- and gender-appropriate medical screening and appropriate immunizations. If you're on the fence about whether or not you should visit a healthcare professional, it's probably a good idea to make an appointment. When it comes to your health, it's better to err on the side of caution.

5. PREVENT and TREAT Addictions

Cut out unhealthy activities that numb your spiritual sensitivities and slow your frontal lobe activity and morally compromising habits that go against your conscience. Replacing any questionable habit with something better is the way to go. If you don't smoke, don't start. If you don't drink alcohol, don't start! If you're already smitten and struggling to quit, don't be dismayed. Get help! The list of diseases and cancers attributed to smoking and alcohol use alone is long, but the suffering their use produces is unquantifiable! However, with God, all things are possible, even deliverance from your addictions. Consider the following when seeking to overcome an addiction.

- Stay away from tempting and enticing situations.
- Identify and avoid the triggers that encourage your addictive behavior.
- Pray and meditate on God and His Word.
- Exercise: physical workouts help decrease addictive urges.
- Turn your attention outward from your body to something else.
- It's important that you get fresh air every day—if you are exercising outside, you will think more clearly and be more self-controlled.
- Place houseplants that you are not allergic to in your living spaces.
- Take a walk in the forest.
- Open the windows of your home and let the sunshine and fresh air in. (Ellen White speaks of the benefits of this quite earnestly!)

Last but not least, in your quest to be healthy and overcome addictions, TRUST God.

- Make intentional time each day to grow your walk with God (as outlined in this book). Spend time meditating on Scripture, on God's promises, and in prayer!
- Cultivate an attitude of gratitude: If you are a complainer, to help start a new habit, challenge yourself to no negative words, or complaining for fourteen days! If you mess up, start the fourteen days over until you succeed. What a difference a new attitude will make.
- Find believers that you can fellowship with to encourage your faith!
- Most of all, cultivate faith in God! Believe that God is good and means to do you good and act in a way consistent with that reality.

Melody loves adding this simple recipe to her daily meals!

Amino Healthy Brain Blast: Mix ¼ cup of each of the following all together, then store in the refrigerator: walnuts (chopped), Brazil nuts (crushed), almonds (slivered), sunflower seeds, pumpkin seeds, sesame seeds, chia seeds, hemp seeds, and date sugar.

Dr. Neil Nedley, the author of the book *Depression: The Way Out*, shares this recipe in his program and recommends that we take 4 level tsp. of the Amino Healthy Brain Blast (two times per day) mixed with soy yogurt or applesauce on top of cereal or blended with juice. This rich brain food helps our mind get adequate sources of tryptophan and omega-3, which help in combating depression.

For more great recipes for healthy plant-based living, consider: *From Plant to Plate*, by Tami Bivens; *The Ten Talents* cookbook, by Rosalie Hurd; *Brighten Up Breakfast*, by Erica Nedley; Weimar Institute's *Newstart Lifestyle Cookbook*; or *Natural Lifestyle Cooking*, by Ernestine Finley.

Zeno Charles-Marcel, MD, is associate director for the Adventist Health Ministries of the General Conference.

Endnotes

Introduction

1. Gerhard Pfandl, "Whose Authority Do I Accept?" *Perspective Digest* 22, no. 2, accessed October 29, 2019, https://www.perspectivedigest.org/archive/22-2/whose-authority-do-i-accept.

2. Wikipedia, s.v. "Forty Martyrs of Sebaste," last modified December 29, 2019, https://en.wikipedia.org/wiki/Forty_Martyrs_of_Sebaste.

3. There are multiple versions of this story and how it transpired. I've gleaned details from several different sources, but I owe my biggest gratitude to my friend Gerhard Pfandl for how I share this story.

4. If you noticed, even within the testimony of the men of Sebaste, there is a certain spiritual inconsistency. While they would not worship any other gods except the one true God (honoring the first commandment), yet these very men were still serving in the army where killing others (which goes against the sixth commandment) was most likely part of their normal duties. Of course, there is disagreement among Christians on whether it's okay to serve in the military, even if one is not bearing arms—I won't tackle that subject. However, there is an excellent book produced by the Biblical Research Committee of the Inter-European Division that deals with this topic that I'd like to recommend. It's called *Adventists and Military Service: Biblical, Historical, and Ethical Perspectives*. It can be purchased from AdventistBook Center.com.

5. Barna Research Group, 1997, cited in William G. Johnsson, "Awash in a Sea of Relativism," *Adventist Review*, NAD Edition, August 1997, 5.

6. Ellen G. White, *The Great Controversy* (Mountain View, CA: Pacific Press®, 1950), 593.

7. Ellen G. White, *The Acts of the Apostles* (Mountain View, CA: Pacific Press®, 1911), 51

8. Frank Hasel, "What Does It Mean to Be a Seventh-day Adventist?" *Adventist Review*, April 30, 2019, https://www.adventistreview.org/1905-48.

Chapter 1

1. Ellen G. White, *Steps to Christ* (Washington, DC: Review and Herald®, 1956), 31.

2. While there are sometimes exceptions where the Holy Spirit is leading, in general we are told that "private sins should be confessed privately and public sins confessed publicly." You can read more about this in Ellen G. White, *The Ministry of Healing* (Mountain View, CA: Pacific Press®, 1942), 228.

3. Ellen G. White, *Selected Messages*, book 1 (Washington DC: Review and Herald®, 1958), 337.

4. Norman Grubb, *Continuous Revival: The Secret to Victorious Living* (Fort Washington, PA:

CLC Publications, 1997), 18.

5. Grubb, *Continuous Revival*, 20–22.

6. Corrie Ten Boom, *The Hiding Place* (New York: Bantam Books, 1974). The Ten Boom family's amazing story is chronicled in this well-known book.

7. Roy Hession, *The Calvary Road: Exploring Christianity* (Sandycroft, Flinshire: CLC London, 1955), 25.

8. Nancy Leigh DeMoss, *Brokenness, Surrender, Holiness* (Chicago: Moody Publishers, 2008), 42.

9. DeMoss, *Brokenness, Surrender, Holiness*, 44.

10. Ellen G. White, *Child Guidance* (Nashville, TN: Southern Publishing, 1954), 468.

11. Lysa Terkeurst, *It's Not Supposed to Be This Way: Finding Unexpected Strength When Disappointments Leave You Shattered.* (Nashville, TN: Thomas Nelson), 2018, 18.

12. While you may not have a hard copy of a Seventh-day Adventist hymnal nearby, the hymnal is available as an application, which you can download on your smartphone. You can also find many of these hymns and songs on YouTube or other sites. I encourage you to sing as you finish each chapter. And pray that the words you sing will become your own. There is so much of the gospel in these songs!

13. I thank Scott Griswold for some of my inspiration in this "Going Deeper" segment. His complete study, "Clearing the Way for the Holy Spirit," can be downloaded from www.revivaland reformation.org.

Chapter 2

1. During these yearly meetings, church leaders and administrators from all around the world come together to make decisions and discuss how to further the mission of the church.

2. Ellen G. White, *Selected Messages*, book 1 (Washington DC: Review and Herald®, 1958), 326.

3. To read this document, visit: https://cdn .ministerialassociation.org/docs/Annual-Council -2010-Gods-promised-gift.pdf.

4. Ellen G. White, *Manuscript Releases*, vol. 5 (Silver Spring, MD: Ellen G. White Estate, 1990), 347.

5. Otto Koning, "The Pineapple Story Series," Embassy Media, Institue in Basic Life Principles, asscessd February 24, 2020, embassymedia.com /series/pineapple-story-series. I recommend the 12-part series where you can hear Otto Koning himself share his story in his earnest and yet humor-filled way.

6. Ellen G. White, *The Desire of Ages* (Mountain View, CA: Pacific Press®, 1940), 300; emphasis added.

7. Ellen G. White, *Steps to Christ* (Washington, DC: Review and Herald®, 1956), 30, emphasis added.

8. Ellen G. White, *Christ's Object Lessons* (Washington, DC: Review and Herald®, 1941), 158.

9. Ellen G. White, *The Ministry of Healing* (Mountain View, CA: Pacific Press®, 1942), 161; emphasis added.

10. White, *Ministry of Healing*, 65.

11. Ellen G. White, *Gospel Workers* (Washington, DC: Review and Herald®, 1915), 365.

Chapter 3

1. *Spurgeon's Expository Encyclopedia: Sermons by Charles H. Spurgeon*, "Holiness Demanded" (Grand Rapids, MI: Baker, 1978), 7:465.

2. Ellen G. White, *Advent Review and Sabbath Herald*, March 28, 1899, 193.

3. Nancy DeMoss Wolgemuth, *Holiness* (Chicago: Moody Publishers, 2004), 2005, 294.

4. "The Holy Spirit and Spirituality," *Adult Sabbath School Bible Study Guide*, no. 487, January–March 2017, 46.

5. Ellen G. White, *Christ's Object Lessons* (Washington, DC: Review and Herald®, 1941), 48.

6. Wolgemuth, *Holiness*, 29, 31, 32.

7. Jerry Bridges, *The Pursuit of Holiness* (Colorado Springs, CO: NavPress, 2016), 4, 5; emphasis added.

8. Nancy Leigh DeMoss, *Brokenness, Surrender, Holiness* (Chicago: Moody Publishers, 2008), 324.

9. Ellen G. White, "Tempted in All Points," *The Bible Echo*, December 1, 1892, 354; emphasis added.

10. In addition to *Pilgrim's Progress,* Bunyan wrote nearly sixty small books as well, many of these being his expanded sermons.

11. The term *christened* means to give (a baby) a Christian name at baptism as a sign of admission to a Christian church.

12. Ron and Dorothy Watts, *The Scripture That Changed My Life* (Nampa, ID: Pacific Press®, 1998), 104.

13. V. Raymond Edman, *They Found the Secret* (Grand Rapids, MI: Zondervan, 1984), 35–37, 39.

14. Charles H. Spurgeon, *Morning By Morning* (Peabody, MA: Hendrickson Publishers, 2006, 269.

15. Paul Washer, *The Gospel's Power and Message* (Grand Rapids, MI: Reformation Heritage Books, 2012), 62.

16. Jerry Bridges, *The Pursuit of Holiness* (Colorado Springs, CO: NavPress, 2016), 22.

17. Ellen G. White, *Messages to Young People* (Nashville, TN: Southern Publishing, 1930), 35.

18. Ellen G. White, *The Desire of Ages* (Mountain View, CA: Pacific Press®, 1940), 25.

19. A. T. Jones, *Lessons on Faith* (Jasper, OR: Adventist Pioneer Library, 2017), 2.

20. Oswald Chambers, *My Utmost for His Highest* (Grand Rapids, MI: Discover House, 1963), July 23.

21. Ellen G. White, *Thoughts From the Mount of Blessing* (Mountain View, CA: Pacific Press®, 1956), 18.

22. Ellen G. White, *Selected Messages*, book 1 (Washington, DC: Review and Herald®, 1958), 324.

23. Ellen G. White, *The Acts of the Apostles* (Mountain View, CA: Pacific Press®, 1911), 532; emphasis added.

Chapter 4

1. This testimony, titled "The Spanish Prayer," was adapted from the book *Story Catcher: Powerful Stories That Will Impact Your Spiritual Journey,* by Richard Duerksen (Safeliz, 2019), 91–93.

2. Ellen G. White, *Christian Service* (Washington, DC: Review and Herald®, 1947), 223.

3. This book is available for download at www.revivalandreformation.org.

4. Gregory L. Jackson, *Surrender: The Secret to Perfect Peace and Happiness* (Hagerstown, MD: Review and Herald®, 1994), 50, 51.

5. Ellen G. White, *Steps to Christ* (Washington, DC: Review and Herald®, 1956), 43.

6. I thank Pastor Gregory L. Jackson for some of the inspiration behind the organization of this chapter. His book *Surrender: The Secret to Perfect Peace and Happiness* can be found in Kindle version at www.revivalandreformation.org.

7. Ellen G. White, *The Ministry of Healing* (Mountain View, CA: Pacific Press®, 1942), 473, 474.

8. Ellen G. White, *Testimonies for the Church* (Mountain View, CA: Pacific Press®, 1948), 8:45.

9. Taking the yoke is actually synonymous with taking up the cross. "The yoke and the cross are symbols representing the same thing, the giving up of the will to God," Ellen G. White, *Our High Calling* (Washington, DC: Review and Herald®, 1961, 100.

10. I thank Nancy DeMoss Wolgemuth for this inspiration, from the back cover of her book *Surrender* (Moody Publishers, 2005).

11. I thank Nancy DeMoss Wolgemuth for this inspiration.

12. Ellen G. White, "Make All Things According to the Pattern," *Signs of the Times,* November 21, 1892, 38.

13. Ellen G. White, *The Desire of Ages* (Mountain View, CA: Pacific Press®, 1940), 172.

14. White, *Desire of Ages,* 324.

Chapter 5

1. Ellen G. White, *Thoughts From the Mount of Blessing* (Mountain View, CA: Pacific Press®, 1956), 142.

2. Pavel Goia shared this testimony during morning worship at the General Conference in the spring of 2019. Millie is not the real name of the woman.

3. Jerry Bridges, *The Pursuit of Holiness* (Colorado Springs, CO: NavPress, 2016), 34.

4. Bridges, *Pursuit of Holiness,* 36. I thank Jerry Bridges for the inspiration behind this section, as I have condensed and adapted some of his thoughts to share here.

5. Bridges, *Pursuit of Holiness*, 41.

6. Ellen G. White, *Steps to Christ* (Washington, DC: Review and Herald®, 1956), 47, 48.

7. Ellen G. White, *Testimonies for the Church* (Mountain View, CA: Pacific Press®, 1948), 5:515.

8. Ellen G. White, *Christ's Object Lessons* (Washington, DC: Review and Herald®, 1941), 96.

9. Ellen G. White, *The Desire of Ages* (Mountain View, CA: Pacific Press®, 1940), 528.

10. White, *Desire of Ages*, 668.

11. Elisabeth Elliot, *The Shadow of the Almighty* (New York: Harper, 1958), 15.

12. White, *Christ's Object Lessons*, 159.

Chapter 6

1. V. Raymond Edman, *They Found the Secret* (Grand Rapids, MI: Zondervan, 1984), 54.

2. Edman, *They Found the Secret*, 55.

3. Edman, *They Found the Secret*, 55.

4. Edman, *They Found the Secret*, 56.

5. Edman, *They Found the Secret*, 52.

6. I thank John Piper for the inspiration behind these thoughts.

7. This is part of the mission statement of John Piper's ministry, Desiring God, https://www.desiringgod.org/about-us.

8. Ellen G. White, *The Acts of the Apostles* (Mountain View, CA: Pacific Press®, 1911), 560.

9. Ellen G. White, *Reflecting Christ* (Hagerstown, MD: Review and Herald®, 2008), 124.

10. Ellen G. White, *The Desire of Ages* (Mountain View, CA: Pacific Press®, 1940), 83.

Chapter 7

1. Ellen G. White, *The Ministry of Healing* (Mountain View, CA Pacific Press®, 1942), 472.

2. While I have not read *Homer's Odyssey*, and do not generally endorse the reading of myths or legends, I thought it was a perfect illustration for the point I wanted to share. I first heard this story years ago when reading the book *When God Writes Your Love Story*, by Eric and Leslie Ludy.

3. Ellen G. White, *Education* (Mountain View, CA: Pacific Press®, 1952), 260, 261.

4. Ellen G. White, *Prayer* (Nampa, ID: Pacific Press®, 2002), 292.

5. Gregory L. Jackson, *Surrender: The Secret to Perfect Peace and Happiness* (Hagerstown, MD: Review and Herald®, 1994), 66.

6. Ellen G. White, *Steps to Christ* (Washington, DC: Review and Herald®, 1956), 70.

7. Ellen G. White, *Child Guidance* (Nashville, TN: Southern Publishing, 1954), 573.

8. Ellen G. White, *Mind, Character, and Personality* (Hagerstown MD: Review and Herald®, 1977), 2:650.

9. Ellen G. White, *The Acts of the Apostles* (Mountain View, CA: Pacific Press®, 1911), 50.

10. Ellen G. White, *The Great Controversy* (Mountain View, CA: Pacific Press®, 1950), 600.

11. Elisabeth Elliot, *These Strange Ashes: Is God Still in Charge?* (Grand Rapids, MI: Revell, 1998), 11.

12. Ellen G. White, *The Faith I Live By*, 135–136.

13. Ellen G. White, *The Desire of Ages* (Mountain View, CA: Pacific Press®, 1940), 677.

14. Ellen G. White, *Christ's Object Lessons* (Washington, DC: Review and Herald®, 1941), 149.

15. Harriet Beecher Stowe and Hudson Taylor, quoted in V. Raymond Edman, *They Found the Secret* (Grand Rapids, MI: Zondervan, 1984), 23.

16. White, *Desire of Ages*, 148.

17. Nancy DeMoss Wolgemuth, "How to Steady Your Heart," December 4, 2013, in *Revive Our Hearts*, podcast, https://www.reviveourhearts.com/podcast/revive-our-hearts/how-steady-your-heart/.

Chapter 8

1. I highly recommend the book *The Heavenly Man*, which shares this full incredible story. While Brother Yun ended up escaping China, and moving to Germany in 2001, his ministry

continues to this day.

2. As of 2019, the full Bible has been translated into nearly 700 languages and parts of the Bible have been translated into more than 3,000 languages. See https://en.wikipedia.org/wiki/Bible_translations (last modified December 18, 2019).

3. Ellen G. White, *Testimonies for the Church* (Mountain View, CA: Pacific Press®, 1948), 6:393.

4. Eric Ludy, "Who Is This Jesus?" Ellerslie, July 15, 2012, https://ellerslie.com/who-is-this-jesus/.

5. Ellen G. White, *Steps to Christ* (Washington, DC: Review and Herald®, 1956), 90.

6. I thank Jerry Page, Frank Hasel, and Jonathan Walter for helping me put these study tips together in condensed form on a bookmark called *Experiencing God's Word*.

7. Ellen G. White, *Christ's Object Lessons* (Washington, DC: Review and Herald®, 1941), 154.

8. White, *Christ's Object Lessons*, 59.

9. Look for this at your local Adventist Book Center or visit: http://aslightlingers.com.

10. Ellen G. White, *Spirit of Prophecy*, vol. 1 (Battle Creek, MI: Seventh-day Adventist Pub. Assoc., 1870), 87.

11. Ellen G. White, *Education* (Mountain View, CA: Pacific Press®, 1952), 190.

12. Ellen G. White, *The Great Controversy* (Mountain View, CA: Pacific Press®, 1950), 593.

13. Frank M. Hasel, "Virtuous Thinking: Loving God With Heart and Mind," *Adventist Review*, January 5, 2018, https://www.adventistreview.org/1801-19.

14. I thank Nina Atcheson for this illustration that she shared in her book *As Light Lingers* (Safeliz, 2018), 83. Since I got to enjoy the experience with her, I added my testimony to hers.

15. Ellen G. White, *The Desire of Ages* (Mountain View, CA: Pacific Press®, 1940), 390.

16. I thank Ken Gire for the inspiration behind these words.

17. Ellen G. White, *Life Sketches of Ellen G. White* (Mountain View, CA: Pacific Press®, 1943), 293.

Chapter 9

1. Dana Olson, "The Scripture Prescription," *Prayer Connect*, January/March 2017, https://www.prayerleader.com/?s=the+scripture+prescription. This source can also be found in the booklet *Solid Foundation: The Power of Praying Scripture*, available for purchase at http://www.prayershop.org.

2. I have taken author's liberties and modified this list slightly from Dana Olson, "The Scripture Prescription."

3. This testimony has been condensed from Dana Olson, "The Scripture Prescription."

4. Ellen G. White, *Christ's Object Lessons* (Washington, DC: Review and Herald®, 1941), 148.

5. Ellen G. White, Letter 31, January 1, 1897, https://egwwritingsorg/?ref=en_Lt31-1887&para=4681.15.

6. White, *Christ's Object Lessons*, 142.

7. Ellen G. White, *Education* (Mountain View, CA: Pacific Press®, 1952), 253.

8. This testimony was taken from the book *The Pastor's Wife*, by Sabina Wurmbrand (Bartlesville, OK: Living Sacrifice Book Company, 2005).

9. Ellen G. White, *The Ministry of Healing* (Mountain View, CA: Pacific Press®, 1942), 65.

10. White, *Ministry of Healing*, 519.

Chapter 10

1. Owen Edwards, "How Thomas Jefferson Created His Own Bible," *Smithsonian Magazine*, January 2012, https://www.smithsonianmag.com/arts-culture/how-thomas-jefferson-created-his-own-bible-5659505/.

2. Eric Ludy, "Rack of Glory," Return of Majesty Trilogy, viewed May 17, 2017, YouTube video, https://youtu.be/bZiBnegXqIg.

3. Ken Gire, *Moments With the Savior* (Grand Rapids, MI: Zondervan, 1998), 64.

4. Gire, *Moments With the Savior*, 65.

5. Personal paraphrase of Matthew 4:9.

6. I thank Ken Gire for the inspiration behind my sharing of this powerful story.

7. Ellen G. White, *Selected Messages*, book 1 (Washington DC: Review and Herald®, 1958, 408, 409; emphasis added.

8. Ellen G. White, "God's Holy Sabbath,"

Advent Review and Sabbath Herald, July 13, 1897, par. 3.

9. The story comes from Nancy DeMoss Wolgemuth, *Holiness* (Chicago: Moody Publishers, 2004, 2005), 363–365.

10. Ellen G. White, *Christian Service* (Washington, DC: Review and Herald®, 1947), 41, 42.

11. Wolgemuth, *Holiness*, 176.

12. Wolgemuth, *Holiness*, 160.

13. Wolgemuth, *Holiness*, 161.

14. Ellen G. White, *Messages to Young People* (Nashville, TN: Southern Publishing, 1930), 109.

15. This book by Ellen White can be accessed online if you do not own a copy. Visit https://egwwritings.org.

16. Ellen G. White, *The Desire of Ages* (Mountain View, CA: Pacific Press®, 1940), 208.

17. Ellen G. White, *Education* (Mountain View, CA: Pacific Press®, 1952), 260.

18. White, *Desire of Ages*, 668.

Chapter 11

1. In fact, if He's truly Lord of your house, He may ask you to throw out that television altogether.

2. Ellen G. White, *Manuscript Releases*, vol. 2. (Silver Spring, MD: Ellen G. White Estate, 1990), 27.

3. Ellen G. White, *Steps to Christ* (Washington, DC: Review and Herald®, 1956), 45.

4. Ellen G. White, *The Ministry of Healing* (Mountain View, CA: Pacific Press®, 1942), 173.

5. John Kitchen, *The Pastoral Epistles for Pastors* (Woodlands, TX: Kress, 2009), 132.

6. Ellen G. White, *Christ's Object Lessons* (Washington, DC: Review and Herald®, 1941), 316.

7. Ellen G. White, *Selected Messages*, vol. 2 (Washington DC: Review and Herald®, 1958), 318.

8. Taken from lectures at a Set-Apart Girl's retreat I attended given by Leslie Ludy in 2005.

9. White, *Steps to Christ*, 57.

10. These questions have been taken and adapted from the chapter "The Heart of Holiness" in Nancy DeMoss Wolgemuth, *Holiness* (Chicago: Moody Publishers, 2004, 2005), 139–154.

Chapter 12

1. This story is based on the testimony shared by Mark Finley at https://youtube/8nAfIne_jUM. Names have been changed.

2. Ellen G. White, *Christ's Object Lessons* (Washington, DC: Review and Herald®, 1941), 415, 416.

3. I've changed Tom's name for safety reasons, as he's working in a closed country.

4. ASAP stands for Advocates for Southeast Asians and the Persecuted. You can learn more about this amazing ministry at www.asapministries.org.

5. Ellen G. White, *The Ministry of Healing* (Mountain View, CA: Pacific Press®, 1942), 485.

6. The title "Virtuous Living in an Unvirtuous World" I have unashamedly borrowed. Original inspiration for these "virtuous living" thoughts goes to Frank M. Hasel.

7. Ellen G. White, *The Desire of Ages* (Mountain View, CA: Pacific Press®, 1940), 301.

8. The first four of the Ten Commandments deal with love for God. The last six deal with love for those around us. Thus the commandments can be summed up in love.

9. Frank M. Hasel, *Living for God: Reclaiming the Joy of Christian Virtue*, (Nampa, ID: Pacific Press®, 2020), 109.

10. Ellen G. White, *Counsels on Health and Instruction to Medical Missionary Workers* (Mountain View, CA: Pacific Press®, 1951), 424.

11. White, *Steps to Christ*, 12.

12. White, *Ministry of Healing*, 161.

Chapter 13

1. Ellen G. White, *Prayer* (Nampa, ID: Pacific Press®, 2002), 249.

2. Ellen G. White, *Christ's Object Lessons* (Washington, DC: Review and Herald®, 1941), 195.

3. Ellen G. White, "Let Us Go Without the

Camp," *Adventist Review and Sabbath Herald*, May 28, 1889, par. 8.

4. I thank Paul Washer and Voddie Baucham for the inspiration behind these thoughts that I heard in a random sermon on YouTube.

5. Ellen G. White, *Child Guidance* (Nashville, TN: Southern Publishing, 1952), 205.

6. White, *Child Guidance*, 149.

7. For guidelines to fasting, visit: https://www.revivalandreformation.org/resources/all/prayer-and-fasting-days.

8. Ellen G. White, *The Adventist Home.* (Nashville, TN: Southern Publishing, 1954), 179.

9. Ellen G. White, *Manuscript Releases*, vol. 10 (Silver Spring, MD: Ellen G. White Estate, 1990), 179.

10. Ellen G. White, *The Ministry of Healing* (Mountain View, CA: Pacific Press®, 1942), 470.

11. Mike Yaconelli, *Wit and Wisdom for Your Life Together* (Oxford, UK: Lion Hudson PLC, 1996), 27.

12. Ellen G. White, *Early Writings* (Washington, DC: Review and Herald®, 1945), 119.

13. Ellen G. White, *Sermons and Talks*, vol. 2 (Silver Spring, MD: Ellen G. White Estate, 1994), 200.

14. Ellen G. White, *Christian Service* (Washington, DC: Review and Herald®, 1947), 206.

15. Ellen G. White, *The Desire of Ages* (Mountain View, CA: Pacific Press®, 1940), 187.

Chapter 14

1. I thank Duane McKey and Adventist World Radio for sharing this amazing story in the February 2019 AWR newsletter. I'm reprinting the story with their permission. To watch more amazing stories with AWR host Cami Oetman, follow this link: https://www.awr.org.

2. This small nonprofit is called www.audioverse.org, and if you haven't discovered it yet, I encourage you to check out the thousands of inspiring messages and sermons found here!

3. Alistair and Deborah's blog can be found at www.SavingtheCrumbs.com.

4. Alistair and Deborah Huong, "3 Better Reasons Why You Should Live Frugally," Saving the Crumbs (blog), May 18, 2014, https://www.savingthecrumbs.com/2014/05/3-better-reasons-why-you-should-live-frugally/.

5. Ellen G. White, *Christ's Object Lessons* (Washington, DC: Review and Herald®, 1941), 352.

6. Ellen G. White, *The Desire of Ages* (Mountain View, CA: Pacific Press®, 1940), 518.

7. Gregory L. Jackson, *Surrender: The Secret to Perfect Peace and Happiness* (Hagerstown, MD: Review and Herald®, 1994), 22.

8. White, *The Desire of Ages*, 519, 520.

9. White, *The Desire of Ages*, 440.

10. White, *Christ's Object Lessons*, 351.

Chapter 15

1. Norman Herr, "Television Statistics" Television and Health, Internet Resources to Accompany The Sourcebook for Teaching Science, accessed February 17, 2020, http://www.csun.edu/science/health/docs/tv%26health.html.

2. George Müller, who lived back in the early 1800's, made the decision to tell only God what his financial needs were, and thus lived a life of complete faith. God rewarded that faith, as Müller was able to provide homes for thousands of orphans. He received millions of dollars over his lifetime, all completely unsolicited.

3. Ellen G. White, *Christ's Object Lessons* (Washington, DC: Review and Herald®, 1941), 342.

4. White, *Christ's Object Lessons*, 342.

5. Ruth Chou Simons, *Beholding and Becoming: The Art of Everyday Worship* (Eugene, OR: Harvest House Publishers, 2019), 9.

6. Liraz Margalit, PhD, "What Screen Time Can Really Do to Kids' Brains," *Psychology Today*, April 17, 2016, https://www.psychologytoday.com/us/blog/behind-online-behavior/201604/what-screen-time-can-really-do-kids-brains.

7. C. S. Lewis, *The Screwtape Letters* (New York: HarperOne, 2001), 60.

8. Tony Reinke, *12 Ways Your Phone Is Changing You* (Wheaton, IL: Crossway, 2017), 193.

9. In the medical world, ADD stands for attention deficit disorder. This is a developmental disorder characterized by symptoms of inattention (such as distractibility, disorganization, or forgetfulness) hyperactivity, and

impulsivity or a combination of these.

10. Ellen G. White, *Testimonies for the Church* (Mountain View, CA: Pacific Press®, 1948), 2:266.

11. White, *Testimonies*, 2:266.

12. White, *Testimonies*, 2:267.

13. John Piper, (@JohnPiper) Twitter, October 20, 2009, 2:02 P.M.

14. Frank M. Hasel, "Unplugged: Disconnect to Reconnect," Revival and Reformation, accessed November 7, 2019, https://www.revivalandreformation.org/resources/all/unplugged-disconnect-to-reconnect. I gratefully borrowed several ideas for the tips in this section from Hasel's article as well. Hasel has written more on the topic in his new book *Living for God* in the chapter titled "The Virtue of Digital Detox."

15. Reinke, *12 Ways Your Phone Is Changing You*, 200.

16. See the helpful app management tips from Tristan Harris, "How to Unjack Your Mind From Your Phone," Medium, January 26, 2016, http://medium.com/thrive-global/distracted-in-2016-reboot-your-phone-with-mindfulness-9f4c8ad46538.

17. Tony Reinke also references his online article "Know When to Walk Away: A Twelve-Step Digital Detox," Desiring God, May 30, 2016, http://desiringgod.org/articles/know-when-to-walk-away.

18. For more information, see Porn Uses and Addiction at "Porn Survey," Proven Men, http://www.provenmen.org/2014pornsurvey/.

19. Ellen G. White, *The Acts of the Apostles* (Mountain View, CA: Pacific Press®, 1911), 530.

20. Ellen G. White, *Steps to Christ* (Washington, DC: Review and Herald®, 1956), 23.

Chapter 16

1. To hear Pastor Doug's full "Cold Confession" testimony, visit: www.audioverse.org.

2. At this point, Doug was eating about 140 pints a year.

3. Ellen G. White, *Testimonies for the Church* (Mountain View, CA: Pacific Press®, 1948), 3:569, 570.

4. Ellen G. White, *Christ's Object Lessons* (Washington, DC: Review and Herald®, 1941), 346, 347; emphasis added.

5. Author's personal paraphrase of Exodus 25:8.

6. White, *Testimonies*, 3:491, 492.

7. Ellen G. White, *Our High Calling* (Washington, DC: Review and Herald®, 1961), 266; emphasis added.

8. Ellen G. White, *Counsels on Health and Instruction to Medical Missionary Workers* (Mountain View, CA: Pacific Press®, 1951), 50, 51.

9. Dan Buettner, "5 'Blue Zones' Where the World's Healthiest People Live," *National Geographic*, April 6, 2017, https://www.nationalgeographic.com/books/features/5-blue-zones-where-the-worlds-healthiest-people-live/.

10. White, *Testimonies*, 3:62.

11. Herbert Douglass, *Dramatic Prophecies of Ellen White* (Nampa, ID: Pacific Press®, 2007), 70.

12. Ellen G. White, *Counsels on Diet and Foods* (Washington, DC: Review and Herald®, 1938), 15.

13. White, *Counsels on Diet and Foods*, 35.

14. White, *Counsels on Diet and Foods*, 32.

15. White, *Counsels on Diet and Foods*, 44.

16. White, *Counsels on Diet and Foods*, 69.

17. Ellen G. White, *The Ministry of Healing* (Mountain View, CA: Pacific Press®, 1942), 310.

18. Ellen G. White, *Temperance* (Nampa, ID: Pacific Press®, 1949), 267, 268.

19. Ellen G. White, *Education* (Mountain View, CA: Pacific Press®, 1952), 201.

20. The acronym NEWSTART was originally developed by health professionals at Weimar Institute to help people remember the simple components necessary for healthy living. To learn more, visit: http://www.newstart.com/newstart2/.

21. White, *Counsels on Diet and Foods*, 153.

Chapter 17

1. This testimony comes from https://www.adventistmission.org/8-adventists-sang-and-a-priest-cursed and was originally written by Andrew McChesney.

2. I thank Tyson Hall for these thoughts from his study on biblical worship.

3. Ellen G. White, *Thoughts From the Mount of Blessing* (Mountain View, CA: Pacific Press®, 1956), 146.

4. To download a copy of these quiz questions with answers, visit www.revivaland reformation.org and search for the "What Is Our Mission?" quiz by David Steward.

5. Ellen G. White, *Testimonies for the Church* (Mountain View, CA: Pacific Press®, 1948), 9:19.

6. Ellen G. White, *The Acts of the Apostles* (Mountain View, CA: Pacific Press®, 1911), 591.

7. Oswald Chambers, *The Complete Works of Oswald Chambers* (Grand Rapids, MI: Discovery House, 2000), 537.

8. White, *Early Writings*, 64.

9. This story was told during a Mock Trial at ARME Bible Camp back in 2015. I've recounted the story from my best recollection.

10. Ellen G. White, *Gospel Workers* (Washington, DC: Review and Herald®, 1915), 299.

Chapter 18

1. Duane McKey, "Reflections From the President—Apr. 2019," Adventist World Radio News, April 15, 2019, https://awr.org/reflections-from-the-president-apr-2019.

2. Visit https://www.awr.org for many inspiring AWR testimonies!

3. Randy Maxwell, *Boot Camp for the Last Days* (Nampa, ID, Pacific Press®, 2016), 52.

4. Ellen G. White, *The Great Controversy* (Mountain View, CA: Pacific Press®, 1950), 390.

5. Ellen G. White, *Early Writings* (Washington, DC: Review and Herald®, 1945), 260, 261.

6. White, *The Great Controversy*, 449.

7. I thank Randy Maxwell for this practical illustration.

8. In *The Great Controversy* we are told, "While the dragon, primarily, represents Satan, it is, in a secondary sense, a symbol of pagan Rome" (438). When we study the prophecies of Daniel 7, Revelation 12, and 13, we find that today's papal hierarchy (otherwise known as the Roman Catholic Church) clearly meets the description of the little horn that received the deadly wound and then was healed. Adventists also believe that the United States fits the prophecy of the lamb-like beast that speaks as a dragon. In other words, in the future, the United States will submit to Rome's religious power once again, thereby creating an image to the beast in the enforcement of Sunday worship. "In order for the United States to form an image of the beast, the religious power must so control the civil government that the authority of the state will also be employed by the church to accomplish its own ends" (443). We are fast on the way to seeing this happen in society today as the pope is already in discussion about how to make Sunday an international day of rest! This might sound nice at first, but eventually it will be forced upon us, and those who refuse and keep the seventh day holy instead of Sunday will be punished.

9. White, *The Great Controversy*, 608; emphasis added.

10. Ellen G. White, *Education* (Mountain View, CA: Pacific Press®, 1952), 57.

11. I thank Charissa Torossian for help in putting this chapter together. If you'd like to learn more about the three angels' messages, listen to her full series: God's Final Call: The Three Angels' Messages—Parts 1–3, which can be found on www.audioverse.org. While Charissa is now married, her series is still found under the name "Charissa Fong."

Chapter 19

1. You can read more about this incredible testimony in the book *The Miracle of the Seventh-day Ox*, by Bradley Booth (Review and Herald®, 2012).

2. Ellen G. White, *Child Guidance* (Nashville, TN: Southern Publishing, 1954), 541.

3. To learn more about how to honor God's Holy Day, consider hosting a Sabbath Delight Seminar in your local church with Dave and Sandy Bostrom. For more information, visit: http://sabbathdelightseminar.org

4. You can read more about this story in Genesis 4.

5. Ellen G. White, *Patriarchs and Prophets* (Mountain View, CA: Pacific Press®, 1958), 72.

6. Dan Lucarini, *Why I Left the Contemporary Christian Music Movement: Confessions of a Former Worship Leader*, (Wyoming, MI: Evangelical Press, 2002), 46.

7. Ellen G. White, *Education* (Mountain

View, CA: Pacific Press®, 1952), 167, 168.

8. Lucarini, *Why I Left the Contemporary Christian Music Movement*, 33.

9. White, *Patriarchs and Prophets*, 360.

10. Ellen G. White, *Testimonies for the Church* (Mountain View, CA: Pacific Press®, 1948), 8:88.

11. Ellen G. White, *The Great Controversy* (Mountain View, CA: Pacific Press®, 1950), 509.

12. Ellen G. White, *Selected Messages*, book 3 (Washington DC: Review and Herald®, 1980), 334.

13. White, *Patriarchs and Prophets*, 594.

14. For more study on the history of music and the Adventist Church, read https://www.facebook.com/notes/brian-holland/why-dont-seventh-day-adventists-listen-to-rock-music/10157134706966686/.

15. *Amoral* means that there is no rightness or wrongness to something.

16. Wolfgang Stefani, "Is Music Morally Neutral?" *Elder's Digest*, January/March 2018, 11, https://cdn.ministerialassociation.org/cdn/elders digest.org/issues/ED%20Q1%202018.pdf.

17. Stefani, "Is Music Morally Neutral?" 11.

18. Confucius in *The Wisdom of Confucius*, Lin Yatang, ed. (New York: Random House, 1938), 251–272.

19. White, *Testimonies*, 5:499.

20. These suggestions are taken from the study "A Biblical Guide to Modern Worship in the Bowman Hills Seventh-day Adventist Church," written and compiled by my friend Tyson Hall. I thank Tyson for the additional inspiration his study gave in writing this chapter.

21. Ellen G. White, *Christian Service* (Washington, DC: Review and Herald®, 1947), 40.

22. Ellen G. White, *Gospel Workers* (Washington, DC: Review and Herald®, 1915), 137.

23. Adam Clarke, "John Chapter 4," *Commentary on the Bible* (public domain, 1831), https://www.sacred-texts.com/bib/cmt/clarke/joh004.htm.

24. White, *Testimonies*, 9:156.

Chapter 20

1. The 777 initiative invited people to pray at 7:00 A.M., and 7:00 P.M., seven days a week for the outpouring of the Holy Spirit. See also "10 Days of Prayer," General Conference Ministerial Association, accessed February 24, 2020, http://tendaysofprayer.org

2. This program was introduced to pray for the Holy Spirit outpouring on our church, specifically during the General Conference Session in San Antonio the summer of 2015. A second 100 Days of Prayer was planned for March–June 2020. To learn about this and or future prayer events, visit www.revivalandreformation.org.

3. I thank Andrew McChesney for his article "Reach the World: It's Personal," *Adventist World*, October 2015, (https://archives.adventistworld.org/images/issues/2015/october/2015-1010-en.pdf), for some of the details I shared in this story.

4. I thank Adventist World Radio for these reports. To see these and other inspiring testimonies on video, visit www.awr.org.

5. If you'd like to become a cell-phone evangelist, visit https://awr.org/training/.

6. Ellen G. White, comments, in *The Seventh-day Adventist Bible Commentary*, vol. 3, Francis Nichols, ed. (Hagerstown, MD: Review and Herald®, 1977), 1152.

7. GYC stands for Generation. Youth. Christ. It is a movement of young people and is a supportive ministry of the Seventh-day Adventist Church. Thousands of young people from all around the world attend its annual conference. You can learn more about this amazing youth movement at gycweb.org.

8. I thank Eric Louw, one of the GYC leaders, for some of the details I shared in this story.

9. Ellen G. White, *Christ's Object Lessons* (Washington, DC: Review and Herald®, 1941), 146.

10. Chris Poblete, "The Power of Prayer: Present Day Departure From Prayer," *The BLB Blog*, Blue Letter Bible, July 31, 2012, https://blogs.blueletterbible.org/blb/2012/07/31/the-power-of-prayer-present-day-departure-from-prayer/.

11. Ellen G. White, *Patriarchs and Prophets* (Mountain View, CA: Pacific Press®, 1958), 203; emphasis added.

12. Ellen G. White, *Last Day Events* (Boise, ID: Pacific Press®, 1992), 188.

13. Ellen G. White, *The Desire of Ages* (Mountain View, CA: Pacific Press®, 1940), 672.

14. The inspiration for this thought comes from the *Adult Sabbath School Bible Study Guide* titled "The Holy Spirit and Spirituality," January–March 2017, 35.

15. Ellen G. White, *The Great Controversy* (Mountain View, CA: Pacific Press®, 1950), vii.

16. I thank Ron E. M. Clouzet for these summary points as shared in *Adventism's Greatest Need* (Nampa, ID: Pacific Press®, 2011), 35. These reflective points come from reading chapter 4 in Ellen G. White, *The Acts of the Apostles* (Mountain View, CA: Pacific Press®, 1911).

17. White, *Acts of the Apostles*, 38.

18. Ellen G. White, *Testimonies to Ministers and Gospel Workers* (Mountain View, CA: Pacific Press®, 1944), 507; emphasis added.

19. V. Raymond Edman, *They Found the Secret* (Grand Rapids, MI: Zondervan, 1984), 103.

20. Dwight L. Moody, *The New Sermons of Dwight Lyman Moody* (New York: Henry S. Goodspeed, 1880), 746, 747.

21. Ellen G. White, *Prayer* (Nampa, ID: Pacific Press®, 2002), 138.

22. Ellen G. White, *Ye Shall Receive Power* (Hagerstown, MD: Review and Herald®, 1995), 10.

23. Ellen G. White, *Selected Messages*, book 3 (Washington DC: Review and Herald®, 1980), 20, 21.

24. David Wilkerson, "A Call to Anguish," May 8, 2009, https://youtu.be/lGMG_PVaJoI.

25. https://egwwritings.org.

Chapter 21

1. Ellen G. White, *The Adventist Home* (Nashville, TN: Southern Publishing, 1954), 542.

2. Ellen G. White, *The Ministry of Healing* (Mountain View, CA: Pacific Press®, 1942), 417.

3. Thankfully, the grim diagnosis we were given that first day did not come true. Since surgery, Karen Holland, my friend and mentor ever since my days at Oklahoma Academy, has been cancer-free. Karen and her husband, Brian, are like a second family to me, and I am in great debt to their mentorship and love, especially during my early young-adulthood years, when I lived in their home for nearly ten years.

4. I wish I could say that every time God has asked this question I have always immediately said, "Yes, Lord, I will trust You!" But sometimes it's taken me a while as I've balked against the pain.

5. Mrs. L. B. Cowman, *Streams in the Desert* (Grand Rapids, MI: Zondervan, 1996), 314.

6. Jerry Page is currently secretary for the Ministerial Association of the General Conference, and Janet is associate secretary for Pastoral Spouses, Families, and Prayer for the worldwide church. This dear couple has made a huge difference in my life and where I am today in ministry.

7. Ellen G. White, *Manuscript Releases*, vol. 2 (Silver Spring, MD: Ellen G. White Estate, 1990), 81.

8. Ellen G. White, *The Desire of Ages* (Mountain View, CA: Pacific Press®, 1940), 224, 225.

9. I thank my friend Vicki Griffin for sharing this note penned by her late husband.

10. White, *Ministry of Healing*, 471.

11. Ellen G. White, *Thoughts From the Mount of Blessing* (Mountain View, CA: Pacific Press®, 1956), 10.

Chapter 22

1. I first heard the story of Polycarp shared by Pastor Joe Morecraft III in an audio sermon titled "Christians Persecution." But more details came from "The Unforgettable Martyrdom," *Christianity Today*, February 21, 2008, http://www.christianitytoday.com/history/2008/february/unforgettable-martyrdom.html.

2. Ellen G. White, *The Triumph of God's Love* (Nashville, TN: Southern Publishing, 1939), between pp. 28, 29.

3. Testimony shared in opening session sermon by Natasha (Neblett) Dysinger at Generation. Youth. Christ. Conference, 2015.

4. My friend D. J. B. Trim writes of many of these forgotten testimonies in his new book *A Living Sacrifice: Unsung Heroes of Adventist Missions* (Pacific Press®, 2019). I strongly encourage everyone to read this inspiring book.

5. Ellen G. White, *The Acts of the Apostles* (Mountain View, CA: Pacific Press®, 1911), 598.

6. The Calverts served in Fiji for eighteen years, during which time they saw much growth in Christianity. Because of their labors, the Fijian king, Seru Epenisa Cakobau, converted to Christianity, renounced polygamy, and for many years afterward lived a consistent Christian life. While the Calverts later returned to England,

James continued to labor for the Nation of Fiji and oversaw the entire Scriptures printed in the Fijian language before his death.

7. Ellen G. White, *The Great Controversy* (Mountain View, CA: Pacific Press®, 1950), 48.

8. Dietrich Bonhoeffer, *The Cost of Discipleship* (New York: Touchstone, 1995), 89.

9. Ellen G. White, *Testimonies to Ministers and Gospel Workers* (Mountain View, CA: Pacific Press®, 1944), 516–520.

10. White, *Acts of the Apostles*, 561.

11. I thank Pastor Tony and Sayuri Rodriguez for always inspiring me that "the best is yet to come!"

12. Ellen G. White, *The Adventist Home* (Nashville, TN: Southern Publishing, 1954), 541–543.

13. White, *Adventist Home*, 542.

Closing Thoughts

1. I thank Eddie Gonzalez for following God's prompting to text me one morning even though he had no idea what was going on, or that I was praying for strength to keep my eyes open after writing all night. His sharing Psalm 77:4 at that precise moment was just one of the many amazing miracles God gave me over the course of writing this book.

2. Fanny Crosby, "To God Be the Glory," 1875, public domain; hymn no. 341 in *The Seventh-day Adventist Hymnal*.

3. Ellen G. White, *The Acts of the Apostles.* (Mountain View, CA: Pacific Press®, 1911), 560.

Appendix 1

1. Ellen G. White, *Last Day Events* (Boise, ID: Pacific Press®, 1992), 192, 193.

2. Nancy DeMoss Wolgemuth, "The Beauty of Brokenness and Humility," Revival and Reformation, accessed February 18, 2020, https://cdn .ministerialassociation.org/docs/2017-New Resources/170%20-%20Beauty%20of%20 Brokenness%20-%20FULL%20VERSION %20MASTER3.pdf, adapted with permission.

Appendix 2

1. Ellen G. White, *Steps to Christ*, 14, 15.

Appendix 3

1. Ellen G. White, *Selected Messages*, book 1 (Washington DC: Review and Herald®, 1958), 109–111; emphasis added.

2. Ellen G. White, *The Great Controversy* (Mountain View, CA: Pacific Press®, 1950), 464.

3. Ellen G. White, *Prayer* (Nampa, ID: Pacific Press®, 2002), 36, 37.

Appendix 4

1. Ellen G. White, *The Acts of the Apostles* (Mountain View, CA: Pacific Press®, 1911), 549.

2. White, *Acts of the Apostles*, 319.

3. Ellen G. White, *In Heavenly Places* (Hagerstown, MD: Review and Herald®, 1995), 95.

4. Jerry and Janet Page, comps., "That We May Be One," Experiencing God Through Prayer and Praise, Revival and Reformation, cropped and condensed for this appendix, accessed February 18, 2020, https://cdn.ministerialassociation.org /docs/Experiencing%20God%20Through%20 Prayer%20and%20Praise/en/2019-10 -28/26_That%20We%20May%20Be%20 One.pdf. To download the full packet, visit https://www.revivalandreformation.org/prayer /experiencinggod.

5. White, *Early Writings*, 119, 120.

Acknowledgements

Above All, May God Be Glorified!

> *Not unto us, O LORD, not unto us, but to Your name give glory, because of Your mercy, because of Your truth.*
> —Psalm 115:1

Writing a book is like putting together a puzzle. I'm not very good at putting puzzles together by myself, but when others help, miracles happen. And that's the story of this book. Really, my name shouldn't even be on the cover, because each piece, each chapter that has come together, is actually the result of the inspiration I've been gleaning for years—from time in God's Word, from mentors in ministry, from friends, from leaders in the church, from the many books and articles I've read, and from all those along life's journey. This book is a testament to God's divine leading, and a tribute to the many beautiful people God has brought across my path—people who have showed me in vibrant living color, what it means to love God and live according to His Word. A few of those people will be mentioned below.

But first, let me begin by saying THANK YOU above all to my **Heavenly Father**! Because of His enabling grace and power, this book is in your hands. While I don't feel like I've done the subject of "living by every word" justice, my prayer is that despite my human weaknesses and inadequacies, God will still be glorified, and that many hearts will be drawn closer to Him as they read this book.

Next let me say thank you to my amazing parent's—**David and Sylvia Mason**. I'm so very grateful for the love, wisdom, prayers and support of my godly parents throughout this long writing process, but also throughout my life. Thank you Mom and Dad for showing me time and time again over the years what genuine, authentic, loving Christianity looks like. Your favorite song, "I Could Never Outlove the Lord," you have lived. Your life has been one of constant sacrificial giving for the sake of others. Mom—even while dealing with your ongoing battle with lung cancer, you've been such an encouragement through this writing process. Thanks for always dropping whatever you were doing to read through a new chapter or give me feedback. I'm forever grateful, and I'm looking forward to heaven with our family!

Brian and Karen Holland—my second family, and home away from home. I have so much gratitude in my heart for all that you've taught me over the years. I'm especially thankful for all your input behind the scenes with writing this book. Thanks for always being available to answer my questions and help me clarify different theological issues, and for making time to do a final quick read-through of my manuscript before it went to Pacific Press.

My life-long forever friends through thick and thin—**Valerie Crosier, Julia O'Carey, Season Smith,** and **Heather Vixie**—These beautiful women know me like few others and have inspired me so much in my walk with God, and in my writing. I can't imagine life without you girls! I love each of you. Thanks for your support and encouragement, and for giving up time together so I could write.

Special thanks to **Melony** and **Jeff Coleman** who took time to read and give input on the original drafts of this manuscript when I first started writing three years ago. Thank you for your continued prayers, especially while I was tackling difficult chapters. What a blessing your support has been!

Tony and **Sayuri Rodriguez**—Thank you for your frequent text messages and pictures reminding me of your personal and specific prayers on my behalf. Your messages always came just when I needed them. Thank you for encouraging me during the tough times that, "The Best is yet to come!" The inspiration for my final chapter subtitle came from *you*!

Rick and Cindy Mercer—I want to say an extra special thank you for stopping to pray for me whenever I texted or called, and especially Cindy for "laboring" with me as we both "birthed" our books at the same time. I remember you telling me, "Push, Melody, Push! You can do this!" And I told you the same. I'm so excited to see your amazing testimony finally shared in your book *Pray Big—God Can Do So Much More!* You once told me laughing, "I hope our babies (books) grow up one day to become friends." Cindy, I'm sure they will be the best of friends, just like you and me!

Dr. Zeno Charles-Marcel and **Marcos Bomfim**—Dear friends and General Conference colleagues, thank you both for your input on my chapters having to do with healthy living and stewardship. Dr. Zeno, I'm especially grateful for how you bent over backwards, even while on a wild speaking itinerary in Africa, to get me the article, "Practical Tips for Growing a Healthy Body," which you wrote just for the appendix of this book. A simple "thank you" does not adequately convey my gratitude!

Frank Hasel—Another friend and respected colleague here at the General Conference. Thank you so much for taking time in your busy schedule to read my manuscript and for your helpful insights and constructive feedback, which prompted the reworking of a few sections in this book. Your input, as well as your own articles, and books have been a tremendous blessing in this writing journey. I've been especially moved and challenged by your new book, *Living for God: Reclaiming the Joy of Christian Virtue,* which gets right to the heart of Christian living in ways that are often overlooked. I will be sharing your book widely.

Thank you to my many additional **General Conference Colleagues**

and friends whose names I don't have space to mention here. Working with the General Conference in prayer ministry these past ten years has been such an amazing privilege. While people talk and opinions are shared, I've been blessed to witness first hand the humility, the Christ-like love, the faithfulness, and the unselfish sacrificial service that often goes on behind the scenes at church headquarters. Even through the challenges I've seen godly Christianity on display in vibrant living color, and what an encouragement this has been. Seeing these living testimonies has strengthened my faith, inspired my writing, and helped me look forward with greater eagerness to Jesus' soon coming, when we all will be able to put aside our struggles and just enjoy unhurried fellowship at Jesus' feet. What a day that will be!

I want to give recognition to some of my **supportive friends and prayer partners,** whose prayers and encouragement have especially boosted my spirits while working on *Daring to Live by Every Word*. Thank you Roman and Raluca Ril for providing a peaceful place to work at your home in Southern Germany as I made the final edits on this manuscript. Thank you Kristin Hutchinson for sharing honest feedback that helped me improve my chapters and make them more readable. Thank you Steve and Stacie Schefka, Steve and Donna Shank, Luis and Tracie Alonso, Alice Scarbrough, Audrey Andersson, Gem Castor, Pavel Goia, Donna McNeilus, Karen Glassford, Cami Oetman, Sue Hinkle, Alyssa Truman (love you AWR girls so much), Dawn Moffit, Kim Goodge, Calvin Kim, Cindy Magan, Kat Taylor, Andy Martinez, Mark Paden, Teri Salvador, Nancy Wilson, Nina Acheson, Esme Ross, Joyce Mulligan, the GC prayer team, and our Tuesday night Bible study group at Gerald and Chantal Klingbeil's home for all your encouragement and persevering prayers. What a blessing to know that when I needed support, you all were praying!

Before I close these acknowledgements, I have to give an extra heartfelt "thank you" to **Jerry and Janet Page** who believed in this book from day one. Thank you for wading through less than ideal early book drafts, and for inspiring me to a higher writing standard, through the power of prayer and the blessing of the Holy Spirit. You both have been such an inspiration in my life, and I know I wouldn't be where I am today in ministry without your support, encouragement and prayers. Thank you for the hours you've spent pouring over this manuscript with me, helping me fine-tune the stories and details for the glory of God. When you get to heaven, there are going to be more stars in your crown than you can imagine!

I can't forget to thank the **Pacific Press Publishing team** for their enthusiastic support of my work and for helping another book become reality. I especially want to thank you, Dale Galusha for your generous accommodation of my publishing needs. And thank you, Miguel Valdivia, for your humble spirit and patient assistance throughout this long process. I will always cherish the special memory of the week of prayer I got to spend sharing with all the Pacific Press staff a couple years ago. What a great team to work with!

And last but not least, I want to say thank you to my many **encouraging and supportive readers** from all around the world who often send me emails, Facebook or Instagram messages, or who greet me at events and share how my first book *Daring to Ask for More* has touched their life. Your testimonies and tears about personal revival, to significant decisions made (like choosing not to have an abortion, to changes in career choices, to trusting God in the midst of suffering, or to pressing forward in faith with some ministry venture), have so encouraged my heart and made all the pain in writing these books worthwhile. So thank you, from the bottom of my heart, for encouraging me to keep writing for God's glory. Here you are—finally—what you all have been waiting for! Book two! Now let us all say, TO GOD BE THE GLORY, great things He has done! My prayer is that this book will lead you closer to the heart of Jesus, and that soon we will all be together, in the clouds of glory, going home.